The Fabric of America

Measuring America
The Code of Love

THE FABRIC OF AMERICA

*How Our Borders and Boundaries
Shaped the Country and Forged
Our National Identity*

ANDRO LINKLATER

WALKER & COMPANY

NEW YORK

Published by Walker & Company, New York
Distributed to the trade by Holtzbrinck Publishers

Art credits Pages vi–vii: Jeffrey L. Ward. Pages 20, 26, 39, 46, 56, 75, 80, 94, 97, 104,
129, 144, 153, 177, 195, 200, 212, 225, 233, 240, 251, 274: Library of Congress.
Page 22: Smithsonian Institution. Page 36: Charles Townsend. Pages 59, 282:
Science Photo Library. Page 70: Massachusetts Historical Society. Page 209:
Wisconsin Historical Society. Page 279: Michele Lee Amundsen.

Library of Congress Cataloging-in-Publication Data has been applied for.

ISBN-10: 0-8027-1533-8
ISBN-13: 978-0-8027-1533-3

Visit Walker & Company's Web site at www.walkerbooks.com

First U.S. edition 2007

1 3 5 7 9 10 8 6 4 2

Typeset by Westchester Book Group
Printed in the United States of America by Quebecor World Fairfield

Contents

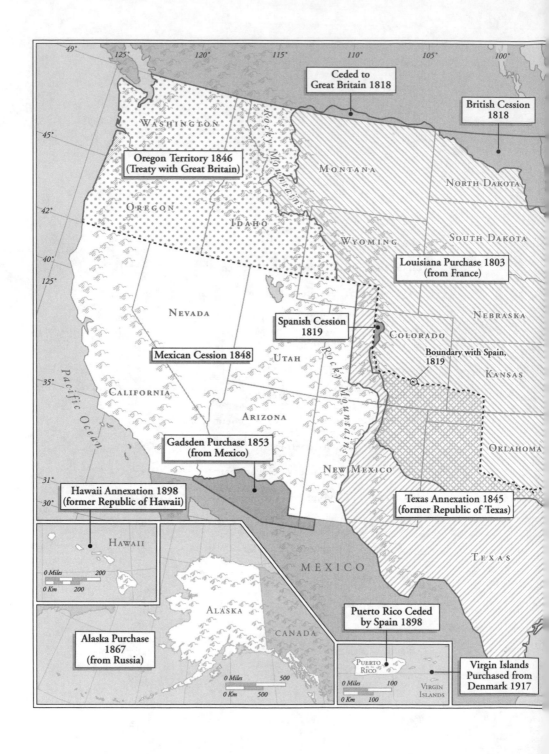

UNITED STATES TERRITORIAL ACQUISITIONS

CANADA

0 Miles 500

0 Kilometers 500

Lake Superior

Great Lakes

MAINE

VERMONT

NEW HAMPSHIRE

Lake Huron

Michigan

WISCONSIN

MASSACHUSETTS

Lake Ontario

MINNESOTA

NEW YORK

Appalachian Mtns.

Lake Michigan

RHODE ISLAND

CONNECTICUT

IOWA

Lake Erie

PENNSYLVANIA

NEW JERSEY

OHIO

Allegheny Mtns.

Mason-Dixon Line parallel
N 39° 43′ 20″

ILLINOIS

INDIANA

WASHINGTON, D.C.

DELAWARE

MARYLAND

WEST VIRGINIA

VIRGINIA

MISSOURI

KENTUCKY

Appalachian Mtns.

Territory of the Thirteen States
(Ceded by Great Britain) 1783

TENNESSEE

NORTH CAROLINA

ARKANSAS

Mississippi River

SOUTH CAROLINA

Atlantic Ocean

ALABAMA

GEORGIA

LOUISIANA

MISSISSIPPI

Boundary with Spain,
1797–1800

FLORIDA

East Florida
(Spanish Cession)
1819

West Florida
(Spanish Cession)
1819

Spanish Cession
1819

THE BAHAMAS

Gulf of Mexico

©2007 Jeffrey L. Ward

FORESIGHT

*The forests and desarts of America are without land-
marks . . . It is almost as easy to divide the Atlantic Ocean
by a line, as clearly to ascertain the limits of those unculti-
vated, uninhabitable, unmeasured regions.*

DR. SAMUEL JOHNSON, *The Literary Magazine*, 1756

TRAPPED IN SIX lanes of traffic, most drivers look impatient or bored
as they inch toward the San Ysidro crossing point between the United
States and Mexico. A few faces appear anxious. Not one expression conveys
surprise. Yet the changes that have happened here in the last few years
should be cause for astonishment. A border, once not much more than a
line of glass-fronted booths, has become a frontier. Everywhere there is
extra security. Black-lensed cameras track the lines of vehicles. Uniformed
patrols check registration numbers against computer records. Unsmiling immigration officers inspect faces and documents suspiciously.

Out in the desert, the signs are more dramatic still: fences, watchtowers,
heat sensors, armed vigilantes, border guards, even detachments of the National Guard. Never before in peacetime has the United States devoted so
much effort and money to the defense of its national frontier. For most of
the last century, the line that demarcates the limits of the nation has hardly
entered public consciousness. As drivers wait in the simmering heat for the
detailed examination of the car ahead to be completed, the paradox suddenly becomes glaringly obvious. What now rates as the most urgent priority on the political agenda is the zone that history forgot.

The moment that the U.S. frontier disappeared from the radar screen can be placed almost exactly. On November 4, 1892, the *Aegis*, a student newspaper published by the University of Wisconsin, carried an article entitled "Problems in American History." Its brash young author suggested that too much attention had been directed by historians to the formal boundaries that divided and delineated the United States. The epitome of the historian he had in mind was Professor Hermann von Holst, who earlier that year had published the seventh and final volume of his monumental work, *The Constitutional and Political History of the United States*.

In his history, Holst concentrated upon the powers contained within state and national frontiers, arguing that the unique character of the United States emerged from the bitter fight for constitutional dominance between state and federal governments. It was this perspective on American history that the article in the *Aegis* attacked. It condemned "the attention paid to State boundaries and to the sectional lines of North and South" and asserted that the United States owed its unique character to the influence of another, less formal frontier, the line of settlement that "stretched along the western border like a cord of union." Seven months later, on July 12, 1893, the writer, Frederick Jackson Turner, professor of history at the University of Wisconsin, presented his thesis to a wider audience, the American Historical Association in Chicago, under a title that was to become famous: "The Significance of the Frontier in American History."

The San Ysidro crossing represents everything that Turner set out to bury. "The American frontier is sharply distinguished from the European frontier—a fortified boundary line running through dense populations," he insisted. "The most significant thing about the American frontier is, that it lies at the hither edge of free land."

It was here that the American character was formed, Turner argued. Whatever their national origin, the settlers became infected with the frontier spirit—"that restless nervous energy, that dominant individualism working for good and for evil, and withal that buoyancy and exuberance which comes with freedom"—and thereby acquired a common identity. In short, it was in "the crucible of the frontier [that] the immigrants were Americanized."

For more than a century Turner's thesis has loomed over the history of the western United States like a battle-scarred colossus. It has been repeatedly assaulted by professional historians for the way that it airbrushes the Native American experience out of the records, leaves unexamined the contributions of women and frontier communities like the Germans and Mormons, and fails to explain why similar experiences on other nineteenth-century frontiers in Siberia, Australia, southern Africa, Argentina, and Canada conspicuously failed to Americanize those pioneers. But however much it is battered, Turner's argument has refused to fall down, if only because the opening up of the west did profoundly affect the rest of the country and did call forth a specifically American response.

In popular consciousness, therefore, Turner's frontier has until now remained unchallenged. The term continues to be automatically attached to such boundless areas as outer space, the Internet, or intellectual property, implying that here are fresh and unlimited opportunities particularly suited to exploitation by American enterprise and adaptability. The spirit it engendered remains the default explanation for what makes America different from the rest of the world.

In the era of terrorism and mass immigration, however, a seismic shift is clearly taking place. It is the older meaning of *frontier* that draws public attention, the line that delineates an area of sovereignty. The history of that frontier began with the first generation of Americans. They had fought to win sovereignty from the British—the right to establish for themselves democratic government and individual liberty. To mark out the scope of that sovereignty, lines had to be drawn in the ground. Among the many consequences of independence, therefore, few were more significant than the curious ritual that took place in the summer of 1784 on top of Mount Welcome, a commanding height in the Allegheny Mountains in what is now West Virginia.

In July of that year, a company of frontiersmen led by a university professor, a geographer, an Episcopalian minister, and an almanac-maker constructed a log cabin on the mountain's peak. To the broad-shouldered axmen and laborers who had hewn the trees and shaped the logs, it must have seemed like a foolish enough enterprise. Part of the cabin's roof was designed to be easily lifted away, and instead of sheltering people armed with rifles, hatchets, and the usual tools of frontier life, it contained nothing but an array of clocks, telescopes, compasses, and sextants. Most days and nights the four leaders spent long hours inside, and their work could only have appeared idle and unproductive, consisting as it did of not much more than peering at the sky through the telescopes and sextants, and jotting down notes of what they saw.

The youngest of the quartet was the almanac-maker, a thirty-year-old, snub-nosed Quaker named Andrew Ellicott. He had left his young wife, Sally, in Baltimore, and was missing her. On July 30, he wrote to tell her about the routine he had to follow.

"We are now living very comfortably on the Top of the highest Mount in this part of the World," he informed her. "Our Observatory is in good order, and Well Stored with Instruments; my Companions are very agreeable Men, and I think we enjoy all the Happiness that people in our Situation could expect."

Ellicott's agreeable companions included the Reverend James Madison, principal of William & Mary College in Virginia and a cousin of the future president; Dr. John Ewing, provost of the University of Pennsylvania; and Thomas Hutchins, geographer-general of the United States and the outstanding mapmaker of his day. Probably no more academically distinguished company had ever before taken out their skills to work on the frontier.

The expertise that Ellicott brought was of a different kind. He had little formal education, and his reputation, such as it was, came from the astronomical observations published in his almanacs. Enthusiasts thought them remarkably accurate. But he was also an instrument-maker of the highest quality—Ellicott's clocks were, and among today's collectors remain, highly prized—and in such high-flown company, it was probably his skill with his hands that seemed most valuable. He himself appeared somewhat in awe of the people around him and astonished by their habits of working.

"The following is a True Picture of Our living," he assured his wife. "We brakefast [sic] between 6 and 7

"Observe the Sun's Altitude between 7 and 10

"Dine between 12 and 1 after which we always drink our two Bottles before we leave the Table

"Then Observe the Sun's Corresponding Altitude

"At 6 we have a large Bowl of Wine Sillybub [a frothy mixture of wine and milk]—

"This rule we never break—We have each of us a Cow—
"We drink our Tea about 7—
"And sometimes *observe the Heavens* the greatest part of the Night."

Apart from the amount of wine required for the astronomy and the caliber of those taking part, the most striking aspect of their work was the cost. Their wages—$6 a day per person—were roughly equivalent to what the governor of Virginia was paid, and the final bill for their work would come to more than $4,000. The purpose of all their endeavors, however, was simply to establish the boundary between the states of Virginia and Pennsylvania.

After seven years of war, both states were burdened by mountainous debts, and in the effort to keep their creditors at bay, they had trimmed every item of unnecessary expenditure from their budgets. Yet on the frontier no expense was spared in the quest to run an accurate line through the uninhabited wilderness. Evidently the seemingly mundane business of determining where one state ended and the other began possessed an importance that may not be immediately obvious today.

The only precedent for what Ellicott and his friends were doing on Mount Welcome had been provided by Charles Mason and Jeremiah Dixon in their epic struggle between 1763 and 1767 to establish the frontier between Pennsylvania and Maryland. The way the two enterprises used the heavens to locate a precise point upon earth was very similar, but Mason and Dixon could claim the distinction of being pioneers. Never before had the newly systematized knowledge of the movement of stars, sun, and moon been combined with the developing technology of telescope construction to establish an artificial boundary. Mason and Dixon, however, were simply dividing the property of William Penn's descendants from that of the Calvert family. The result of all their meticulous work merely increased the financial value of Pennsylvania and Maryland to their colonial owners.

The boundary run by Andrew Ellicott and his fellow scientists on top of Mount Welcome had a wider purpose: to define the limits of two states. Its consequences would inevitably shape the economic and political growth of Pennsylvania and Virginia, creating a sense of sovereignty that grew with the power of the states. These two states were not alone. In the years after independence, every other state took steps to demarcate the extent of its territory, both by natural features like rivers and mountaintops, and by lines of latitude and longitude. On a map, the result of the boundary-makers' work might appear to be nothing more substantial than a carefully inked line, but it carried a political and constitutional weight that has reverberated through the history of the United States.

To establish a frontier was to create an area of separate jurisdiction. Within it, a specific framework of laws, of government, and eventually of values would be formed. How separate and distinct was the jurisdiction that grew up behind a state's borders posed a question that would give rise to eighty years of constitutional friction and the bloodiest of civil wars. It would also produce the most sophisticated guarantees of individual freedom and democratic government that human society has yet seen. To a degree unknown in previous nations, the United States was the product of the formal divisions that the boundary-makers marked in the wilderness.

The need for such boundaries, between states, properties, and individuals, was inseparable from American history. As the editors of the authoritative western history *Under an Open Sky* put it, "Boundary setting is so inclusive a frontier and regional process that it encompasses all the others; all social life is in some sense a struggle to define the difference between ours and theirs, mine and yours, self and other." The process began with the arrival of the first colonists.

From the other side of the Atlantic, eighteenth-century commentators like Dr. Samuel Johnson habitually referred to colonial America as a desert or an ocean where no clearly defined boundaries existed. Its "unmeasured regions" made a contrast with Europe, whose national frontiers had evolved over generations through warfare, the growth of population, and the influence of religion. Except in time of war, these boundaries were generally recognized and respected. Even when some major adjustment of them took place, such as the partition of Poland in 1772 between the neighboring powers of Russia, Prussia, and Austria, the rivers that constituted the new borders were well-known and clearly mapped.

The New World lacked this essential feature of European politics. Skirmishing between the colonial powers was endemic because, as a governor of Nova Scotia put it, "there hath never as yet (properly Speaking) been any

Adjustment of Limits." The royal charters creating British colonies attempted to specify their borders, but the vagueness of the wording betrayed their authors' ignorance. The 1665 charter issued for the new colony of Carolina, for example, stated baldly that it would extend from "thirty six and thirty Minutes, Northern latitude, and so West in a direct line as far as the South Seas [meaning the Pacific Ocean]; and South and Westward as far as the degrees of twenty nine, inclusive, northern latitude; and so West in a direct line as far as the South Seas."

On the basis of this phrase, an independent North Carolina would claim all of what is now Tennessee. Connecticut used similar wording in its charter to justify occupying parts of Pennsylvania, while Virginia's various charters allowed the state to argue that it should possess everything west of the Appalachians between the Great Lakes and the junction of the Ohio and Mississippi rivers.

The need to mark out on the ground exactly what the charters were attempting to describe became of such importance that blood was shed, fortunes were lost and centuries-long lawsuits were conducted to establish a line of latitude or the position of a river. The reason was simple. Unlike the Portuguese, who came in search of spices, and the Spaniards, who were seduced by gold, and the French, who traded in furs, the constant preoccupation of the English was how to own the soil before them.

"Many good religious devout men have made it a great question, as a matter in conscience, by what warrant they might go and possess those countries which are none of theirs but the poor savages," wrote John Smith in his *Advertisements for the Inexperienced Planters of New England*, published in 1631, and offered several reassuring answers. Most were the stock ones of seventeenth-century colonizers—that the land belonged to England because she had discovered it, that settlement was justified by the need to spread Christianity among the heathen, that disease had already cleared the original inhabitants from much of New England, and that from Florida to Canada there was enough space for everyone, natives and newcomers alike. But then he added another that specifically answered any would-be colonist's doubts about title to his American land. "If this be not a sufficient reason for such tender consciences," he wrote offhandedly, "for a copper knife and a few toys as beads and hatchets, [the Indians] will sell you a whole country; and for a small matter their houses and the ground they dwell upon."

On the Southampton dockside, as John Winthrop's company of settlers were about to depart for Massachusetts Bay in 1630, the Puritan preacher John Cotton preached an entire sermon on their divine right to the land, assuring them, "Where there is a vacant place, there is liberty for the sons of Adam or Noah to come and inhabit, though they neither buy it nor ask their leaves." And Winthrop himself reinforced the message by pointing out that the few indigenous inhabitants had no real claim to the land, at least by the standards of English owners, whose property was exactly surveyed, neatly hedged in, and well grazed. "As for the Natives in new England," he argued, "they inclose no Land, neither have any setled habytation, nor any tame Cattle to prove [their title to] the Land by . . . and Soe if we leave them sufficient for their use, wee may lawfully take the rest."

There was, however, a more violent method of acquiring land. In Jamestown, the colonists had originally been guided by John Smith into buying the land from the Powhatan confederation, but relations deteriorated as the colony became better established. In March 1622 the confederation turned on the colonists in outlying villages and massacred more than 350 of them, almost a third of the colony's population. The Virginians' reaction, after the first horrifed shock had passed, was unexpected—a desire not just for revenge, but for something more.

"Our hands which before were tied with gentleness and faire usage, are now set at liberty by the treacherous violence of the Sauvages," wrote one colonist in a pamphlet entitled *The Relation of the Barbarous Massacre in Time of Peace and League, treacherously executed by the native infidels upon the English*, "So that we . . . may now by right of Warre, and law of Nations, invade the country, and destroy them who sought to destroy us, whereby we shall enjoy their cultivated places, turning the laborious mattacke into the victorious sword . . . and possessing the fruits of others' labours."

The principle that conquest in a just war gave a country legitimate possession of enemy territory was universally accepted, and for almost a century afterward force became the principal means in New England and the South for acquiring fresh territory. By the early 1700s, the Powhatan confederation and other Algonquian-language nations around the Chesapeake Bay had been almost obliterated by a combination of outright violence and disease. Then the Piedmont territory occupied by the Tuscarora and Yamasee was cleared as far as the Blue Ridge Mountains after a series of campaigns that lasted from 1711 through 1716. In New England, the 1637 Pequot War and the greater destruction of King Philip's War from 1675 to 1676 achieved the same end.

Dispossessing the original inhabitants was not enough. English law also required the land to be within the area specified by the royal charters. "No colony hath any right to dispose of any lands conquered from the natives," ran a royal decree in the 1660s, "unless both the cause of the conquest be just and the land lye within the bound which the king by his charter hath given it." Thus the vague phrases so confidently used in London had to be given an exact reality in America soil. But even then one more step was required by English common law. To convert the newly acquired territory into individual parcels of lawful property that had a value and could be legally bought and sold, their boundaries had to be surveyed, and a description with a plat or outline map needed to be registered with the colony's government.

So important was this final stage that the ability to survey a parcel of ground became an essential part of every settler's education. Rufus Putnam, Washington's chief engineer at the siege of Boston in 1775, who asserted that "I never Saw the inside of a School house except about three weeks," learned how to survey, as did the immaculately educated Charles Carroll of Maryland, America's richest colonist, who attended the best schools on both sides of the Atlantic. The value of a reliable surveyor was such that even as an apprentice, George Washington could boast of his ability to earn more than $100 a week. "A doubloon [approximately $15] is my constant gain every day that will permit my going out" he told a friend, "and sometimes six pistoles [approxmately $22.50]."

Boundaries of all kinds—imperial frontiers, colonial borders, property limits—were inseparable from the development of colonial America. When the people of the independent states declared their intention to assume "a separate and equal station" among the powers of the earth, the need for clearcut boundaries was as obvious to them as the right to life and liberty.

By far the longest clause in the Articles of Confederation and Perpetual Union drawn up by the states in 1777 dealt not with representation of the people or defense or finance, but with border disputes between one state and another, and the methods of solving them. With the exception of Rhode Island, every state from New Hampshire in the north to Georgia in the south had a quarrel with its neighbors over its borders. In addition, four states, Massachusetts, New York, Virginia, and South Carolina, were confronted by breakaway movements engaged in sometimes violent struggles to draw new boundaries that would end in the creation of Vermont, Kentucky, and Tennessee. And until 1781 Maryland refused even to sign the Articles of Confederation in protest against Virginia's claims to include huge territories beyond the Appalachians within her limits.

So deep did the tensions run that violence always threatened to break out. The danger was made clear by one major conflict that occurred in the middle of the Revolution. In December 1775, when they might have been fighting the British, seven hundred Pennsylvanians instead fought a pitched battle with three hundred Connecticut settlers in a boundary quarrel known as the Yankee-Pennamite War. Without a stronger central government to resolve territorial disputes peacefully, Alexander Hamilton argued in the *Federalist Papers*, the states would inevitably turn against each other, and the sword would become "the arbiter of their differences." Thus the most immediate purpose of the boundary-makers on Mount Welcome was to keep the peace, hence its importance. But there were other, longer-lasting consequences that were inseparable from the act of establishing a frontier.

More than a century before the American colonists declared their independence, the long, bloody conflict of the Thirty Years War between Protestant and Catholic nations, which had torn Europe apart, ended in the Peace of Westphalia in 1648. In a series of treaties, the European powers recognized that within their own realms, rulers had the exclusive right to exercise jurisdiction over their citizens regardless of the claims to interfere asserted by outside agents, such as the pope or Holy Roman emperor. Constitutional philosophers like the seventeenth-century Dutch authority Hugo Grotius had long argued that a nation consisted primarily of people joined by similar race and culture under the jurisdiction of one ruler, and only secondarily of territory. But the Westphalian agreement changed the emphasis. In future, the extent of the nation and the jurisdiction of the ruler was increasingly defined not by its people but by its territory. And in the words of Emmerich de Vattel's *Law of Nations*, it was now important that "to prevent every subject of discord, every occasion of quarrel, the limits of territories ought to be marked out with clearness and precision."

Until 1776, Britain's colonies fell within the jurisdiction of the home country, and so, when Americans first asserted their independence, European powers like France and the Netherlands, accustomed to the obligations of the Treaty of Westphalia, refused to offer military aid or financial loans. They required evidence that the former colonists now constituted a separate entity. Consequently, when the Continental Congress tasked Thomas Jefferson's committee with producing the document that would become known as the Declaration of Independence, it did so not simply out of patriotism but because, as Jefferson explained in his autobiography, "a Declaration of Independence alone could render it consistent with European delicacy to treat with us, or even to receive an Ambassador."

However, neither the Declaration nor the Articles of Confederation made clear whether one nation or thirteen had been created. Each state retained "its sovereignty, freedom and independence" but also delegated some of its jurisdiction to "the United States in Congress assembled." What the founding documents left ambiguous, the founding geography began to make clear.

Pennsylvania and Virginia already possessed the rights to issue their own currencies, set their own tariffs, and negotiate their own treaties with Native American nations. The line that Ellicott and his fellow commissioners ran through the mountains with such painstaking attention to accuracy created a frontier that defined the extent of the states' jurisdictions as understood by the Treaty of Westphalia. The states, in short, were acquiring most of the characteristics of nationhood.

Since Andrew Ellicott's career was spent in that unmapped territory that Turner would later describe as "the frontier," they present two views of the way the land was settled that are in direct conflict. "The frontier is productive of individualism," wrote Turner. "The tendency is anti-social. It produces antipathy to control, and particularly to any direct control. The tax-gatherer is viewed as a representative of oppression." But wherever the boundary-makers' lines ran, they introduced government, law, and taxes to areas where little or none had existed before. They also paved the way for the operation of land speculators who might, and often did, buy up the farms worked by the pioneers without ever setting eyes on them. A century before Turner pictured the romantic freedom of the frontier, the work of Ellicott and the other boundary-makers had introduced a reality that undermined his central thesis.

At the heart of Ellicott's character lay a contradiction, between his deep-seated desire for regularity and a tendency to emotional extravagance. A career devoted to mapping the unmapped expanse of the wilderness often seems to have been the only way that he could satisfactorily reconcile two conflicting impulses.

As the eldest child in a Pennsylvania Quaker family, he came from a background firmly grounded in order and method. His father was a clockmaker, his uncles designed and constructed technologically advanced water mills, and having learned at his father's side the meticulous skills needed to build accurate timepieces, Ellicott became a surveyor of the utmost reliability before devoting his life to astronomy.

Yet as he demonstrated in a remarkable series of letters written to his wife, Sally, he was also a man convulsed by passionate desire and agonies of remorse. Throughout thirty-five years of marriage, he invariably addressed her by such endearments as "Dearest of all Earthly Beings," "My Love," and "My Darling," and whenever he left her side, he would write to her with undisguised longing, as he did in 1785 from the Alleghenies, "many are the waking Hours I spend in my Tent, in the dead of Night, anticipating my return to your Arms and once more enjoy the Charmes of your Mind and conversation." He worried ceaselessly over the health and education of their numerous children and was devastated by the death of the youngest in 1784, and yet, as he exclaimed to Sally, "I love our children, but I adore you."

Despite this powerful inducement to stay at home, a cocktail of motives drove him from her arms to earn a living on the frontier. One ingredient, as he explained to an unfeeling secretary of state, was "[my desire] to support a government I venerate, and my pride to serve faithfully a country which I love, the country in which I was born, and which contains everything I hold dear." Another, and no less deeply held, was his devotion to the science involved in running a boundary.

To draw a straight parallel from east to west across a curving globe with reliable precision required an accumulated body of astronomical knowledge, a command of mathematics, and an accuracy of observation that simply did not exist until the mid-eighteenth century. In his lifetime, Ellicott became the acknowledged master within the United States of each stage in the process, from the first delicate construction of a telescope through the final rugged work of clearing a path through the undergrowth. Wherever he went—and his lines helped define the shapes of no fewer than eleven states and the District of Columbia, as well as the southern and northern frontiers of the United States—he took a profound satisfaction in the scientific underpinning of his work. Even if his boundaries were "lost by the carelessness, or destroyed by the caprice or wickedness, of man," he once commented, "[they] may be accurately renewed so long as astronomy shall be understood, and the sun, moon and stars continue to shine!"

Ellicott never made any secret of his conviction that government was essential to stop men from behaving capriciously or wickedly. Encountering the notorious icon of frontier justice, Captain William Lynch, Ellicott listened with horror to the handsome old man—"he has the appearance of an antient [sic] athlete"—telling how he and his Lynchmen would first whip a suspected lawbreaker until he confessed to the crime of which he was accused, then tie him to a horse with a rope suspended from a branch round his neck, and wait for justice to be administered when the animal moved away. "These punishments were not unfrequently inflicted upon the innocent, through spite or in consequence of answers extorted under the smarting of the whip," Ellicott noted with astonishment. "It seems almost incredible that such proceedings should be had in a civilized country governed by known laws."

Wherever a state or a national boundary was established, however, the law followed. Before Ellicott died in 1825, Secretary of State John Quincy Adams negotiated treaties with Britain and Spain extending the limits of the United States along the forty-ninth parallel in the north as far as the Rockies, and in the south from the Gulf of Mexico to the Pacific Ocean. Less than a generation later, the borders had been pushed out to include the entire coastline from northern Oregon to southern California. Within that national frontier, U.S. common law, strengthened by legislation specifically concerned with the distribution of public lands, enabled settlers to acquire landed property not only by purchase or by credit, but by clearing the ground and often simply by occupation. However far west the creaking Conestoga wagons traveled, their intrepid passengers knew that their desire to own the land was backed by the Constitution and the entire panoply of law. Thus, contrary to Turner's picture of the pioneer at odds with government and legal contraints, every new wave of settlers had a vested interest in introducing government, and law and order, to the wilderness as quickly as possible so that their claims could be recognized as property.

"Here, every citizen, whether by birthright or adoption is part of the government, identified with it, not virtually but in fact," declared Morris Birkbeck, one of Illinois' pioneer settlers, in 1824, ending his tribute with the embarrassing gush, "I love this government."

What made the immigrants American was not the frontier experience but the context in which their experience took place. During the nineteenth century, most of the world's grasslands, from the Russian steppes to the Argentine pampas, were seized from their original occupants, and the newcomers all faced challenges similar to those on the U.S. prairies.

Turner himself implicitly acknowledged the universality of the frontier spirit when to describe the restless, adventurous impulse that inspired American pioneers, he quoted lines from a poem called "The Song of the English" by his favorite poet, Rudyard Kipling:

> We were dreamers, dreaming greatly, in the man-stifled town;
> We yearned beyond the skyline where the strange roads go down.

Had he wanted, Turner might have found equally appropriate, though less poetic, lines in the tribute paid to Australian pioneers by Banjo Paterson, the nineteenth-century bard of the outback:

> 'Twas they who rode the trackless bush in heat and storm
>   and drought;
> 'Twas they who heard the master-word that called them
>   farther out;
> 'Twas they who followed up the trail the mountain cattle
>   made,
> And pressed across the mighty range where now their bones
>   are laid.

Or he could have spread his net wider. In 1821, Alexander Pushkin evoked the wild appeal of Russia's frontier in *The Prisoner of the Caucasus*, setting a trend that was followed by some of the great examples of frontier literature, such as Mikhail Lermontov's *A Hero of Our Time* and Leo Tolstoy's *The Cossacks*. Throughout the nineteenth century, Russia's eastward push into Central Asia evoked responses so similar to the excitement produced by the United States' westward expansion that when Fyodor Dostoevsky tried in 1881 to explain what the Asian frontier meant to Russians, he used an analogy that would surely have resonated with Turner: "Asia for us is that same America which we still have not discovered. With our push towards Asia, we [too] will have a renewed upsurge of spirit and strength."

What distinguished the American pioneers in their covered wagons was not their resilience and enterprise, but the rewards open to them for their resilience and enterprise. Russia's pioneers occupied the land either as peasants with no ownership rights or as gentry holding it as part of the imperial government's administration. In New France and New Spain, land was distributed to the colonizers within a fundamentally feudal framework. Even in Canada, where property rights grew from the same basis of English common law as in the United States, the land was sold subject to the government's overriding jurisdiction in a way that profoundly affected the availability of frontier territory. To put it crudely, what made the frontier experience described by Turner uniquely American was the fact that it took place inside the American frontier.

In the aftermath of 9/11, the frontier of the United States suddenly appeared desperately vulnerable. With the pressure of immigration, legal and illegal, adding to the threat of terrorism, many commentators have chosen to portray the border as all that divides a healthy, democratic society from a hostile world. The desire to protect this seemingly fragile line of defense has become a driving force in foreign and domestic policy.

The history that made the frontier tells a different story. The intrinsic strength of any boundary is what lies behind it. Today's national boundary is only the outermost layer in a pattern of lines that make up the political fabric of the United States. These lines represent a unique constitutional system. They evolved from the clash of sectional interests and competing visions of the way American society should develop. They contain within them values of personal liberty and public democracy that were hammered out as the nation grew. And they began with that first precisely calculated line that Andrew Ellicott helped draw through the Alleghenies.

CHAPTER I

THE FIRST FRONTIER

*Nothing will produce Bad History more directly nor bru-
tally, than drawing a Line, in particular a Right Line, the
very Shape of Contempt, through the midst of a People,—
to create thus a Distinction betwixt 'em,—'tis the first
stroke.—All else will follow as if predestin'd, unto War
and Devastation.*

THOMAS PYNCHON, *Mason & Dixon*, 1997

THE SUMMER OF 1784 was unusually cool, and it followed an exceptionally cold winter. Benjamin Franklin noted that the strange
weather had begun in the fall of 1783 and occurred not just in North America but throughout Europe. Its most peculiar aspect was a grayish film that
colored the sky.

"This fog was of a permanent nature," he commented. "It was dry, and
the rays of the sun seemed to have little effect towards dissipating it, as they
easily do a moist fog, arising from water. They were indeed rendered so faint
in passing through it, that when collected in the focus of a burning glass
they would scarce kindle brown paper."

With typical insight, Franklin conjectured that the atmosphere might
have been polluted by a volcanic eruption, although the only one he knew
of had occurred in 1768. In fact the Icelandic volcano of Laki had exploded
in five massive eruptions during the summer of 1783 and continued to pump
out huge quantities of sulfur and other acid fumes until February 1784. As
temperatures plunged, almost one quarter of Iceland's population died from

starvation, the Thames froze over in London, and high in the Allegheny Mountains, heavy clouds and lingering fogs delayed the work of demarcating the boundary between Pennsylvania and Virginia.

For day after day the commissioners were unable even to see the sky, and at night the fog obscured the stars. Once, a party of men were trapped in thick cloud and had to spend a night out on the mountaintop. The next morning the swirling vapor remained so thick that those in camp needed to fire guns to guide the lost scientists back. In his journal, Andrew Ellicott commented wearily on the constant rain and mist that prevented them from observing the heavens. "If we can have clear Weather for two Days, we shall compleat our opperations for this season," he wrote in the fall of 1784. "The sun has shined but twice this week, and then but for a few minutes."

Their task made it essential to be able to see the sun and stars. Surrounded by an uncharted wilderness of steep, tree-covered mountains, they were in effect mariners required to establish both the longitude and latitude of their position in the midst of an expanse without landmarks or charts. Unlike sailors who needed only to know their position to within a few miles, however, the boundary required an accuracy measurable in yards. Their only guide through the trackless wasteland was the hazily drafted charter issued to William Penn in 1681 that decreed that the province of Pennsylvania was "to extend westwards five degrees in longitude" from the Delaware River.

To establish the exact distance on the ground, however, depended on being able to tell the time accurately. Because the spin of the earth carries it through 360 degrees in twenty-four hours, or fifteen degrees in one hour, the time at the most westerly point in Pennsylvania was bound to be exactly twenty minutes later than on the Delaware River. Thus, it was necessary to be able to compare the times in both places at the same exact moment, and that meant using the stars and planets as a heavenly clock. Consequently the eight boundary commissioners appointed by Virginia and Pennsylvania to run the line had split into two teams, one to take observations from the summit of Mount Welcome, estimated to be approximately the right distance from the Delaware, and a second to work on the river itself.

The expertise in celestial timekeeping was still new. It depended upon the remarkable *Nautical Almanac*, compiled annually in Britain from 1766

by the Reverend Nevil Maskelyne, the astronomer royal. This contained tables showing where the moon would be at different times of day and night
relative to the sun, the planets, and thirty-six different stars throughout the
coming year. In theory, an observer had only to note the time when the
moon was a given distance from a particular planet, and to look up the time
when the moon and planet would be in the same relative position at London's port of Greenwich—the point from which Maskelyne made all his
calculations—to work out how many degrees he was to east or west.

In practice, however, repeated observations were needed to reduce errors.
Then complex calculations had to be made to allow for atmospheric distor-
tion and for the distance of the observer from the center of the earth. The
British Board of Longitude estimated that all the figuring would take four
hours to complete after the time spent taking the initial lunar observations,
but with good instruments, with repeated measurements to average out errors,
and with unremitting care over the mathematics, it was possible to achieve an
accuracy measurable not in miles but yards or even feet (see appendix).

Blessed with formidable gifts of concentration and clear thought, and
cursed by an almost neurotic fear of failure, Andrew Ellicott might have
been born for such a task. To belong to the Ellicott family was to carry a desire for precision in the blood.

The first Ellicotts, including an earlier Andrew, arrived in America in the
1730s, and, as Quakers, almost inevitably settled in Pennsylvania. Like
other members of the Society of Friends, he and his family fitted easily into
the orderly structure created by William Penn for the colonists. Solebury
Township in Bucks County, where they lived, could have served as a show-
piece for his "holy experiment" in harmonious living.

In 1681, within weeks of receiving a charter from King Charles II awarding
him an area of land in North America named Pennsylvania, Penn had ordered
his agent "to buy land [round the future Philadelphia] of the true owners
which I think is the Susquehanna people." As a result, Pennsylvania, which to
Charles II was no more than a map reference to pay back a debt owed to Penn's
father, appeared to most foreign observers as the ideal example of benign colonization. In the years ahead, the great Swiss philosopher Emmerich de Vattel,
whose 1758 textbook on international law, *Droit des gens; ou, Principes de la loi*

Andrew Ellicott

naturelle (Law of nations or Principles of natural law), was taken by the Founding Fathers as the ultimate authority on the subject, would cite Penn as the "laudable example" of how title in a new land should be transferred.

Other colonial proprietors followed the same policy, most notably Roger Williams in Rhode Island and the Calvert family, who owned Maryland. Indeed the importance of having clear title to the land they took from Native Americans pushed all governments into coming to some form of agreement involving purchase. The sale of this property to settlers was needed to pay the costs of administering the colony. Until the eighteenth century, the land offered for sale was confined to the coastal regions and rivers, and the number of immigrants was so small that colonial governments could restrict settlement to those territories. In Maryland, Virginia, and the Carolinas, settlers were required to choose their property, then have it surveyed and registered in the colonial land office before they could buy title to it. Governments in New England and Pennsylvania and, sometime later, in Georgia adopted a different method—pre-surveying the land, usually in rectangles, before selling it. Permission to settle beyond the surveyed area was rarely given.

Like other colonial governments, Penn's imposed its own conditions on would-be settlers. They were required to buy property that had already been bought from the Indians and measured out in neat rectangles by Penn's surveyor, Thomas Holme, a condition that virtually restricted early immigrants to Philadelphia and two other counties on the banks of the Delaware River, Bucks and Chester.

"Our townships lie square," Penn explained to potential migrants in 1685, "generally the Village in the Center; the houses either opposite or else opposite the middle, for near neighbourhood . . . so that the neighbours may hold one another in a Christlike manner and praise God together, and that they may accustom their children to do the same."

Solebury Township followed this pattern exactly with its forty-acre, rectangular common at the center, and four houses arranged on each side close to one another, while the fields and meadows spread out behind in a broadening wedgelike shape. The Ellicotts would have paid the Penn family a quitrent of six shillings per hundred acres or about twenty cents a year for their land and, like their neighbors, formed part of a society dominated by Quaker morality and ruled by edicts such as those against selling alcohol and bearing arms that emerged from the Friends' monthly and quarterly meetings. The colonial assembly representing the interests of the colonists was controlled by this Quakerocracy.

The Ellicotts had good reason to feel grateful for Quaker values. Ellicott's father, Joseph, and two uncles were all left destitute as children by the death of their parents and were farmed out to be raised by other Quaker families. Proof that craftsmanship was in their genes came when all three turned out to have a gift for making machinery. Originally apprenticed to a weaver, Joseph's true talents emerged when he went to work for a millwright named Samuel Blaker in Bucks County. Although a family history described Joseph as "a smart, active boy and a good weaver, but his mind ran wholly on mechanics," the records of the local Society of Friends indicate that his mind must occasionally have been diverted from engineering. In the summer of 1753, Blaker's daughter, Judith, was reported at the quarterly meeting to be pregnant, and that Joseph Ellicott had admitted to the "misdemeanour."

They were married in December, a month before the child was born, and although this regularized the situation officially, in the conventional society of Bucks County the sight of an eight-months-pregnant bride must have produced gossip as remorselessly as a stream turning a mill wheel. Whatever her character was like before, as a mother Judith Ellicott showed herself to be anxious and demanding to a degree that left an indelible mark on her first child, Andrew.

Ellicott was born in January 1754, and proof that he had inherited his father's engineering skill comes from a remarkable musical clock, now kept in the Smithsonian Museum, that he helped Joseph to build. It not only told the time, but displayed the movement of the planets and played a selection of twenty-four popular tunes. Looking at the rows of tiny cogs and wheels provides a sobering reminder that, until the first machine tools arrived in America in the nineteenth century, each one had to be

Joseph and Andrew Ellicott's clock

cut and ground by hand, and that Ellicott was just fifteen when they were made.

This masterpiece was the forerunner of more than a hundred other clocks on which father and son worked together, and the collaboration suggests a close relationship between them. Their intimacy stood in sharp contrast to Ellicott's chilly relations with his mother. It is difficult to know how Judith Ellicott managed to alienate her sons. All four left home as soon as they could, and the few writings of hers that survive are filled with recriminations against them for failing to write or visit her. "As thou art the only son of 4 that seems to retain me in their remembrance," she wrote bitterly to her third boy, Joseph, "I would wish thee therefore to write often—I should be very glad to hear from David Ellicott [her second son] as he has never yet favourd me with one single line. I have nothing particular to write."

Her driven personality was presumably responsible for the anxious tone that appears like a trademark in Ellicott's reports, so that even late in life, he often sounded more like a boy accused of laziness than a respected astronomer. "I never was caught in bed by the sun," he protested when questioned about the time he took over his surveys, and referring to his months running the line of the Spanish frontier, "I never went to bed before midnight and was up every morning, one excepted, at five o'clock."

That double impulse toward perfectionism—craftsman's pride compounded by underlying anxiety—was an essential ingredient in Ellicott's mastery of celestial observation. Every aspect of it, from the initial adjustment of clocks through measuring the relative positions of different stars and the final comparisons with existing records and astronomical tables, required a relentless, even finicky attention to detail that he possessed to an inordinate degree. But as he showed when he first left the civilized society of the coast in 1784 to begin work in the mountains, he detested disorder.

"I do not like the Country," he told his wife, Sally, in a letter from Oldtown, Pennsylvania, or, as he put it, "the Very Border of the Wilderness." He was repelled by the untamed country, by the bug-infested inn, and by the lawless behavior of the inhabitants, epitomized by a shoot-out with a gang in which "one of their Company was Killed in Robbing a House in the neighborhood where I was."

Experience would change his hostility to such affection that he could not refuse any chance to escape into the wilderness, but that first encounter was significant. It was impossible to grow up in eighteenth-century Pennsylvania, even in the harmonious surroundings of Bucks County, without being aware of the disorder that convulsed the western part of the colony.

Before the Ellicotts first arrived in Pennsylvania, immigrants from Germany and northern Ireland, attracted by its policy of religious toleration, were beginning to flood into the foothills and the valleys of the Alleghenies, far beyond Penn's squares. In 1724, James Logan, one of the Penn family's lieutenants, wrote in exasperation of "these bold and indigent strangers, saying as their excuse when challenged for titles [to property], that we had solicited for colonists and they had come accordingly." Others were ruder, calling them *banditti* or "Goths and Vandals" or, most plainly of all in Benjamin Franklin's phrase, "those mad People on the Frontier."

They quickly exposed one of the major shortcomings of Penn's colony— no one knew its true extent. As specified in its royal charter, its boundaries were to extend as far north as "the three and fortieth degree," somewhere beyond Albany, New York, and as far south as the fortieth degree of latitude (north of Maryland's present northern boundary), where it would intersect "a Circle drawn at twelve miles distance from New Castle [on Delaware Bay]." Although this might have looked clear enough in London, it bore no relation to the realities of American geography. Drawn out on the ground, Pennsylvania's southern border would have left Philadelphia deep inside Maryland.

Pennsylvania was not unique in being overwhelmed. In the Carolinas, the proprietorial system of surveys gave way under the flood of incomers in the 1720s, and as Carolinians moved south into Georgia in search of uncontrolled land, they then brought down James Oglethorpe's idealistic dream of building a society there for veterans and poor farmers around pre-surveyed property. Similar strains emerged in New York as new arrivals clashed with well-established patroons over the extent of their manors and their powers in the Hudson Valley, and on the New England frontier the governments of Massachusetts and New York found their power flouted by settlers moving into what would become Maine and Vermont. But nowhere did the impact of immigration occur more dramatically than in Pennsylvania.

No one exploited the confusion of Pennsylvania's frontier to better effect than Thomas Cresap, the founder of Oldtown. It pointed to the change in

Ellicott's feelings about the wilderness that when he next passed through the settlement, he called on the man who was a legend among the frontier's banditti, and living testament to the importance of clearly defined boundaries. "He is now more than 100 Years Old," Ellicott reported with admiration, "he lost his Eye sight about 18 months ago, but his other faculties are yet unimpaired, his sense Strong and Manly, and his Ideas flow with ease."

By most accounts, Cresap was in fact ninety-one and would live another five years, a tribute to the healthiness of the outlaw's life. From his arrival in 1710 as a sixteen-year-old from England, his past was a history of eighteenth-century America. He came as part of the flood of immigrants that overwhelmed the colonial governments' plan to settle them within defined limits. For the first time, most of the immigrants to British America were not English and were quite prepared to defy the English common law that underpinned the ownership of land in the colonies. People with names like Paxton, Crockett, and Houston from northern Ireland, and German-speaking Wetzels and Weisers from the Rhine Valley, simply ignored the law and divided up the western land themselves.

Taking advantage of the confusion, Cresap made a specialty of registering in Maryland claims to land that lay in Pennsylvania and selling it to German immigrants whose lack of English left them unsure of what was happening. In his home state of Maryland his activities earned him the name the Border Ruffian, but elsewhere he was more generally known as the Maryland Monster. He farmed one such claim himself, close to Oldtown and lying well inside modern Pennsylvania. In 1736, when Pennsylvania settlers who had bought the same land from the Penns arrived to claim their property, Cresap drove them off at gunpoint. The settlers retaliated by bringing in Sheriff Samuel Smith, from Lancaster, Pennsylvania, but he was greeted by bullets flying round his ears. On his next visit, the sheriff took the precaution of arriving with a posse of fifty-five heavily armed farmers and succeeded in cornering Cresap and fourteen companions in his house.

According to Smith's deposition, when called upon to surrender, "Cresap, with several horrid oaths and the most abusive language against the proprietor and people of Pennsylvania, answered that they should never have him until he was a corpse." A furious gun battle broke out, and as the sheriff later recalled, "They would not surrender but kept firing out 'till the House was set on fire." Despite his defiant promise, Cresap was among the outlaws who eventually gave themselves up, singed but unrepentant. As he was marched in chains through the streets of Philadelphia, he exclaimed to his guard, "Damn it, this is one of the prettiest towns in Maryland!"

Released from his shackles, Cresap decided to settle legally in what would become Oldtown. According to his own account, he used to offer such hospitality to the Indians who came into western Pennsylvania to trade furs that they called him the Big Kettle. The seventeen-year-old George Washington, who took shelter with Cresap in 1749 on his way to survey Lord Fairfax's five-million-acre estate across the border in Virginia, recorded being "agreeably surpris'd by the sight of thirty odd Indians coming from War with only one Scalp. We had some Liquor with us of which we gave them Part. It elevating there Spirits put them in the Humour of Dauncing of whom we had a War Daunce."

The war party almost certainly came from the Iroquois federation in the north, who were then engaged in long-term hostilities with the Catawbas

A memorial to Thomas Cresap in Cumberland, Maryland

in the Carolinas. But the contact with the Europeans was not untypical of what modern historians call "the borderland," the ill-defined area where squatters, natives, fur dealers, and missionaries lived and bred, absorbing each other's culture, and forming an uneasy, mutually rewarding, self-adjusting society.

What none of them could have known was that the arrival of the apprentice surveyor working on behalf of his patron, Lord Fairfax, presaged the end of the borderland. The huge Fairfax property, almost amounting to a separate colony, stretched across the northern neck of Virginia up to the Maryland and Pennsylvania boundary. The previous year his lordship had employed Thomas Lewis and Peter Jefferson, father of the future third president, to map the southern boundary of his gigantic holding. With its outer limits defined, the task of his new team of surveyors, including Washington, was to establish who was living on the Fairfax estate and how many acres they were working. Squatters paid no rent, and Fairfax's kingdom had to turn a profit. Within a few years of Washington's survey, dozens of illegal settlers had either been evicted or had signed ninety-nine-year leases paying a rent of about $5 annually for one hundred acres. Fully surveyed, the Fairfax property might produce as much as $250,000 a year. The lesson did not go unheeded.

"The greatest Estates we have in this Colony," the young Washington confided to a friend, "were made   by taking up & purchasing at very low rates the rich back Lands which were thought nothing of in those days, but are now the most valuable Lands we possess." In 1752, at the age of twenty, he purchased 1,459 acres in the Virginia Piedmont, the first step in a career of land-dealing that eventually made him owner of more than 52,000 acres spread across six different states.

Washington was not alone. A growing number of speculators had come to the same electrifying conclusion that immigration was pushing up the value of land. In 1751, Benjamin Franklin predicted that the population of the colonies would double to 2.6 million by 1775. The logic was inescapable, and it led to the formation of more than a score of land companies to survey and register claims to unowned territory. The soaring value of property left no room for Cresaps or other banditti. In colonial legislatures throughout British America, landowners, speculators, and proprietors brought pressure to bear to impose order in the backcountry. New counties were created, new county surveyors were appointed to register properties—among them George Washington for Culpeper County, Virginia—and new county sheriffs were sent to exact taxes.

From the point of view of the eastern politicians and speculators, this was no more than a restoration of government. To western farmers forced to travel up to one hundred miles to pay taxes or appear in the new county courts, it appeared like tyranny. Thus during the critical years before 1775, when resistance to London's attempt to impose taxes on its colonists began to create a distinct sense of being American, two different struggles for democracy were building against two different governments—the colonies against Britain, and western farmers against east coast authority.

In Pennsylvania, the attempt by Penn and his heirs to regain control from Cresap and his fellow banditti began with a prolonged legal battle in London to have the boundaries in their royal charter drastically revised. Not until 1732, long after Penn's bankruptcy and death, did they succeed in persuading the Court of Chancery in London, the senior English court dealing with equity and contracts, to shift the entire commonwealth of Pennsylvania south. The northern boundary was now to be the forty-second degree, and the southern was to run exactly fifteen miles south of Philadelphia along a line that did intersect the arc round New Castle.

Once more, what seemed clear-cut on a map proved impossibly complicated on the ground. For thirty years the difficulties of drawing straight lines, arcs, and tangents across the curvature of the earth and getting them to meet at the right point bamboozled the best surveyors in the colonies. Eventually Penn's heirs agreed with the Calverts, the earl of Baltimore's family who owned Maryland, to share the enormous cost of having a definitive boundary run by the eminent British astronomers Charles Mason and Jeremiah Dixon.

The pair had already worked together on the world's first great international scientific project, the observation of the 1761 transit of Venus across the face of the sun, an enterprise that involved scientists from most of the nations of Europe. Although they had successfully viewed the phenomenon from Cape Town, the restless, inquisitive Mason, forever striking up conversations with strangers and traveling, as he put it, "for curiosity to see the country," appeared to be an odd match with the dour, concentrated Dixon, who rarely stirred far from his precious telescopes. Nevertheless, in the four years from 1763 to 1767, the two of them not only untangled the geometrical confusion around Philadelphia, but more impressively solved the problem of running an accurate parallel or line of latitude due east-west, a feat never before accomplished in North America, and probably not in Europe.

Although the United States' longest frontier is a parallel, as are the top and bottom borders of many states, it is easy to overlook the fiendish challenge each presented its maker—to draw a straight line across the rounded surface of the globe. At sea, mariners would simply follow a constant compass bearing—270 degrees to head due west—but on land ordinary compasses became too unreliable due to magnetic variation, the presence of mountains, and the action of other distorting forces. Until the invention of the solar compass in the 1840s, a boundary-maker intent on the utmost accuracy had to rely on celestial navigation. But then, a second, more horrible predicament presented itself—on the surface of the three-dimensional earth the shortest line between two points lying east and west of each other is not straight but, paradoxically, a curve, known as a Great Circle or a circumference of the globe (see appendix).

The complex solution found by Mason and Dixon was to run a Great Circle from one observation point to the next, a distance of about a dozen miles, then track back along the line of the parallel. Close to a week of star sightings was required at each point, and the use of the finest scientific instruments in the British empire. The combined wealth of the Penns and Calverts had purchased for them a six-foot-tall, vertically suspended telescope known as a zenith sector, a transit and equal-altitude instrument, and a Hadley quadrant, all constructed in brass and mahogany with achromatic lenses by John Bird, instrument-maker to King George III. On April 5, 1765, accompanied by more than one hundred surveyors, chainmen, axmen, and laborers, Mason and Dixon set out with these instruments from Alexander Bryan's farm, exactly fifteen miles south of Philadelphia, to run Pennsylvania's boundary along the line of latitude 39 degrees 43 minutes 18.2 seconds (39° 43′ 18.2″) north of the equator.

More than two years and 230 miles later, their star-derived line reached another, older boundary high in the Appalachians, the Catawba warpath. This one, established by violence and bloodshed, marked the limit of the influence of the Six Nations, who had guaranteed their safety, and the beginning of Delaware and Shawnee territory. On October 9, 1767, Mason noted in his journal that their Six Nations guards "would not proceed one step further westward," and so, on a bluff overlooking the Monongahela River, a mound five feet high was built to mark the end of what would become known as the Mason-Dixon Line.

The effects of the new boundary were immediately apparent. Both the Penns and the Calverts began to survey and sell land near the border, and squatters already there were forced to buy or rent, and most significantly to pay tax. A principle had been established that would last throughout American history and remains strictly applicable to present-day problems on the border with Mexico—a clear-cut boundary is government's first weapon in the control of its citizens.

When delegates from Virginia and Pennsylvania met in 1779 under the auspices of the Continental Congress to resolve the problem of their undefined border, they decided to take the Mason-Dixon Line as their starting point. There were practical reasons for the choice—the line already covered about two thirds of what would be the southern boundary of Pennsylvania—but it also recognized that the states were now heirs to many of the colonies' concerns. They too needed clear-cut borders not just to keep the peace between them, but to enable each to govern efficiently, to register property, to tax citizens, and to enforce law and order. But the colonial governments had been able to call upon the huge scientific resources of Britain built up around the Royal Society since its foundation in 1660, and to make use of the most advanced scientific instruments from London manufacturers who were supported by royal patronage and the demands of the industrial revolution, while the states had to find their own homegrown scientists who were often forced to rely on instruments they had made themselves.

The long apprenticeship that Andrew Ellicott had served as a clockmaker was essential to his later success as an astronomer. The skills in one field transferred easily to another, and Ellicott's craftsmanship as an instrument maker is still evident in some beautifully made telescopes that he built and that are now held in the Smithsonian Institution.

He owed his interest in the subject to the chance arrival in Solebury of an intense young Irishman called Robert Patterson, whose talents led soon after to his appointment as professor of mathematics at the University of Pennsylvania. For a brief period, however, he ran a school in the area. In June 1769 when the planet Venus made a transit across the face of the sun, Patterson supervised his fifteen-year-old student's observation and timing of the event and evidently mixed instruction on the astronomical significance of the occasion—in theory it would allow the distance to the sun to be calculated—with his own political feelings of hostility to the British and affection for his new country.

"You were in your young days my preceptor," Ellicott wrote Patterson much later. "It was under your guidance that my mind was directed to the love of my country and to science. If I have been useful, you are entitled to the credit, if not it has been my own fault."

The depth of Patterson's influence was apparent when the Revolution broke out, and in defiance of his family's pacifist beliefs, Ellicott volunteered for military service. By then the entire Ellicott clan—Joseph, his two brothers with their families, and their children's families—had moved south to Maryland in search of a site where they could build new, more powerful mills. Barely ten miles from the rapidly growing port of Baltimore, they found the perfect position on the fast-running Patapsco River, and the successful flour-milling operation they set up would eventually grow into Ellicott City, now part of the conurbation of Greater Baltimore.

Newly married to Sarah Brown, invariably known as Sally, the dark-haired daughter of a Bucks County farmer, Ellicott joined the clan reluctantly. "[Pennsylvania] is my native country," he used to insist, "and I love it above any other." His time on the Patapsco was cut short by his decision to serve in the Maryland militia. This evidently caused such a painful rift in the family that in 1779 Ellicott chose to move away with his wife to live in Baltimore. In the end he was not called upon to fight, but his father died before they could be reconciled, and by the time peace came, Ellicott had made a reputation in a quite different field from milling.

In October 1780 the *Maryland Journal* announced the publication of a pamphlet with the compendious title of *The Maryland, Delaware, Pennsylvania, Virginia, and North-Carolina Almanack, And Ephemeris, For the Year of our*

Lord, 1781. Below this came a cover line stating, "The Astronomical Part of this Almanack was calculated by the ingenious Andrew Ellicott, Esq; of Baltimore-Town."

Almost from their first appearance in 1639, almanacs were, in the words of a critic, "the most despised, most prolific, most indispensable of books, which every man uses, and no man praises." Their popularity came from telling people what they needed to know. Weather forecasts, the times that the sun rose and set, and the dates of the full moon were mixed in with the sort of useful wisdom about romance and good manners that would once have been passed on by word of mouth. Old folk sayings such as "Where there's Marriage without Love, there will be Love without Marriage" and "Fish & Visitors stink in three days" were retailed, as though new minted, in Benjamin Franklin's *Poor Richard's Almanac*, earning him a name for sagacity, not to mention sales of ten thousand copies a year.

The *Maryland Almanack* followed the usual pattern, but Ellicott's ephemeris, literally a calendar showing the predicted movements of the stars, planets, and moon through the year, was exceptional in the detail it offered. The times of sunrise and sunset were exact enough to set an unreliable clock by, and those who wanted to travel by the light of a full moon, like those who believed the weather turned at the new moon, could find the information they needed. But there was more esoteric information, the positions of all the known planets at different times of the year, eclipses of Jupiter's moons, and the longitude of Baltimore.

The following year Ellicott felt confident enough to produce on his own *The United States Almanack for the Year of our Lord* 1782, which, coupling science with patriotism, he explained was also *the Second after Leap-Year and the Sixth Year of American Independence*. Letting rip with the astronomy, he not only offered the usual "motions of the sun and moon, the true places and aspects of the eight planets, the rising and setting of the sun, and the rising, setting, southing and age of the moon," but a forthcoming transit of Mercury across the face of the sun and, what could only have been of interest to the most expert navigators, "lunations, conjunctions, [and] eclipses." Many of these figures were based on calculations in Maskelyne's *Nautical Almanac*, but checking the sightings and adjusting the values for Baltimore required the exact observation and meticulous mathematics of a genuine astronomer. Apart from Patterson's initial instruction, his expertise was self-taught.

Readers of the *United States Almanack* were also given a recipe for pickling ham, a forecast of "hard thunder" on June 13, an indispensable money-changing table for converting the different currencies of Pennsylvania, New-Jersey, Delaware, and Maryland, and a prophecy that "[Britain] will be forced to acknowledge this year, in the fullest manner, the Independence of these United States, which will be recognised by all the powers of Europe." This was a shrewd prediction, but it was the accuracy of the astronomical predictions that gave the Ellicott almanac its authority. It was sold in cities across the middle states, and by the time that peace came, its compiler's reputation had spread beyond Maryland, to Philadelphia and to Richmond, Virginia.

The invitation from James Madison to become one of Virginia's boundary commissioners reflected the rarity of astronomers in the state. Although Ellicott was also a surveyor—he earned the bulk of his income from the practice—it was his ability to calculate his exact position from the stars that made him indispensable on the frontier in 1784.

Always careful to the point of anxiety about the accuracy of his work, he had loaded his mules with tents, a chest of clothes, a *Nautical Almanac*, and his instruments—a Dollond telescope, a Hadley's sextant, and several Ellicott chronometers—everything that he deemed necessary for the job of running the border. But compared with what a real Virginian would have taken, he was traveling light.

The boundary commissioners' column that crossed the Monongahela River in July to set up an observatory on the highest mountain in the area might have served a small army. Led by a score of axmen to hack a path through the forest, the four commissioners were accompanied by four surveyors, an indeterminate number of laborers, servants and slaves including a dairymaid, and a line of horses and mules carrying beds, tables, chairs, chinaware, tea, wine, and rum, and some of the finest scientific instruments in the United States wrapped in feather-down quilts, as well as a small herd of cows. This last item was recommended as a prophylactic against scurvy by the medical expert William Buchan, who wrote that "milk alone will frequently do more in that disease than any medicine." He said nothing about whipping up wine with the milk to make a frothy syllabub, and since the plain-living Pennsylvanians would hardly have entertained such an idea, it must have been another Virginian extravagance.

Differences of temperament triggered tensions between the restrained Ewing, a stern Presbyterian minister renowned for preaching the virtues of prudence and economy, and the exuberant Madison, soon to be an Episcopalian bishop and notorious for his eagerness to embrace whatever was new in science, economics, and politics. He won plaudits for teaching the first course in political economics in the United States based upon Adam Smith's *The Wealth of Nations*. But respectable folk like Ewing felt Madison went too far when he celebrated escape from King George's rule by amending the second sentence of the Lord's Prayer to read "Thy republic come, thy will be done" and by preaching not about the kingdom of heaven but about "that great republic where there is no distinction of rank and where all men are free and equal."

As the days dragged on, and the expense rose, the heads of the two delegations began to quarrel about money—"The old Gentleman had always too much the Idea of a *good Bargain* about him," the outgoing Madison complained of Ewing's Pennsylvanian stinginess. But nothing could be done until Ellicott and Thomas Hutchins had made a sufficient number of observations synchronized with timed eclipses of Jupiter's moons. They required two months to make about forty usable sightings. By late September, no amount of wine and syllabub could keep the warring academics out on the cold mountain any longer, and both abruptly left for the warmth of their college fires.

The bad weather put the whole expensive project at risk. All through the gray summer and foggy fall, the second team of boundary commissioners on the Delaware River had been engaged in the same work as those on the mountain. To establish the five degrees of distance between them precisely, the observations of both teams had to be made at exactly the same moment, hence the need to time them not simply by chronometers, but in relation to the regular eclipses of Jupiter's moons that were visible on the river and on the mountain. The second team enjoyed two advantages: down by the river the weather was clearer and warmer, and their observations were supervised by Pennsylvania's David Rittenhouse, the outstanding astronomer in the United States, whose genius, according to Thomas Jefferson, was comparable to that of George Washington and Benjamin Franklin. "We have supposed Mr Rittenhouse second to no astronomer living," he wrote in

Notes on the State of Virginia, "and that in genius he must be the first, because he is self-taught."

The critical test of Ellicott and Hutchins's work came in September 1784, when Rittenhouse and the Virginia mathematician Robert Andrews came west from the Delaware River to compare results. The Delaware team had managed to make almost sixty observations timed against Jupiter's moons, nearly twice as many as those made on cloudy Mount Welcome, and there must have been some anxious moments as they checked their figures. Fortunately a sufficiently large number of observations were found to be synchronized exactly for the scientists to calculate their relative positions.

The results showed that the Mount Welcome observatory was plotted a few hundred yards too far west. Having made adjustments for the error and for the exact distance that Rittenhouse's observatory had been from the Delaware River, the commissioners put down a temporary marker. Then the cavalcade of axmen, laborers, wagons, and cows descended from the mountains to begin marking out the line westward from where Mason and Dixon had left off in 1767.

They used the same laborious method of determining the line as their predecessors, following a Great Circle and tracking back along the parallel. But barely two months later, on November 12, having labored half the summer and all the fall, Ellicott, Rittenhouse, and the others arrived at the summit of yet another mountain "of a most stupendous height" and allowed themselves a look back at the long, straight line they had cut through the trees. "The Prospect is noble and romantick," Ellicott confessed to his journal. "From this mountain we could Trace our Parallel of Latitude for 40 Miles, which to a Mathematician is a prospect the most pleasing of any other."

Just four days later this was followed by another triumphant entry. "Today we fixed the South West Corner of Pennsylvania which is a Squared White Oak Post," he wrote, as though the state had until then been something loose and liable to blow away. "The Completion of this Business has given me the greatest Satisfaction possible, not merely on account of the Accuracy, but the prospect of a speedy return to my Affectionate Wife and Family who are continually on my mind."

Today a global positioning system can work out almost instantly what took Ellicott and his fellow commissioners close to five months, but he had good reason for satisfaction. Rather than relying on binary oscillations within

The stone demarcating the southwest corner of Pennsylvania from the northwest corner of
Virginia (now West Virginia), laid by Thomas Hutchins in 1785

a silicon wafer to mark the passage of time, he had built his own pendulum
clocks and checked their accuracy against the sun at midday and the
eclipses of Jupiter's moons at night. Instead of electronic signals bounced off
artificial satellites, he had deduced his position by observing the eccentric
passage of the moon in relation to the stars, then checking its position
against the established locations contained in complex astronomical tables.
The result was a neat line roller-coastering through the valleys and mountains of the Alleghenies that left no doubt where Pennsylvania ended and
Virginia began. Proof of its accuracy comes from modern GPS observations
indicating that the square post was hammered in just twenty-three feet too
far to the west.

CHAPTER 2

THE BOUNDARIES OF POWER

*So great moreover is the regard of the law for private prop-
erty, that it will not authorize the least violation of it; no,
not even for the general good of the whole community.*
WILLIAM BLACKSTONE, *Commentaries on the
Laws of England*, 1765–69

IN THE EARLY summer of 1785, Ellicott and Rittenhouse returned to the
frontier to define the western boundary between Pennsylvania and what
is now West Virginia. Ewing and Madison had decided not to repeat their
uncomfortable experience on the frontier, leaving the two astronomers as
the senior commissioners for Virginia and Pennsylvania. Since they agreed
totally on the supreme importance of exactness, there was little chance that
the fractious atmosphere surrounding the southern boundary would be repeated. But for a technical reason, the 1785 expedition turned out to be one
of the happiest in Ellicott's experience.

The new line began at the squared post hammered into the ground in
November 1784 and ran due north to the Ohio River. Running a meridian,
or north-south line, posed none of the complications of a parallel. Because
meridians pass through both north and south poles making a circumference
of the earth, they are automatically Great Circles. Thus a straight line
heading due north on the globe will also be the shortest distance between
two points. The astronomy and calculations that went with establishing due
north were equally straightforward.

The critical observation was the moment that the Pole Star and the star

Alioth in the constellation of the Great Bear were directly aligned one above the other. In the course of a given interval of time, worked out again by the *Nautical Almanac*, the Pole Star would then move to exactly true north. To craftsmen such as Rittenhouse and Ellicott, achieving exactness in this operation was simply a pleasure. Their celestial observations and calculations were repeated every few miles so that the compasses used by the surveyors responsible for cutting the path of the boundary through the forest were constantly corrected for the most minute local deviations.

"The greatest Harmony possible subsists among us," Ellicott told Sally in June 1785, a month after setting out. "Mr Rittenhouse in perticular frequently complimented me which I confess has somewhat raised my Vanity because he is commonly sparing but where he conceives there is real Merit."

Enthusiastic as ever, Madison had insisted during the winter that William & Mary College should award Ellicott a degree as master of arts, despite his lack of formal education. He was immensely proud of the honor, but in the presence of David Rittenhouse, he recognized that he stood on a lower level.

At the age of fifty-two Rittenhouse was at the height of his fame. Modern commentators downplay Jefferson's estimate of him as one of the world's leading scientists, regarding him rather as a superb observer and craftsman, but in the context of his time, working in a new society without public funds or patronage to support him, he stood supreme. Not only had he constructed two elaborate orreries, he had organized Pennsylvania's observation of the 1769 transit of Venus with meticulous attention and been appointed professor of astronomy at the University of Pennsylvania after the Revolution. To Ellicott he was a hero, the epitome of the speculative, open-minded scientist, and he set himself to emulate Rittenhouse's emotional detachment and attention to detail. What he could never match was his hero's whimsical, inventive humor.

Rittenhouse's health was always delicate, "never absolutely well nor absolutely ill," by his own description, and his character had developed a self-absorbed, solitary edge. Although his chief employment was secretary to the Pennsylvania Treasury, he had seized the chance as a boundary commissioner to exchange "the plagues of office" for the solitude of the mountains. To his irritation he discovered that they were filled with axmen, chainmen, and surveyors who "hindered me from enjoying a lonely walk or some passage in

David Rittenhouse

Milton—or perhaps a loll on my bed. Nay, even our fellow-commissioners, the Virginians, I mean; I sometimes wish their wine was better and flowed more plentifully: not that I might enjoy it with them; but that I might enjoy myself the more alone, alone."

From this general condemnation, he allowed one near exception—"I could almost call Mr Ellicott a congenial soul," he admitted—but it was hardly as warm as Ellicott's reference to "my wise and learned friend, the ingenious Mr Rittenhouse." Nevertheless, they often hiked off into the mountains together to search for fossils and to explore rivers to their source or, in Rittenhouse's words, until it was decided "we should proceed no further for if we did, we should in all probability find some of the water-goddesses—perhaps stark naked and fast asleep."

In the unexplored wilderness of the Allegheny Mountains, Ellicott and Rittenhouse steered through a mountainous sea whose waves were fifteen hundred feet high and stretched to the horizon. "Conceive a Country composed of an infinite number of very High Hills, narrow at the Top, and only seperated by narrow Crevices or Chinks, as for Vallies, there is none," Ellicott told his wife. "These Hills are Inhabited at present by Bears, Wolves, Deer, &c. and covered by Tall Timber and Weeds; among the latter are many Serpents, particularly the Rattle Snake." Even today the dirt roads in west Pennsylvania follow the chinks east to west, and anyone who tries to follow the commissioners' trail has to negotiate the steep waves on foot, scrabbling up through the undergrowth and tightly packed trees, and skidding down the pebbly slope on the other side.

They lived from what the land provided, sometimes eating well off venison and bear meat, followed by gooseberry tart, and sometimes surviving on bread and water. The insects stung and bit as viciously then as now, but in far greater numbers. "When we leave our Tents, we have to muffle up our Faces and keep Gloves on our Hands to oppose their attacks," Ellicott noted. Clouds of horseflies tormented their horses until they broke free of their tethers and ran into the smoke of the campfires for relief. Poison ivy was everywhere, and Ellicott, who had been allergic to it since childhood, found his hands gloved in blisters.

If it was bad for the scientists—and gazing at a dawn star while mosquitoes whined and gnats stung demanded superhuman concentration—the conditions were tougher still for the axmen. Taking down trees in the virgin forest was both hard and dangerous work, and every few days limbs were crushed and broken by falling trees. When William Cross died after being hit by a heavy branch, Ellicott recounted, "We buried him in the Middle of the Line, and raised him a Monument of Logs—such a Circumstance in the Wilderness is attended with an uncommon degree of Solemnity."

In the face of such hardship, the axmen grew rebellious, but like commanders of a ship at sea, the commissioners could not afford to show weakness. "This evening we discovered a mutiny among our People," Ellicott wrote on June 7, "but for prudential reasons did not give any intimation of the discovery." Ellicott had appointed his younger brother Joseph as surveyor, a position that made him responsible for the axmen. Although both Joseph and Benjamin, the youngest brother, had been trained by Andrew in the use of sextant and chronometer, and could make satisfactory telescopes and compasses, neither had their eldest sibling's flair. Throughout his life, however, Joseph Ellicott enjoyed a reputation as a man who drank and worked hard, and he took no prisoners in such a situation. "Early this morning, one Brown who was the soul of the Mutiny received a severe cudgelling," Ellicott noted in his journal, "and several others [were] discharged—we then went with the remaining hands and began work."

Approaching the Ohio Valley, where the population of settlers and squatters was rapidly growing, they recruited more axmen, and the work accelerated. On August 24, Ellicott wrote to his wife, "We now lie encamped on the Banks of the Ohio and intend Crossing it Tomorrow. The Boundary Line between the States of Virginia and Pennsylvania was compleated on the 23rd Day of this Month. It makes a most beautiful appearance from the Hills being between 60 and 70 Miles due North and cut very wide and perfectly streight."

The result of their grueling work was dramatic. Ever since Fort Pitt had been erected in 1759 on the fork of the Ohio and Monongahela rivers, the entire surrounding territory had been regarded as belonging to Virginia. Lord Dunmore, the last royal governor of the colony, had garrisoned the fort with Virginia militia, and settlers registered their claims with the Virginia Land Office and paid Virginia taxes. The beautiful, straight line cut by Ellicott and Rittenhouse changed all that. It crossed the Ohio River almost thirty miles downstream from Pittsburgh, opposite the modern city of East Liverpool, thereby transfering thousands of settlers and several hundred square miles of territory to Pennsylvania.

This was more than an administrative adjustment. For both government and governed, the establishment of a secure border had a profound impact. For Pennsylvania, it marked the start of a process of definition that would free it from claims to its territory by Virginia, New York, and Connecticut and see its area grow by about fifteen million acres, approximately 20 percent larger than its size as a colony. As the limits of its jurisdiction were defined, the state would behave like its colonial predecessors, surveying territory, establishing new counties, taxing inhabitants, and selling unoccupied land to pay its debts. In the gilded drawing rooms of Philadelphia where politicians and financiers gathered, this would appear to be a highly desirable outcome.

In the Ohio Valley, the new boundary took on a different aspect. Although it changed nothing in the crumpled landscape or the harsh living conditions, it radically altered the lives of frontier families by placing them within Pennsylvania's jurisdiction. The new state's taxes were higher than Virginia's, and the burden of them much harsher because Pennsylvania, unlike Virginia, was short of hard currency with which to pay. On the frontier, people were accustomed to grow or hunt most of what they needed and to barter for the rest. But taxes had to be paid in cash, and lack of coins and bills forced many to sell the livestock and tools on which they depended for survival. "Very few in this Town can procure Money to go to market," a Pittsburgh merchant complained in 1786. "And as to pay . . . a Debt, it is out of the question."

Yet if they failed to pay, county courts issued orders to seize property, and the county sheriffs who executed them charged the debtors a heavy fee for the service. Resentment against Pennsylvania's government soon began to grow in the western counties that were created inside Pennsylvania's new state boundary. By the late 1780s, the farmers were beginning to fight back, digging up the roads and felling trees to prevent law and revenue officers from entering the counties. It was not the first time that the backcountry had staged a revolt against eastern governments.

In 1765, North Carolina's western farmers found themselves enclosed within the extensive new counties that the colonial government created in its drive to impose order in the backcountry. Forced to travel long distances to the county courts to register properties and pay taxes, the farmers were further incensed by the actions of unpaid county sheriffs, who charged often outrageous fees for duties such as serving subpoenas and collecting fines. To regulate the activities of these officials, "these cursed hungry caterpillars, that are eating and will eat out the bowels of our Commonwealth," as George Sims of Granville County described them, and to force the eastern-based government to listen to their demands, the western farmers organized themselves into armed bands called Regulators. In language strikingly reminiscent of that of Samuel Adams in Boston lambasting British taxation in the name of liberty, the spokesman for the Regulators, Herman Husband, appealed to his followers, "How long will ye in this servile Manner subject yourselves to Slavery? Now shew yourselves to be Freemen, and for once assert your Liberty and maintain your Rights."

Wherever colonial governments moved to establish their control of the western lands, they adopted similar tactics and encountered similar resistance. The struggle focused on the county because, except in New England, where township meetings ran affairs, government for the backcountry happened at the county level. The colonial legislatures created huge new counties to cover the backcountry, then appointed county justices of the peace to administer the law, county surveyors to register and measure out property, and county sheriffs to ensure that lawbreakers were arrested, justice was done, roads were maintained, taxes were paid, and men of military age showed up for service in the militia.

Significantly neither in North or South Carolina, where Regulators were also formed in reaction to the corruption and ineffectiveness of county officials, nor in western Pennsylvania, where the "Paxton Boys," a force of around fifteen hundred western farmers, rode east out of the Appalachians to terrorize Philadelphia in 1764, nor in upstate New York, where the Green Mountain Boys drove government surveyors off their land at gunpoint, nor in the other colonies where resistance occurred, did the frontiersmen want less government. What they demanded was better representation in the colonial legislatures to give them parity with the east coast, and at county level, more efficient courts, less oppressive officials, and fairer taxes.

The independence that the American states won from London's government did not remove the backcountry farmers' resentment against eastern rule. State governments in general, and Pennsylvania's in particular, might be more democratic than their colonial predecessors, but power was still weighted toward the eastern elite, and the taxes bore even more heavily on western farmers. There were just twenty-eight hundred taxpayers in Westmoreland County, one of the new counties created inside Ellicott and Rittenhouse's frontier, but in six years the county court issued no fewer than sixty-one hundred orders to sequester their goods and land for nonpayment of taxes. Such pressures soon brought the backcountry revolution to life again.

The lines that Ellicott and Rittenhouse were drawing had another effect that went far beyond Virginia and Pennsylvania and was to dominate U.S.

politics for generations to come. The boundary not only promoted greater administrative efficiency and social injustice within the states, it was helping to transform them into nations.

This was an unintended consequence, yet an inevitable one given the amorphous nature of "the United States of America" as constituted by the Articles of Confederation and Perpetual Union. Neither seven years of warfare nor military victory had resolved the contradiction implicit in the title of the founding document—was the new entity to be a confederation or a union? It left a constitutional vacuum that the increasingly powerful states threatened to fill.

The United States, by contrast, barely existed except in the Articles of Confederation and the Declaration of Independence. Given Hugo Grotius's definition that the people constituted the nation, it was significant that someone as ardently patriotic as Thomas Jefferson should have consistently referred to Virginia as "my country" in *Notes on the State of Virginia* in 1782. Even in the deepest crisis of the war, New Jersey troops reporting for duty at Valley Forge had initially refused to swear allegiance to the "United States of America" because, as they said, "New Jersey is *our* country."

In peacetime, the very word *American* began to lose the popularity it had gained in the lead-up to hostilities when people used it primarily to distinguish themselves from Loyalists. But it had never appeared in the Declaration of Independence or the Articles of Confederation. The adjective commonly used by Congress to denote a national identity or collective purpose was *Continental,* as in Continental Congress, and only to distinguish the new national force created in 1783 from Washington's old Continental Army was it given the name of the First American Regiment.

In December 1783 when George Washington resigned his command after supervising the army's dissolution, the substance of the confederation was reduced to little more than the score or so of delegates then meeting in Maryland's Senate chamber in Annapolis, a near bankrupt Finance Department, several overseas delegations arranging trade agreements or foreign loans, and the U.S. post office. "The United States of America" had borrowed money from foreign bankers, exchanged ambassadors, won a war, and accepted the Treaty of Paris, by which the British conceded defeat, but the title represented the multiplicity of states rather than a single entity.

Although the territory between the Appalachians and the Mississippi had been ceded by the British to "the United States," most of the southern half was claimed either by Georgia, or by settlers pouring out of North Carolina and Virginia into what would become Tennessee and Kentucky. North and west of the Ohio River the land was threatened by British and Spanish forts and occupied by hostile Native Americans, and in Congress influential voices held that it belonged to each of the thirteen states rather than to the central government. Without a physical presence to represent the idea of "the United States," and a frontier to define its extent and power, it was hardly surprising that when people spoke or wrote the phrase, they used the plural tense rather than the singular.

Were it not for Thomas Jefferson, "the United States" would have had no territory in which to create a national identity to rival that being created for the states. In a few tumultuously creative months, he not only gave the concept a physical reality but mapped its future territorial expansion until it did indeed become the United States of America.

In the fall of 1782, Jefferson's thirty-three-year-old wife, Martha, died giving birth to their sixth child, and he was overwhelmed by a paroxysm of grief. His daughter Patsy vividly recalled how he "was led from the room [where she died] in a state of insensibility by his sister, Mrs. Carr, who, with great difficulty, got him into his library, where he fainted, and remained so long insensible that they feared he would never revive. The scene that followed I did not witness, but the violence of his emotion, when almost by stealth, I entered his room at night, to this day I dare not trust myself to describe."

For weeks afterward, he could scarcely bring himself to talk to anyone, and the smallest reminder of her death left him overcome. "I ever thought him to rank domestic happiness in the first class of the chief good," wrote his kinsman Edmund Randolph, astonished at the extent of his misery, "but scarcely supposed that his grief would be so violent as to justify the circulating report of his swooning away whenever he sees his children."

The very violence of his emotion, however, throws a light on the inner being of this most private, enigmatic character, "the Great Sphinx of American history," as his biographer Joseph Ellis termed him. It indicates better than Jefferson's public explanation the depths of passion that drove his political commitment, a passion he did his best to conceal. His preferred guise was to present himself not as a politician or statesman, but as a scientist. "Nature intended me for the tranquil pursuits of science, by rendering them my supreme delight," ran one typical explanation, "but the enormities of the times in which I have lived have forced me to take a part in resisting them and to commit myself on the boisterous ocean of political passion."

There was enough truth in this to make it plausible. His command of botany, the most highly developed science of the time, was evident in his *Notes on the State of Virginia* and spilled over into his magpielike hunger for information about anthropology, agriculture, and meteorology. He took huge pride in succeeding Franklin as president of the American Philosophical Society. And to a degree unmatched by the other Founding Fathers, he saw democracy and the new United States of America as opportunities for experiment.

In June 1783 he accepted an appointment to fill a vacancy as one of Virginia's representatives to the Continental Congress, and the ferocious energy Jefferson brought to bear on the vexed question of the territory beyond the Appalachians would only have surprised someone ignorant of the ex-

Thomas Jefferson

treme passion of which he was capable. Among the ideas he wished to test out were the advantages of a decimal system of measurement and a decimal coinage, the abolition of primogeniture or inheritance of property by the eldest child, the guarantee of religious liberty, the restriction of ownership of property to one generation, the limitation of contracts to a period of thirty years, the universal provision of free education, and many others more or less practicable. The most far-reaching of his theories, however, concerned the distribution of land and its effect upon society.

His model was an image of Saxon England, before the Norman conquest in 1066. Instead of the Normans' feudal belief that the land fundamentally belonged to the king and that all his subjects merely held their share of it from him, the Saxon system was based on alodial law, which held that the person who worked the land owned it outright. "The opinion that our lands were allodial possessions is one which I have very long held," Jefferson told his friend Edmund Pendleton in August 1776. Just as the Norman system was conducive to monarchy because it concentrated ownership of the land in one person, the Saxon structure created democracy by making ownership available to everyone. "Is it not better now that we return at once into that happy system of our [Saxon] ancestors," he suggested to Pendleton, "the wisest & most perfect ever yet devised by the wit of man?"

In the model he envisioned, the political structure would be built up from the community based on the local "hundred" or county with its own court and administration. And its values would be derived from the independent-minded yeomen farmers who owed no allegiance or obligation for the soil they worked and owned outright.

When he was elected governor of Virginia in 1779, Jefferson immediately took advantage of the opportunity to try out his ideas. In a general reform of its system of government, he presented to the legislature a bill based on the Saxon system that, he explained, "proposed to lay off every county into hundreds of townships of 5. or 6. miles square," each of which would be a center of government with a school, a court, constables, and elected officials. The bill failed, but he never deviated from this basic model. Thirty years later he still insisted, "These little republics would be the main strength of the great one . . . Could I once see this I should consider it as the dawn of the salvation of the republic, and say with old Simeon, 'nunc dimittas Domine.'"

Most delegates thought of the western lands simply as a source of funds. They could be offered as collateral, Thomas McKean suggested in a letter to Samuel Adams in 1782, arguing that Dutch bankers would be prepared to lend more money "if we can obtain an indisputed title to the Western lands that belonged to the Crown of Great Britain." Jefferson, by contrast, was determined that they should also provide the structure for his republic of yeomen farmers. "It is the manners and spirit of a people which preserve a republic in vigour," he wrote. ". . . While we have land to labour then, let us never wish to see our citizens occupied at a work-bench, or twirling a distaff."

Constitutional thinkers from the Roman poet Virgil to Vattel had suggested similar ideas, and the social thinkers of the Scottish Enlightenment, whose books bulked large on Jefferson's shelves, made the same argument. In the words of Francis Hutcheson, doyen of the group and Adam Smith's teacher, "Lands must be dispersed among great multitudes, and preserved (thus dispersed) by agrarian laws, to make a stable democracy."

What made Jefferson's ideas different from those of every theoretician before him was not their originality but the staggering opportunity that independence presented for putting them into practice. Once the British had ceded their land between the Appalachians and the Mississippi, he and other delegates to the Continental Congress faced the challenge of dealing with four hundred thousand square miles of territory. No scientist could have asked for a better chance to experiment.

In the winter of 1783–84, Congress met in the elegant, azure-painted surroundings of the Senate chamber in Maryland's State House in Annapolis, a space not much bigger than a schoolroom, but easily large enough for the twenty or fewer delegates who usually attended. There, seated in four rows at plain wooden desks, they settled the business of the Union. In any company, Jefferson's vision and intellect would have stood out; in that small circle he was exceptional. And in those months, perhaps more than at any other time in his life, he was driven to bury in public business the private agony of Martha's death. "I can accept all of the economy of life," he once confessed to John Adams, "and all of human activities and human nature except one thing: what is the use of grief?"

Amidst a mass of other work ranging from the ceremonial to be observed when General Washington came to resign his commission as commander in chief through reports on the Treaty of Paris and the organization of central government—by his estimate it could be run by just forty-eight employees at an annual cost of $68,525.33—Jefferson found the time and energy to formulate the pattern for the territorial growth of the United States. It is no exaggeration to say that his three reports on the western lands rank alongside his role in writing the Declaration of Independence and his negotiation of the Louisiana Purchase in terms of their impact upon the long-term development of the United States.

To have a value, the backlands had to be transformed into property. Every delegate understood the process of purchase, survey, and sale, but disagreed about the way each step ought to be carried out. Should individuals be allowed to buy land from the original inhabitants, or only the states, or even the United States alone? Was it to be surveyed before being sold, or afterward? And should the shape of the property be determined by the seller or the buyer?

Quick answers were urgently needed. Both the states and the United States had run up huge debts during the war and looked to the western lands as their one source of capital. But already lines of wagons and convoys of flatboats were carrying pioneers westward to occupy lands without paying anything for them. Their occupation threatened not only the United States and the individual states, but the claims of more than a dozen speculative land companies that had been granted the right before the Revolution to survey and acquire most of what is now Kentucky, Ohio, Indiana, Illinois, and Michigan. Despite the urgency, all the players faced an immovable obstacle that Jefferson himself had created.

In 1781, while Jefferson was governor, Virginia had ceded to the United States its charter claims to the vast expanse of territory beyond the Ohio River that fanned out to the north and west as far as the shores of Lake Superior. The purpose was to persuade Maryland to sign the Articles of Confederation, and later that year Maryland did indeed finally join the other twelve states in the Union. One condition was attached to Virginia's cession—the territory was to become national domain, with the United States alone possessing authority to make treaties with the native inhabitants and acquire land from them. Since this would rule out the claims of other states and of the land companies, the overwhelming majority of dele-gates in Congress wanted the Virginia delegation to drop its condition.

Instead of backing down, Virginia's delegates decided, as Jefferson put it, to "leave it to [the other delegations] to come forward and tell us they were ready to accept." The stalemate lasted until February 1784, when the Vir-ginians upped the stakes. The next time they were asked to give way, Jeffer-son noted, "We replied, 'No,' if the lands are not offered for sale the ensuing spring, they will be taken from us all by adventurers; we will, therefore, put it out of our power, by the execution of a deed to sell them ourselves, if Congress will not."

Fearful of losing the backcountry altogether, the other delegations agreed to accept Virginia's conditions on March 1, 1784, a date that marks the creation of the first U.S. Territory. Amongst the rapid sequence of events that saw the Revolution's explosion of ideas solidify into nation-hood, the importance of giving physical expression to the idea of a single United States has often been overlooked. In the short term, the national domain beyond the Ohio River simply offered the central government the prospect of a source of income, but in the long term it was to be the arena in which an American identity was formed.

Beyond the borders of the thirteen states now lay an area where an inde-pendent jurisdiction would have to be created, with laws and values outside their control. Eventually too this territory would have to have its own bor-ders, because, like William Penn, the United States needed to retain con-trol of the distribution of its land. The solution that Jefferson proposed was as draconian as that of any colonial proprietor. In March and April 1784, two committees under his chairmanship produced reports on the way the central government's land was to be surveyed and sold, and the steps by which its frontier communities were to become new states.

The committee on the disposal of land drew up a draft ordinance recom-mending that before the land was sold, the United States should survey it in squares with the lines running north-south and east-west. This shape was simple to measure out and easy for the would-be purchaser to check—or in Jefferson's words, "the democratic principle is contained in the dimension of the units which facilitated for persons of ordinary attainment the computa-tion of area." It would then be given to veterans in exchange for military warrants or sold on the open market but in a way that prevented speculators from making a profit. In other words, only true settlers would be enabled to buy. And not only would the land beyond the Ohio be pre-surveyed, it was to be preboundaried into states. Jefferson's committee on the Western Lands proposed eleven of them, boasting exotic names such as Cherronesus, Pelisipia, and Polypotamia, with boundaries as straight-lined and rectangular as boxes except where the Mississippi or some other river offered a more convenient frame.

When the population within any of these squared-off Territories reached twenty thousand, the inhabitants could apply to join the Union as a state, but Congress alone could decide upon their admission. Until then the Territories were to be ruled by officers appointed by Congress. The new states were to be admitted subject to five provisions. They would "forever remain a part of the United States of America," and their inhabitants and territory were to be subject to "the Government of the United States in Congress assembled." They would have to shoulder a proportion of the huge wartime debts incurred by the original states. Their government had to be "republican in form," and "after the year 1800 of the Christian aera, there shall be neither slavery nor involuntary servitude in any of the said states."

That Jefferson, the great champion of state and county government, should have proposed these authoritarian measures is a deep irony, for nothing did more to increase the strength of the federal government as the nation exploded across the continent in the nineteenth century. Their prescriptive nature made possible the orderly expansion of the United States, but it also fueled the rivalry between slave and free economies to win control of the increasingly powerful federal government with its iron command over the newly established Territories. To both sides, the survival of slavery in the years before the Civil War seemed to depend on Congress's capacity to prescribe the conditions under which a new state was to be admitted to the Union.

The renewal of his appointment to be minister to France in mid-1784 ended Jefferson's annus mirabilis as congressional representative. In his absence his colleagues stripped his program of some of its decoration—the great state of Cherronesus hit the cutting-room floor as did his attempt to have the backlands measured out in newly invented decimal units, and most fatally of all, the proposal that slavery should be abolished after 1800 was voted down. Nevertheless, on May 20, 1785, when the Congress passed into law the "Ordinance for ascertaining the mode of disposing of Lands in the Western Territory," the substance of Jefferson's scheme was preserved—the squares, the progression of frontier communities into states, and the draconian steps to instill democracy and republicanism within the boundaries of what were now to be "not less than three nor more than five States."

CHAPTER 3

THE STATE AS NATION

The Westphalian system had its limits. For one, the princi-
ple of sovereignty it relied on also produced the basis for ri-
valry, not community of states; exclusion, not integration.
NATO SECRETARY-GENERAL JAVIER SOLANA,
Symposium on the Treaty of Westphalia, 1998

IN NOVEMBER 1785, Andrew Ellicott arrived in Philadelphia to stay
with his friend David Rittenhouse. Compared to Baltimore, whose fourteen thousand citizens lived for the most part in wooden houses fronting un-
paved streets, Philadelphia was a metropolis. It boasted a rapidly growing
population of forty thousand people, and such modern services as a public
library, fire engines, a public hospital, a university. The grid of streets that
Thomas Holme had laid out between the Schuylkill and Delaware rivers
were not only cobbled but swept clean. Even Thomas Jefferson, who decried
the "disgusting monotony" of its brick houses, did not hesitate to recom-
mend its shape for the future capital of the United States.

The purpose of Ellicott's visit was to seek election to the American
Philosophical Society, the leading scientific body in the United States, and
he was received, as he proudly noted, "with particular marks of distinction"
by his old frontier acquaintance, the university provost Dr. John Ewing, and
the professor of mathematics Robert Patterson, who had first introduced
him to astronomy. A still greater accolade was an invitation from the
seventy-nine-year-old Benjamin Franklin, founder of the Philosophical Society, to spend the day in his little house and tell him about the "Western

Country." Evidently overcome by the honor, Ellicott could remember nothing of their hours together except that "this venerable Nestor of America"
had insisted on shaving himself, commenting that happiness at his age consisted in not having to rely on others to do the job for him.

These tributes to his expertise made the edgy temper he displayed during
his visit all the more surprising. His unease arose partly from financial pressures. "I expect my pay this Season," he had optimistically assured his wife
during the summer, "will enable me to put Affairs in such a situation that
Money will never have charms sufficient to draw me from you another Season." But Virginia's generous wages had quickly been eaten up by his large
family. In nine years of marriage, six children had been born, and although
one died from yellow fever—to the family's profound but stoical grief—Sally's
attraction and her husband's passion had their inevitable consequences.
Pregnancy promised to restore the number of children by December. To
support them, he had to work harder than ever through the winter months,
not only producing the annual almanac with all the astronomical calculations involved, but taking a job as professor of mathematics in the first public academy to be opened in Baltimore.

The contrast between his harried existence in the provincial confines of
Baltimore and that of Rittenhouse living comfortably on a state treasurer's
salary, with two grown-up daughters from a previous marriage helping their
stepmother tend to all his needs, aroused Ellicott's envy. "Although my
Family are constantly in my mind whenever I am distant from them," he
confided to his journal when it was time to return to the sound of wailing
babies in Baltimore, "I nevertheless cannot help feeling some emotion leaving a Family where I have lived with so much ease and satisfaction."

More generally, Philadelphia's wealth evidently brought to the fore the
underlying insecurity that was an integral part of Ellicott's character. When
a longtime acquaintance, John Fitch, inventor of an early steam-driven boat,
stopped him in the street to ask for his help in promoting the idea, Ellicott
angrily dismissed the request as "persecution." A few days later he became involved in an absurd altercation in a bookshop. He was browsing through the
shelves when he overheard a fancily dressed young man—"a Maccarony
looking fellow," in Ellicott's opinion—complain to the storekeeper that
Americans had no taste for "the fine arts." At this, Ellicott waded in because,
as he put it, "I conceived myself aimed at by the general reflection."

"Upon my word, sir," he recalled himself saying to the man, "it is very Extraordinary to pass a general reflection upon all the Natives of the United states—to condemn the whole Continent for want of a taste in the 'fine Arts' as you term them. If you had a genious for visiting our seminaries of Learning and possessed one degree of Candour, you would freely Acknowledge your Mistake." Standing over six feet tall, weather-beaten and hardened by six months in the wilderness, an irritated Ellicott must have been a daunting proposition because the young man took one look at his unexpected adversary, "saw my ill-nature and left."

In some circles in Philadelphia, however, the young man's sophistication would have been applauded. Wealth had produced a definable aristocracy in the city marked out by their fine carriages and matched horses, their extravagant parties, and a studied form of superiority known as "English manners." "If you are not in fashion," Lord Chesterfield had written in *Letters to His Son*, "you are nobody," and the book's popularity in Philadelphia showed that high society there paid heed to its snobbish wisdom.

It was the Revolution that had allowed this circle to grow wealthy, and many were connected to the Philadelphia trading house of Willing and Morris. This was the conduit used by the Committee of Secrecy set up by Congress in 1776 for the purchase of strategic materials, and from the first season of fighting when the company had made a risk-free gain of nearly $50,000 on a contract for supplying gunpowder, the profits had poured in. The accumulation of money allowed Robert Morris to lend directly to Congress and underwrite other wartime loans, a situation that led to his appointment as superintendent of finance in February 1781. Three months later, Congress granted him a charter to set up the Bank of North America with other Philadelphia merchants, and from then on disentangling private interests from public became impossible.

Robert Morris's partner, Thomas Willing, was the president of the bank, and other friends and business colleagues, such as Judge James Wilson and John Swanwick, were directors. The most glittering couple in Philadelphia's social set, William and Anne Bingham, belonged to the same network. Anne's father was Tom Willing, and William had been sent to the West Indies with government funds to buy materials for the war effort and had come back so wealthy that he could afford to build himself a Pennsylvania house modeled on a duke's mansion in London.

By Chesterfield's definition, Ellicott's poverty and provincialism made him a nobody, hence no doubt his crossness with the "Macarrony." But between Philadelphia's wealthy aristocracy and the unfashionable nonentity, there was this connection—when peace came, the city's moneyed classes piled into land speculation, and the boundaries that Ellicott drew were, for a time, to make them wealthier than ever. The process had already begun in the west. In the summer of 1786 it moved to the north, allowing Pennsylvania to establish its jurisdiction over the most fiercely disputed frontier in the United States.

The long and bloody quarrel over the Wyoming Valley in northeast Pennsylvania began in the 1760s when the Connecticut-based Susquehanna Land Company sold land there, based on Connecticut's charter granting it all the territory westward from Narragansett Bay to "the South Sea." Well-watered with good pasture, the valley was an oasis of farmland straddling the Susquehanna River, and customers had quickly moved in. The land lay within the territory of the Six Nations, the confederation of Native Americans headed by the Iroquois who held sway over a gigantic swath of terri-

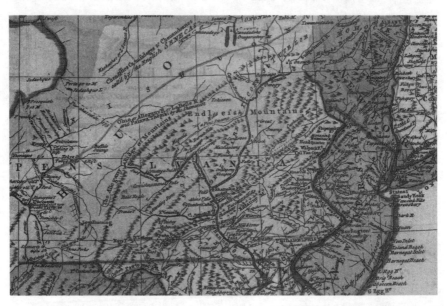

The Wyoming Valley in northeast Pennsylvania, separated from Connecticut
by New York Territory

tory south of Lakes Erie and Ontario. Both the land company and the Penn family claimed to have bought the valley from the Six Nations, and when farmers from Pennsylvania tried to move in during the 1770s, the Connecticut settlers drove them off at gunpoint.

Belatedly, Connecticut asserted that the valley lay within its jurisdiction, ignoring the hundred miles of New York that lay in between. An enraged Pennsylvania sent in six hundred militia to assert its authority, and with the United States already at war with Britain, they fought a daylong battle with the settlers in December 1775. Fearful that the strife would spread, the Continental Congress issued a grave warning of the danger of civil war breaking out "between the inhabitants of the colony of Pennsylvania, and those of Connecticut." Under intense pressure, the two sides agreed to allow Congress to adjudicate, and in 1782 it decided that the valley belonged to Pennsylvania, a verdict Connecticut was persuaded to accept in exchange for almost five million acres in the territory beyond the Ohio River.

The settlers were not so easily won over. In 1784, their anger erupted into armed rebellion when Pennsylvania's commissioner declared that titles to land registered in Connecticut were invalid. Whatever Congress might decide, on the ground the Wyoming Valley would remain contested land until it was established beyond doubt that it lay within Pennsylvania's northern boundary. In accordance with the amendment to Penn's charter, the line was to run due west from the Delaware River along the parallel forty-two degrees north.

Where astronomy was concerned, Ellicott's insecurities vanished. When Virginia's boundary with Pennsylvania reached the Ohio River in August 1785, his job as the state's boundary commissioner abruptly ceased, because at that point Virginia's northern frontier followed the Ohio down to the Mississippi. The western edge of Pennsylvania, however, was to continue northward until it reached Lake Erie. Summoned back to Philadelphia by the demands of the state treasury, Rittenhouse demonstrated his confidence in Ellicott's skills by recommending him as his replacement. Thus, as they crossed the river, Ellicott immediately became a Pennsylvania boundary commissioner, a change he welcomed, because as he wrote in his diary "[Pennsylvania] is my native Country, and I love it beyond any other."

For ten more weeks, Ellicott continued to push Pennsylvania's western border north toward Lake Erie until, in November, he and his assistant, Andrew Porter, were halted by boggy ground and freezing weather. The simplicity of running a meridian meant that the final miles to the lake could be run the following year by Porter alone. Ellicott's expertise was needed for the demands of running a parallel, the line that separated Pennsylvania from New York.

His solution to the complexities of demarcating an east-west parallel was to make Ellicott's reputation as the leading boundary-maker of his day. He not only dispensed with Mason and Dixon's elaborate method of combining the Great Circle and parallel, he also replaced the magnificent, six-foot-long zenith sector they and the 1784 boundary commissioners had used. Although its huge magnifying power offered incomparable accuracy, it was cumbersome to transport and operate—suspended vertically, it required the observer to lie on the ground to view stars directly overhead—and in 1786 the cash-strapped states could afford neither the time nor the money.

The method that Ellicott suggested as an alternative possessed the American virtues of simplicity and practicality. It depended upon his growing expertise as an astronomer, and a more convenient telescope. Instead of following a carefully navigated Great Circle with the inevitable delays of setting up the six-foot sector, he proposed to run a speedy guideline, also known as a random line, due west for twenty miles with a surveyor's compass in approximately the right direction. Then, using a more portable zenith sector, Ellicott planned to establish their exact longitude and latitude with a barrage of moon and star observations—he would carry out more than fifty on average at each stopping point—after which the necessary corrections would be made to bring them onto the parallel (see appendix). From there, the actual boundary could be run back along the parallel to the starting point, with markers inserted at mile intervals.

His growing authority was demonstrated when he convinced both Rittenhouse and New York's boundary commissioners, including the highly regarded young Simeon de Witt, the state's surveyor general, to adopt this untried procedure. But de Witt's agreement came with a reservation. "He says they must depend on us for the necessary Instruments," Rittenhouse reported. They needed in particular a zenith sector that would be more easily managed than Bird's delicate monster, but still powerful enough to see stars as they reached their highest point in the heavens at any time of night or day.

A zenith sector

The solution lay close at hand. Rittenhouse had constructed a five-foot sector, but it lacked an achromatic lens, which was needed to eliminate the rainbow flare that plain glass produced. Manufacturing such a lens was beyond the capacity of American technology, but at his own cost Ellicott bought one imported from England by an amateur astronomer in Philadelphia and adapted Rittenhouse's instrument to take it.

The work delayed their start until July, and the tensions over Ellicott's impending departure continued to build until, for the only time in their marriage, his wife broke down completely. By then Sally was pregnant again and already caring for six children under the age of eleven. She was evidently in tears when Ellicott left, and the letter he wrote the day after his departure suggests the sort of strain that running a boundary inflicted on both of them.

"My dear, In consequence of your distresses and anxiety about my journey and absence," he wrote, "my mind is agitated beyond anything I have experienced before, and had not my honour and reputation and perhaps liberty depended upon the execution of this business, I should have returned home to breakfast. We are both young and have a young family to provide for, you have won more than your part, and I am desirous to do mine. If you knew how much my happiness depends upon your peace of mind, I think you would be reconciled to this little, temporary separation."

Ellicott's sympathy was unmistakably genuine, but it was not just financial pressure that drove him out into the wilderness. This boundary was his project. The zenith sector that he had bought from Rittenhouse with magnificent disregard for the family's rocky finances was his. Most important, the method was his. Indeed, the way in which the Pennsylvania–New York boundary was run would become the prototype for nearly all subsequent east-west borders in the United States, including its immense frontier with Canada.

The advantages of Ellicott's method were immediately apparent. In 1786, the commissioners succeeded in running the first ninety miles of Pennsylvania's northern border from the Delaware River as far west as the Tioga River in less than three months. Clearly marked "with substantial milestones," it showed beyond doubt that the disputed Wyoming Valley was part of Pennsylvania. Their progress was accelerated by the effectiveness of the Rittenhouse sector, which proved to be a masterpiece of craftsmanship. Incorporated into it was the maker's own device for making the crosshairs in the focal lens. Instead of the usual strands of silk thread, which, however fine to the naked eye, appeared ropelike to astronomers trying to measure star locations precisely, Rittenhouse used the thread from a spider's web, an innovation that allowed unprecedented refinement of observation. When a survey team went over their line in 1881 using modern instruments, it found that Ellicott's system had tracked the parallel with exceptional accuracy.

The political consequences were immediate. The Pennsylvania assembly promptly created an immense administrative area, named Luzerne County, between the Delaware and Tioga rivers, including the Wyoming Valley. Then it sent in surveyors and a new set of commissioners to supervise the election of an assemblyman, sheriff, and other law officers. The commissioners were headed by the stern disciplinarian Colonel Timothy Pickering, formerly Washington's adjutant general, and when Ellicott returned in 1787 to continue the boundary, he was delighted to find that Pickering had already opened the county court and set in motion the administration of the newest part of Pennsylvania.

"This circumstance must be one of the most pleasing kind to the honest, well-disposed People of this unhappy District which has constantly been in a state of anarchy and confusion since its first settlement," he wrote approvingly to Sally. "General Pickering has great merit for his exertions in bringing the Connecticut claimants to a quiet submission to the jurisdiction of the State."

Not everyone agreed. To Ellicott's annoyance, anti-Pennsylvania rebels broke into the stables and stole the boundary commissioners' bridles and saddles. But he was correct in supposing that there was a strong inducement for Yankee settlers, legal and illegal, to metamorphose into Pennsylvania farmers, however unappealing the prospect of paying taxes and accepting the authority of sheriffs and revenue men and county courts. The classic answer came from John Locke in the second of his *Two Treatises on Government*: "The great and *chief end* therefore, of Mens uniting into Commonwealths, and putting themselves under Government, *is the Preservation of their Property*."

No doubt the Butlers—by far the most numerous family living in the Wyoming Valley—remained more inclined to reach for their rifles than their books when they saw the Pennsylvania judges coming, but their actions illustrate vividly the truth of Locke's diagnosis. So long as Connecticut laid claim to the valley, the Butlers had nominally accepted its authority and registered their titles to valley land with the state. But once Ellicott had run his line, the Butlers and most of their valley neighbors were persuaded to accept government from Philadelphia when Timothy Pickering promised that their title to the land would be confirmed by Pennsylvania. To put the matter crudely, the settlers' allegiances followed their title deeds, and those were now being registered in the Land Office of Pennsylvania.

The other side of Locke's equation was the price that government exacted for securing its citizens' property, and Pennsylvania's protection did not come cheap. The distress suffered by farmers in the newly created western and northern counties was caused not only by the shortage of cash in circulation, but by the power that the state possessed to enforce its demands.

The fashionable set in Philadelphia would surely have agreed with Ellicott's assessment of the benefits that Pickering brought to the Wyoming Valley. In their eyes, government was undoubtedly for the good of all honest people—but it was especially good for those with money.

What gave Robert Morris and his friends a head start in the race to make money when peace came was the simple fact that they had access to large quantitites of gold and silver while the rest of the population had to make do with paper money. To finance operations in the Revolutionary War, all thirteen states and the Continental Congress had issued paper currency in staggering quantities, as much as $400 million in the course of the war. It came in every guise, from interest-bearing bonds to military warrants entitling veterans to hundreds of acres of land. One Philadelphia dealer advertised for sale no fewer than twenty-two different types of bills, warrants, bonds, and certificates. Putting such a flood of money in circulation created galloping inflation. By the end of 1780, the index of wholesale prices in Philadelphia had risen a hundredfold in five years, and the bills themselves had lost up to 80 percent of their face value.

"I lent the old Congress £3000 [about $10,500] hard money in Value, and took Certificates promising interest at 6 per cent," Benjamin Franklin moaned after the war, "but I have received no Interest for several years, and if I were now to sell the principal, I could not get more than 3s 4d [just under 60 cents] for the Pound [about $3.50] which is but a sixth part."

The drop in value prompted many holders of paper money, especially desperate veterans who had been paid in military warrants, to take the loss and sell. Since they were sold for cash, these different forms of currency were soon concentrated in the hands of the wealthy, who bought them for as little as ten cents on the dollar. Of the $4.8 million that Pennsylvania issued in paper money, much of it in interest-bearing bonds, no less than 96 percent was owned by just over four hundred individuals, and fifty percent ended up in the hands of Robert Morris's circle. It was an investment that quickly paid dividends.

Alarmed by the threat of economic meltdown, the states and Congress made desperate efforts from 1780 onward to reduce the amount of paper in circulation. In the space of just five years, wild inflation turned to deep deflation as the supply of money was choked off. New U.S. bills with guaranteed interest payments of 6 percent were offered in exchange for forty old ones, and similar deals were made by the states. To ensure that the interest was paid, taxes were raised to a level where receipts were up to 300 percent higher than in the colonial era. Pennsylvania, for example, took in an average of $205,000 annually in the late 1780s compared with less than $70,000 before the war.

So great was the interest burden, however, it is estimated that up to three quarters of the revenue that states raised went to pay the bondholders. If taxpayers lacked money to pay, county courts would issue orders for the seizure and sale of their goods, which the sheriffs were expected to execute without delay. Shylock-like, the holders of the new bonds insisted upon their interest. "Issue the Executions," demanded one bondholder when a state treasurer was slow to pay the interest he was due. Since $1,000 worth of bonds, purchased for as little as $200, produced an annual income of $60, they were an excellent investment.

Devalued bills could, however, be put to still more profitable use. In every state, land offices were created to sell vacant territory, and they were authorized to accept, in partial payment at least, paper money at face value. Instead of an annual but belatedly paid 6 percent return, a speculator could make an immediate profit of up to 80 percent by exchanging devalued bills for land.

Boundaries were essential to the operation. Apart from confiscated Loyalist properties, the bulk of the vacant land was situated at the extremities of the states far from the populated coast. Hence the pressing urgency to define their landward borders. And what Ellicott and Rittenhouse did for Virginia and Pennsylvania was replicated by other boundary-makers—Simeon de Witt for New York and New Hampshire, Thomas Hutchins and Rittenhouse again for Massachusetts and New York, Richard Henderson and Thomas Walker for North Carolina and Virginia, William Houstoun and John Habersham for Georgia and South Carolina.

The states could not afford to delay. Even in the midst of the war, Virginia decided it was worth trying to run the state's southern border with North Carolina because, as its commissioner explained, "a number of people were settling to westward who imagined they were in North Carolina while we thought they were on the lands reserved for our officers and soldiers." The new Virginia–North Carolina border was supposed to run due west to the Cumberland River along the parallel 36 degrees 30 minutes north, a line that would also divide Kentucky and Tennessee fifteen years later. In their haste, the commissioners failed to solve the problems of running a parallel, and two wavering lines several miles apart were drawn, causing Cresap-like confusion for generations to come. But once the division was in place, Virginia went on a land-selling binge, disposing of three million acres in the west before Ellicott and Rittenhouse had finished establishing its northern border.

North Carolina acted in the same way. "These lands might enable us to pay off a great part of the State debt," her delegates told Congress, "or such debts as have been contracted for Militia service in the State." In 1783, the state sold four million acres of its western land in just seven months, most of it in exchange for military warrants. Altogether more than half the land involved in these two sales, most of it in what would be Kentucky and Tennessee, ended in the hands of big-city speculators or other forms of absentee landowners.

Nevertheless, it was in Pennsylvania that the connection between the boundary-making and the sale of land was most obvious. Even before Ellicott and Porter had completed the western border to Lake Erie, the Pennsylvania Assembly authorized its northwestern territory to be surveyed from "the point where the western boundary of the State crosses the Ohio river." Half of it, termed Donation Lands, was to be allocated to holders of military warrants, and the rest, Depreciation Lands, to holders of the state's devalued currency. In similar fashion, once the northern border reached the Tioga River in 1786, the state's land in Luzerne County was put on sale, bringing the total sold in two years to more than one and a half million acres.

"All I am now worth was gained by speculations in land," Timothy Pickering told his sister in 1796. "In 1785 I purchased about twelve thousand acres in Pennsylvania which cost me about one shilling [about 75 cents] in lawful money an acre . . . The lowest value of the worst tract is now not below two dollars an acre."

Once Philadelphia's moneyed élite began transferring their paper money assets into land, Pickering's investment appeared modest. According to its prospectus, Robert Morris's North American Land Company purchased one million acres in Pennsylvania out of a portfolio that was said to total six million acres. William Bingham acquired another million acres. James Wilson and George Clymer joined Pickering in buying tens of thousands of acres. But all these were dwarfed by the activities of the state's comptroller general, John Nicholson, who eventually owned, through a variety of different companies, some 3.7 million acres.

The injustice of it infuriated Pennsylvanians of all kinds, but especially western farmers. Dozens of petitions were lodged with the legislature denouncing the corruption of a system that promoted gross inequalities "incompatible with the nature of our government." The very heart of the revolution, claimed another petition, was betrayed by the policy of "selling Back Lands in great quantities to companies . . . [a policy] destructive of an essential principle in every republican government: the equal division of landed property."

Their anger and sense of betrayal was shared by frontier farmers throughout the northern states, all of whom suffered from the lack of ready currency. As supplies of both paper and coin slowed and then dried, it produced such a sharp deflationary effect that by 1785 the index of wholesale prices tumbled from above 10,500 in 1780 to close to the 1775 baseline figure of 100. Prices plummeted for all goods but especially farm produce.

In Hampshire County in western Massachusetts, the local newspaper, the *Hampshire Herald*, commented in 1784 that tax collectors had "taken and exposed to sale cattle, and other property, belonging not merely to the poorer people, but to substantial farmers," and reflecting the growing fury among farmers, it warned, "Is there not danger that the powers of Government, stretch'd beyond a certain tone, will burst asunder?"

The crisis was less severe in the southern states where export crops such as tobacco, indigo, and rice brought in cash, and an aggressive policy of selling public lands succeeded in reducing state debts and the amount owed to bondholders. In 1786, taxation in Virginia and Maryland could even be cut. North of the boundary drawn by Mason and Dixon and Ellicott, however, the realization was spreading that the money of the poor was fattening the purses of the rich and thereby creating what one furious writer in Massachusetts called "a self-created nobility."

Seen from the drawing rooms of Philadelphia, however, the states had proved remarkably efficient at squeezing revenue from their citizens without provoking outright revolt. In 1790, figures issued by Alexander Hamilton, secretary of the treasury, indicated that, even in the midst of the recession, with harvests hit by two bad summers, the states had managed to pay off up to half of what they owed in just six years. In addition, the three richest states, Virginia, Pennsylvania, and New York, had bought around $9 million of Continental bills, effectively taking on that amount of U.S. debt.

Clearly defined, ruthless to their citizens, and increasingly powerful, the states pursued their own independent interests with growing disregard for the Union. In 1786, Pennsylvania simply ignored a ruling by Congress that tried to overturn a judgment by the state's courts on the distribution of prize money from the capture of a British vessel. New Hampshire attacked Massachusetts for charging duty on goods imported through Boston, while Massachusetts accused Connecticut of betrayal when it welcomed to its ports British ships that Massachusetts had wanted to keep out. In each case, Congress proved powerless to act. A low point was reached in early 1787 when New Jersey complained that New York was charging harbor fees on vessels from the state, and Congress could do nothing more than advise New Jersey to retaliate. Compared to the vigorous progress of the states, the government of the United States was regressing from ineffectiveness to irrelevance.

Dissatisfaction with the Continental Congress had been apparent from the first days of peace. It had always been difficult to secure a quorum of representatives to conduct business—New Hampshire's delegates arrived late and left early, Georgia's and North Carolina's appeared sporadically, and many simply absented themselves. In 1783, the Treaty of Paris could not be ratified for weeks because the necessary minimum of nine states were not represented, and between October 1785 and January 1786 Congress had a quorum for just ten days.

Its constitutional frailty quickly created a financial problem. The Articles of Confederation prevented Congress from raising money directly and enabled the smallest state, Rhode Island, to veto a proposal supported by a majority of the others to give Congress the right to raise revenue from customs dues. Forced to rely on requisitions from the states, Congress was helpless to prevent its financial demands from being placed a long way behind their domestic concerns. Although part of its requisitions on the states could be paid in paper money, some had to be paid in coin so that international creditors could be paid interest on the loans that they had made to the United States. In 1783, less than 12 percent of the cash requested was paid, and the situation deteriorated as the decade wore on.

In its despairing report of 1786, the Board of Treasury declared that "almost the whole of the Specie required by the Requisition of the 27 September [1785] which amounted to One Million of Dollars is still unpaid." Only seven states even bothered to pass legislation authorizing the taxes needed to raise the money. New Jersey, Delaware, and North Carolina followed Connecticut's example in ignoring the requisition completely, and from South Carolina, which had defaulted completely the year before, the Treasury sadly concluded "no payment can be expected."

Without some other form of income, the United States appeared doomed to default on its payments. And so like the states themselves, it looked to make up the shortfall from land sales. In May 1785, Congress passed a Land Ordinance putting into effect Jefferson's proposal for surveying the western territory beyond the Ohio in squares, and selling it off to the American public. The U.S. Public Land Survey, as it was known, was to begin at the point where the Ellicott and Rittenhouse line cut across the Ohio River, and their former colleague Thomas Hutchins was selected to be in charge of the task.

Signifying that the land strictly belonged to all the states, Hutchins had nominal charge of thirteen surveyors, one from each state in the Union, and an uncounted number of chainmen and axmen to clear a path through the steep, wooded hills beyond the Ohio River. Compared to running a straight boundary across a curved globe, the task could not have been simpler—"grunt survey work" in the words of a modern land surveyor. Hutchins's team was to measure out squares, six miles by six, and subdivide them into thirty-six smaller squares, each covering one square mile or 640 acres in area. There was no need for spherical trigonometry. Because the distances were so small—six miles rather than the hundreds of miles covered by a boundary—they could assume the earth was flat, and so only the most basic instruments were needed, a sextant and a compass for measuring direction, and the surveyor's standby, a twenty-two-yard-long, Gunter's chain, for measuring distance.

The procedure too was straightforward. Two teams of surveyors found due west and due north by compass and by sextant sightings on the Pole Star, then, once the directions were known, took bearings on distant marks, then ordered the axmen to clear paths toward them. When the way had been opened up, the chainmen went to work, measuring the distances to create a grid of squares, each identified in the north/south column as a township and as a range in the east/west row. To avoid the distortions of magnetic north, the surveyors were supposed to take sightings from the Pole Star, but a compass bearing was good enough to establish due west.

With thirteen teams each covering a mile a day, they might have laid out more than six townships in a week. But less than a month after starting, rumors of an Indian attack sent Hutchins and his teams scurrying back to the shelter of Pittsburgh, having covered just four miles. They did not return until the following year, when their rate of work was hardly quicker. In 1787, after two seasons, the land they had measured out was put up for sale. At a time when each state was used to selling more than a million acres of land each year, the United States sold fewer than one hundred thousand acres and raised just $117,108. The consequences of such a failure had been spelled out clearly enough by the Board of Treasury in 1786.

"Nothing occurs as a probable mode of relief, but a Sale in Europe of part of the Western Territory, which has been ceded to the United States," the Board warned. "The more our Reflections are employed on this Subject, the more we are impressed with a Conviction, that nothing [else] can rescue us from Bankruptcy, or preserve the Union of the several States from Dissolution."

In the opinion of many New Englanders, such as Rufus King of Massachusetts, the dissolution of the United States would not have been such a disaster. If the seven northern states separated from the others, he argued, they "would not only remedy all their Difficulties, but raise them to a degree of power and Opulence which would surprize and astonish." Theodore Sedgwick of Connecticut went further, declaring in 1786, "Even the appearance of a union cannot long be preserved." By February 1787, the supreme defender of the United States, James Madison himself, was ready to acknowledge that talk of "a partition of the Union into three more practicable and energetic Governments" had become common enough to be discussed in newspapers.

For at least two years Madison had immersed himself in the study of other forms of government—Poland's elected monarchy, the Swiss republican confederation, the United Kingdom's constitutional monarchy, among others—with the specific intention of reforming the Articles of Confederation. From an initial agreement in 1785 between Virginia and Maryland on common borders and trade in the Potomac River and Chesapeake Bay, he had brought about a meeting of five states at Annapolis in September 1786 to arrange more commercial cooperation at a state level, and better supervision by the central government. This had ended with a decision to discuss reform of the Articles in May 1787 at a convention in Philadelphia, but with no further aim than trying to reform the existing confederation to keep it in existence.

Not all the states were neglectful of the needs of the United States. When Congress requisitioned $3 million from the states in September 1785, most of the middle and southern states, including the Carolinas, Pennsylvania, New York, and New Jersey, let it be known that they did not intend to pay the whole of the cash demand. But the New England states initially budgeted for higher taxes to meet their obligations. For the region's hard-pressed taxpayers, this was the last straw. It was not simply the payment that made them desperate, but the prospect of the cash going directly to foreigners and fat-cat bondholders.

In Rhode Island, the popular revolt brought about the election of a new assembly with a mandate to issue paper money for payment of taxes. Connecticut's legislature voted to ignore Congress's requisition altogether, while violent resistance led to the tax being postponed in New Hampshire. Only Governor James Bowdoin of Massachusetts insisted on exacting the full amount in coin.

Behaving as they had in the Revolution, Captain Job Shattuck of Groton, Massachusetts, and other veterans set up committees to become part of a network of resistance. But the name they adopted, the Regulators, and their demands for easier taxation, a more responsive legislature, and reform of the system of fee-taking county officials—"Deputy Sheriffs [be] totally set aside, as a useless set of officers in the community"—harked back to a still older struggle. "We fought for liberty but despots took it, whose little finger is thicker than George's loins," declared Ely Samuel in northern Massachusetts. "O that George held the claim still! For, before the war, it was better with us than now."

When Captain Daniel Shays, a much decorated war veteran, took command and marched on the federal arms depot in Springfield in the winter of 1786, there seemed a real possibility of a popular uprising. But the Regulators, as their name implied, were never revolutionaries. They wanted

1787 Massachusetts broadside proclamation following Shays's Rebellion

government to be reformed, not overthrown, and when a force of militia, paid for by Boston's moneyed elite, confronted Shays's force at Springfield, they scattered.

Nevertheless, they got what they wanted. On a small scale, the shock of their revolt was the main reason that Bowdoin was replaced as governor by popular John Hancock, who promptly reduced the tax—a decision made possible by money raised from the sale of state property—but what they could never have imagined was the large-scale impact on state government.

From New England, General Henry Knox, secretary of war, wrote in alarm to George Washington in November 1786 that up to fifteen thousand men were ready to rebel, and "they are determined to annihilate all debts public and private and have agrarian Laws [sympathetic to farmers], which are easily effected by means of un-funded paper money which shall be a tender in all cases whatever . . . This dreadful situation has alarmed every man of principle and property in New England. They start as from a dream, and ask what has been the cause of our—delusion? what is to afford us security against the violence of lawless men?" Knox's answer was unequivocal. "Our government must be braced, changed, or altered to secure our lives and property."

The effect of this letter on Washington was electrifying. Always aware that the British regarded the Revolutionary War as only a temporary setback, he took Knox's news as evidence that the United States was "fulfilling the prediction of our transatlantic foe! 'leave them to themselves, and their government will soon dissolve.'" Days after receiving the letter, he wrote in turn to James Madison: "We are fast verging to anarchy and confusion . . . Thirteen Sovereignties pulling against each other, and all tugging at the foederal head will soon bring ruin on the whole; whereas a liberal, and energetic Constitution, well guarded and closely watched, to prevent incroachments, might restore us to that degree of respectability and consequence, to which we had a fair claim, and the brightest prospect of attaining."

Thus perversely, the states' very efficiency in administering their territories and paying their debts succeeded in producing an impression of chaos. The 1787 convention at Philadelphia, originally intended only to reform the Articles of Confederation, now suggested itself to a determined number of delegates as the scene for a wholesale reform of government. And alarmed by the narrow escape from anarchy, the savior of the Revolution, General George Washington himself, proposed to lend his authority to their efforts.

CHAPTER 4

THE BULLYING STATES

The rule of law is always rule over a defined territory.
Morality may be without borders, but law's rule begins
only with the imagination of jurisdiction.
    PAUL KAHN, *The Cultural Study of Law*, 1999

IN THE EXTRAORDINARY summer of 1787 when fifty-five delegates
from twelve states met in Philadelphia to hammer out a new constitution
for the United States of America, Andrew Ellicott was running the last half
of Pennsylvania's northern border. At the heart of the deliberations in the
city lay a question that bore directly on Ellicott's work in the northern
fringe of the Allegheny Mountains—how much independence did a state
retain within its borders?

Eventually the delegates preferred to leave the matter unresolved, thus
setting up what would be the defining struggle of the nineteenth century
between individual states and the federal government. But even as the matter was being discussed, the urgent need for an answer was underlined when
a band of Seneca warriors surprised Ellicott and his boundary commissioners on the banks of the Allegheny River.

The Senecas had evidently watched their activities with growing
suspicion—the astronomers peering through their telescopes, the surveyors
with compasses in hand directing the clearing of a path through the woods,
and the chainmen measuring out the ground. By the 1780s Native Americans east of the Mississippi knew that this sort of activity could only signal
one thing. As the Moravian missionary John Heckewelder testified, they

had learned that the arrival of surveyors "with chain and compass in their hands, taking surveys of the tracts of good land" led inevitably to an invasion of settlers, and "when they had ceded lands to the white people, and boundary lines had been established—'firmly established!'—beyond which no whites were to settle, scarcely was the treaty signed, when intruders again were settling and hunting on their lands!"

Taking Ellicott's men for unauthorized surveyors marking out potential property, the Senecas' initial move, blocking access to the canoes, was aggressive. Nevertheless, as one of the nations in the Six Nations federation, they were accustomed to following the ritualized deliberations required by their federal constitution before any important decision was taken. During the formal exchanges, the leaders of the group warned Ellicott of the dangers of continuing his survey. Their hot-tempered young men were angry at the surveyors' intrusion and might turn to violence if the work did not immediately cease.

Patience was not one of Ellicott's virtues, and the hardship of running Pennsylvania's northern border exacerbated his irritation. Having left the Wyoming Valley in June, he and his fellow Pennsylvania commissioner, Andrew Porter, together with their New York counterparts, had been forced by falling river levels to abandon the heavy canoes and deck boats carrying their instruments and transfer their cargo to already laden packhorses. Climbing through steep hillsides covered in pine and oak forests, past gigantic slabs of fallen rock, they had run their lines, random and true, due west straight across every obstacle. Every twenty miles they had carried the tent serving as an observatory to the top of the highest summit together with the zenith sector, the clocks, and the compasses so that sun- and star-sights could be made.

In the summer heat, men and animals had suffered terribly. The overloaded horses began to founder, but were driven on until in the bleak words of Ellicott's official report to the Pennsylvania assembly, the harsh treatment "killed and rendered useless two thirds [of them]." At last the team passed the watershed from where the rivers began to flow westward, and with their few remaining animals almost at a standstill, they had come across a branch of the Allegheny River.

"We immediately set about making canoes," Ellicott reported, "and by the spirited exertions of our men, with no other implements than three falling

axes, two or three Tomahawks and a Chisel, we compleated in six days for the use of our Pennsylvania party 5 excellent Canoes, two of which are between 40 and 50 feet in length." They had dragged these hollowed-out logs down to the stream and bumped them half-floating over the rocks for ten miles until they reached the main Allegheny River.

At that point the Senecas stopped them, and Ellicott's anger showed in his response to the threat of violence from their young men. "You talk of danger," he exclaimed, "but remember we are now doing the business of the whole state and not the business of a few people, and the least injury done to our men will be considered as done to all the people of Pennsylvania." The purpose of their line was to show that "all the land to the north of it belongs to the Indians, and the land on the south from the river Delaware to the Lake Erie belongs to the People of Pennsylvania." And it was land, he added with irritation, for which they had always paid the Indians generously.

In Ellicott's tirade lay the grounds of the struggle between the states and the United States, on which the fate of the Six Nations would depend. It arose from the fact that three sovereignties were in play. From colonial times, the Native Americans had been regarded as nations as much under the Crown's protection as the colonies, a relationship made plain in 1763 when King George III prohibited settlement beyond the Appalachians so that "the several Tribes or Nations of Indians who live under our Protection . . . should not be molested or disturbed in the Possession of such Parts of Our Dominions and Territories . . . as are reserved to them." Only the Crown and its representatives in North America, the colonial governments, were permitted to buy land from them.

In similar fashion, under the Articles of Confederation the United States alone was deemed to have the right of "regulating the trade and managing all affairs with the Indians." This was exercised as early as 1784 at the Treaty of Fort Stanwix, when the Six Nations federation was forced to accept punishment for the support that four of their nations gave the British during the Revolution. The treaty confined them to the east of a line that ran from modern Buffalo "to the north boundary of the state of Pennsylvania," and in the words of its critical clause, "the Six Nations shall and do yield to the United States, all claims to the country west of the said [line]." Thus the parallel that Ellicott was attempting to run with so much difficulty was cer-

Detail of 1771 map showing northwest Pennsylvania, Lakes Ontario and Erie,
the Six Nations homeland, and Presqu'isle

tainly carving out what belonged to Pennsylvania, but north of the line the land could legally be claimed by the Six Nations, New York, and the United States.

The fertility of the Six Nations homeland below Lakes Ontario and Erie was legendary. Except for the winter months when the water froze over, the climate was benign, warm enough to grow grapes, peaches, and apples, with grazing rich enough for cattle to give gallons of creamy milk. Gently terraced hills sloped up from the shoreline, and along the wide valley bottoms lay a fine alluvial soil, easily worked and productive of corn, apples, pumpkins, and squashes. The higher land stretching as far south as the Ohio Valley was managed as a hunting ground, but that was less attractive to speculators than the farmland.

In 1786, with only the first part of the New York–Pennsylvania boundary in place, Governor George Clinton of New York forced the three eastern nations in the federation into treaties yielding up their lands to the state for sale to land speculators. Once the line was run all the way to Lake Erie, the remainder of this bountiful land, occupied primarily by the Senecas, would also fall within New York's boundaries. Clinton did not have long to wait.

Having bribed the Seneca band with two of his surviving horses, Ellicott and his teams of surveyors and axmen were allowed leave, floating downstream in their dugout canoes into lush flatlands, where at once their work became easier. The instruments were canoed to the observation points, guidelines were cut and measured with speed, and in place of the carved rocks that served as milestones, they hammered posts into the rich soil surrounded by mounds of earth.

On October 12, 1787, a triumphant letter was dispatched to Philadelphia datelined "Lake Erie." It announced that the guideline had been run to the lake, and that the final observations were being made in order to calculate the true line. "Considering the unexpected difficulties we had to encounter for want of a competent knowledge of the Geography of the Country, the death of our Horses, time taken up in making Canoes and treating with the Indians, our business has gone on beyond our most sanguine expectations." Both the Andrews, Ellicott and Porter, put their names to this, but the author was certainly the former. Only he would have explained their working methods with typically Ellicott exactness about the number of astronomical observations made—no fewer than 336—immediately followed by a typically Ellicott defense against the unspoken accusation that he could have done more. "Neither attention nor exertions have been wanting on our parts," he insisted, "towards Scientific and permanent completion of the business entrusted to us."

Almost a century later when his boundary markers had to be restored, the new boundary commissioners paid tribute to his methods. Comparing Ellicott's feat using a handmade zenith sector, clocks, and compasses with their own findings based on late-nineteenth-century instruments machined and ground to an accuracy of one ten-thousandth of an inch, they concluded, "The operations of the early Commissioners do their memory great credit. The variation from the true geographic parallel is small [considering] the difference in precision between the instrument of that day and this." The science, however, produced consequences unimaginable to the scientists. The most destructive fell on the Six Nations, but to the United States the most significant was the defeat it suffered at the hands of New York.

. . .

For more than a century, the Six Nations had played a strategic role balancing the competing pressures imposed by British and French colonial powers. Writing of their values, the French Jesuit missionary Father Charlevoix described "these Americans" in terms that the new Americans would have used of themselves. They were, he said, "perfectly convinced that man was born free, that no power on earth has a right to infringe his liberty, and that nothing can repay him for the loss of it."

To accommodate that conviction with the need to live together, the federation of six nations, around fifteen thousand strong, organized their government through a constitution that reconciled differing ambitions by a sophisticated set of checks and balances that some modern apologists argue must have served as a model for the United States. Each individual nation had responsibility for a different administrative role, consultation was required on all decisions and unanimity on major choices, and decision-making alternated between men and women. Although the federation was formed through war, with ultimate authority being wielded through elected male chiefs, women selected the leaders, and as the constitution declared, "Women shall be considered the progenitors of the Nation. They shall own the land and the soil. Men and women shall follow the status of the mother."

The Revolution destroyed this cohesive arrangement. The Mohawks under their leader Joseph Brant chose to fight with the British and drew in three other nations, the Seneca, Cayuga, and Onondaga, with them, while the Oneida and the Tuscarora, influenced by the missionary Samuel Kirkland, supported the Americans. In 1779, General John Sullivan attacked the Six Nations homeland below Lakes Erie and Ontario in retaliation for a raid on the Wyoming Valley. His troops not only destroyed crops, but brought back with them news of the richness of Six Nations land, making it a prime target for settlers and speculators alike.

When peace came, New York's claim to almost twelve million fertile acres of Six Nations land was challenged by Massachusetts, under the terms of its royal charter granting it possession of "the Maine lands from sea to sea." This border dispute only ended in December 1786 when the two states reached the compromise agreement known as the Hartford Treaty, leaving jurisdiction with New York, but giving Massachusetts the right to buy two thirds of the land, approximately eight million acres, from the Six Nations. Almost at once Massachusetts sold its right to two New York speculators, Oliver Phelps and Nathaniel Gorham, for $1 million, a sum that exactly equaled the state's entire annual budget. The down payment of one third of the price immediately allowed Governor John Hancock to remove the crushing burden of taxation from western farmers. Had the border been established earlier, Shays's Rebellion might never have taken place, and the history of the Constitution would have followed a different course.

The treaty also left the Six Nations to the tender mercies of Governor Clinton once Ellicott had completed demarcating the border with Pennsylvania. To keep the transaction cheap, Clinton negotiated for leaseholds rather than outright purchase and, following a policy suggested by General Philip Schuyler, restricted the state to acquiring farmland only. This left the much larger hunting grounds untouched, but as Schuyler had correctly predicted, the settlers quickly began to clear off the game anyway, eventually allowing the state to acquire all the Indian land cheaply.

Leasing the land was attractive to the Six Nations, not simply because it left ultimate ownership with them, but because their sachems, or leaders, were by then convinced that they had to learn the ways of the Americans, and that it was useful to have their teachers living in their midst. But the difference between leasing and selling was buried in the horse-trading of the Hartford Treaty, and the speculators sold the land as though it were owned outright. "[Governor Clinton] did not say, 'I buy your Country,'" the Oneida sachem Good Peter protested in 1788. "Nor did we say, 'We sell it.'" But Clinton paid no heed, insisting that the three nations with whom he had signed agreements should move into smaller reservations close to the Canadian frontier.

The state might be ruthless, but the arrival of a new player in the form of the U.S. government offered the Six Nations sachems a slim hope of holding on to their land and legal rights. As immediately became clear, the new president took a very different view of Indian rights.

The election in 1789 of General George Washington as president provided the clearest possible symbol of the overriding authority of the United States. Not only was his election unanimous, he was the incarnation of the Union.

No one else could have welded the disparate forces of the states into a national army so that, as he said when he bade them farewell, "Men who came from the different parts of the Continent, strongly disposed, by the habits of education, to despise and quarrel with each other . . . instantly became but one patriotic band of Brothers." The broad chest, the towering height, the wide-socketed blue eyes, the boldly jutting chin made more formidable by the need to clamp shut his jaws against his spring-loaded false teeth, all gave him the appearance of a leader, but he was more than a symbol.

Washington came to the presidency with an agenda, and that was unity. The full force of his prestige, personality, and shrewdness was concentrated upon the belief that "it is in our United capacity we are known, and have a place among the Nations of the Earth. Depart from this, and the States separately would be as unknown in the World and as contemptable (comparatively speaking) as an individual County in any one State." To the last day of his presidency, he did not deviate from the belief that the states should accept a subordinate role within the Union because "all the parts combined cannot fail to find in the united mass of means and efforts greater strength, greater resource, proportionably greater security from external danger."

So formidable has the stature of "the Father of the Nation" grown in history, together with that of the two great figures Thomas Jefferson and Alexander Hamilton, who served him as secretaries of state and the treasury, it is difficult to grasp how gossamer thin the federal power really was, whatever the Constitution said, and how easily it could be defied by powerful state governors. Its weakness was cruelly exposed in the battle over the disposal of the Six Nations land north of Ellicott's border.

The new federal Constitution gave the United States the power "to regulate Commerce with foreign Nations, and among the several States, and with the Indian Tribes." One of the federal government's earliest pieces of legislation was the 1790 Indian Trade and Intercourse Act, which made clear that Indian land was only to be acquired by treaty with the United States. The act was passed specifically to give the president power to deal with William MacGillivray, the leader of the Creeks in Georgia and Florida, but within weeks of its passage, Washington dispatched Timothy Pickering, as someone who was familiar with the area, to inform a Seneca delegation preparing to meet the Pennsylvania negotiators "that all business between them and any part of the United States is hereafter to be transacted by the general Government."

Encouraged by the entry of the United States into the negotiations, the Seneca sachem Cornplanter immediately set about enlisting the new president's assistance, using political skills honed by long sessions in his own confederation. In November 1790, Washington agreed to meet Cornplanter in person and gave his word that Seneca ownership of their lands would be guaranteed by the federal government, which alone had the right to negotiate for their sale. "Here then is the security for the remainder of your lands," Washington promised Cornplanter. "No State nor person can purchase your lands, unless at some public treaty held under the authority of the United States. The general Government will . . . protect you in all your just rights."

By allying himself to Washington, Cornplanter showed himself to be the most pragmatic of the Six Nations' sachems. His rivals for paramount influence among the Six Nations, the warlike Brant and the eloquent Red Jacket, counseled complete opposition to the inexorable hunger of American settlers for land, but Cornplanter recognized that this was a force that

Cornplanter

could not be opposed, only diverted. Washington himself took an equally realistic view of the Six Nations.

His Indian policy was intended to persuade potential enemies to live peaceably within the United States. As a major land speculator himself, he had no qualms about acquiring their land. In 1795 he would buy three thousand acres in New York's Mohawk Valley, using money borrowed from Governor George Clinton, and resell quickly for a profit of $6,000 on the deal. But self-interest demanded that all dealings be done equably without stirring up hostility. "It will be fortunate for the American public," he declared in early 1791, "if private Speculations in the lands, still claimed by the Aborigines, do not aggravate those differences, which policy, humanity, and justice concur to deprecate." Whatever the difficulties, unity always remained the ultimate prize.

From a federal perspective the need to avoid unnecessary hostility was obvious. In the northwest, Brant and the British were encouraging a western alliance among tribes such as the Delaware, Wyandot, and Miami against further white settlement in the Ohio Valley. In the southwest, Cherokee anger at incursion by settlers from North Carolina and Georgia had already turned to sporadic violence, and it could easily spread by way of the Chickasaw to the Creek in the far south.

Yet for all that the Constitution, the Congress, and the Father of the Nation might say, within his own frontier Governor Clinton continued to pursue his own program of forcing the Six Nations to exchange lease rights in their former lands for outright ownership of smaller reservations close to the Canadian border. The eight million acres of the Phelps and Gorham purchase were freed up through these arrangements, as were four million acres bought later by Alexander Macomb. The evidence that New York was acting on behalf of speculators regardless of the greater good of the United States drove Washington to a furious outburst to Alexander Hamilton.

"The States individually are omitting no occasion to interfere in matters which belong to the general Government," he wrote in April 1791. "It is not more than four or five months since the Six Nations or part of them were assured (through the medium of Colonel Pickering) that thence forward they would be spoken to by the Government of the United States *only* and the same thing was repeated in strong terms to the Cornplanter at Philadelphia afterwards . . . To sum the whole up in a few words: the interference of

States, and the speculations of Individuals will be the bane of all our public measures."

Whatever New York could do for its speculators, Pennsylvania was about to do better. What made this second defiance more humiliating for Washington was that it concerned a tract of land in the extreme west of Six Nations territory, known as the Triangle, that clearly belonged to the United States.

The Triangle got its name from a curious gap left by Ellicott's line. Under the terms of New York's 1780 cession to the United States of its claims to western lands, the state's western border was deemed to be the meridian running north-south through "the western extremity of Lake Ontario." Ellicott's parallel clearly extended westward of this line. Thus the triangular area between New York's western limits, Pennsylvania's northern boundary, and the shores of Lake Erie could only belong to the United States. Within this area Seneca land was unequivocally guaranteed to them by the president.

The most important feature on the southern shoreline of Lake Erie was a spit of rock and sand called Presqu'isle that thrust out like a fishhook into the lake creating a safe and well-protected harbor. That harbor was vital to speculators hoping to interest customers in the potential of the Six Nations land because it would allow farmers to ship their produce to markets in the east. The two principal speculators were Nathaniel Gorham, who owned eight million acres of New York, and to the south, John Nicholson, who laid claim to nearly four million acres of Pennsylvania.

Nicholson had one overwhelming advantage that Gorham for all his eminence lacked—he had almost unlimited control over his state's financial affairs. Appointed to the newly created post of comptroller general in 1782 at the age of twenty-five, he had kept Pennsylvania financially afloat at a time when the state was struggling under the emergency of a war economy and the violent antagonisms stirred up by a democratic government fundamentally opposed to the imposition of new taxes. His financial policy of direct taxation supplemented by the issue of paper money backed by the Depreciation and Donations Lands schemes benefited the super-rich, but they repaid him by buying all the bonds the state issued, thus keeping Pennsylvania solvent. It drove the state's western settlers to the point of rebellion, but the trick that Nicholson carried off was to keep them from outright violence while maintaining investor confidence in the value of his paper money. The clearest sign of his success was a report in the *Pennsylvania Gazette* on August 14, 1784, that "treasury notes, state money, and public securities of all kinds, pass daily in stores and shops, in town and in the country at their *real* value."

His weapons were charm, ruthlessness, and a spongelike capacity for information that he welcomed from tavern landlords and surveyors as much as from bankers and senators. Those who could not follow his financial wizardry, he deemed "asses, dupes or blockheads" and saw no reason to enlighten them. From 1782 to 1794 about $27 million of public money passed through his hands from tax receipts, land sales, excise duties, and the issue of paper money. No one was sure how much he managed to divert into his own pockets because his supporters defeated an attempt to impeach him in 1794, but he owned public land in every one of Pennsylvania's thirty-nine counties. And in his rivalry with Nathaniel Gorham, the resources of the state, financial and legal, were at his disposal.

In 1788, Pennsylvania offered to buy the Erie Triangle from the United States at a high price on condition that a survey be undertaken to establish that Presqu'isle would be included. Gorham retaliated by arguing that the Triangle stood inside New York's borders and that Pennsylvania's boundaries had been improperly extended to Lake Erie without any relation to its charter. To counter these charges, Pennsylvania sent Ellicott to New York to testify before Congress in the hot summer of 1789 that the Keystone State's rectangular shape was based on interstate agreement and impeccable astronomy.

Sharp-eyed and fleshy-faced, Gorham made a formidable opponent. Like many of the biggest land speculators, he had made his fortune during the war when he was responsible for provisioning Massachusetts' militia. Elected to the Continental Congress, he had served a term as president, then helped bring the Constitution into being, first as chairman of crucial debates and later as chief advocate in persuading his home state to ratify it. "This Mr Gorham, my opponent, is the greatest man in all new England, and formerly President of Congress," Ellicott told Sally after facing his hostile questioning through humid days and fetid, candlelit evenings. "[It] has been the most severe contest I have been engaged in, and has employed my whole attention both by night and day."

On the other hand, Ellicott himself was no longer a nobody. That year he was appointed geographer-general of the United States following Hutchins's death, and passing through Philadelphia he asked Benjamin Franklin for an introduction to the newly elected president. In friendly fashion Franklin replied that it was his policy never to bother Washington with personal applications and instead provided Ellicott with a certificate of recommendation: "I have long known Mr Andrew Ellicott as a Man of Science, and while I was in the Executive Council had frequent Occasions, in the Course of Public Business, of being acquainted with his Abilities in Geographical Operations of the most important kind which were performed by him with the greatest Scientific Accuracy." To have his work endorsed by the eighteenth century's outstanding experimental scientist soothed even Ellicott's thin-skinned pride, as did the manner in which the great man ended his letter: "I am dear friend yours most affectionately B Franklin."

The most effective proof of his standing, however, came in August when Congress accepted his testimony and overturned Gorham's objection to Pennsylvania's right to buy the Triangle. "I carried my point in the lower House of Congress," Ellicott wrote in triumph. "The art and cunning of the new England people exceed anything that I had any idea of, but in this case they were defeated by perseverance and solid argument." That fall after the Senate had approved the contract, Ellicott was commissioned by the United States to run the border between the Triangle and New York.

The task depended on establishing the longitude of Lake Ontario's most westerly point, then plotting where the same meridian cut across Lake Erie's southern shore. But Ontario lay within Canada, and a team of Americans mapping and measuring so close to the border was not welcomed by the British. To Ellicott's irritation, the frontier guard turned them back until permission for their presence was given by the governor of Canada. The delay and the onset of winter meant that the first part of their survey was not completed until January 1790.

On his return from the wilderness, Ellicott immediately sent the president a report on what he had done. Typically it managed to be both boastful and defensive, asserting that all existing "geography of the Country about the Lakes [is] very erroneous"—on most maps Lake Erie was located almost two hundred miles too far south—and blaming the British for any delays and extra expenses he had incurred. In fact over half the report had nothing to do with geography but consisted of a verbatim account of his argument with an obstreperous British officer at the Canadian frontier. The officer first denied Ellicott the right of entry, then invited his American military escort to lunch while blandly informing Ellicott, "You may retire to the Tavern in the Bottom, and purchase such refreshments as you may want." Rubbing salt into the wound made in Ellicott's always vulnerable psyche, the officer refused point-blank to allow him to return by way of the Niagara Falls with the excuse that "too many people have seen the falls already."

Nevertheless the map that Andrew Ellicott provided for the president made any sensitivities of temperament irrelevant. He calculated for the first time the true location of Lake Erie and the United States' northern border, which on previous maps had floated as much as twenty miles too far north or south of its proper position. On top of that he took advantage of the British governor's permit to measure the distance of the Niagara River from Lakes Erie to Ontario, and to make the first accurate calculation of the 162-foot height of the falls. For good measure he provided an accurate plan of the strategically important ground beyond the border, including "the whole British settlement of Nassau." It made a sharp revenge for the insult of the tavern lunch.

The survey also established that New York's border lay almost twenty miles east of Presqu'isle, and that the natural harbor therefore fell within the Triangle. Thus the chief beneficiary of Ellicott's science turned out to be John Nicholson.

To secure the Triangle, Pennsylvania had agreed to pay the United States seventy-five cents an acre, but as comptroller general, Nicholson made sure that when the deal went through in 1791 most of it was paid in the form of old certificates issued by the Continental Congress, which were once thought worthless but with interest were valued at almost $90,000. It was a good deal for the state, but a better one for Nicholson, because within a few months of its title being confirmed, Pennsylvania sold most of the Triangle to various buyers, nearly all of whom turned out to be either John Nicholson under different aliases or associates connected with his newly created Pennsylvania Population Company.

Just as Clinton had defied the United States in the interests of Gorham and Macomb, so Pennsylvania's governor, Thomas Mifflin, ensured that the state supported its premier speculator. Once the Triangle passed from U.S. jurisdiction to that of Pennsylvania, Cornplanter and his associates were bribed by state officials with money and three thousand acres on the Allegheny River to sign a document giving outright ownership of Seneca land in the Triangle to Pennsylvania. This extinguished the rights of Seneca ownership that Washington had personally guaranteed would not be transferred without the involvement of the United States. Not only did it defy both the president and the federal government, but it produced exactly the result that Washington had feared would come from not treating the Indians with "humanity and justice."

The sense of outrage among the majority of Senecas who repudiated the agreement immediately spilled over into the western alliance of Native Americans in the Ohio Valley. Seneca warriors joined the force assembled by the Miami general Michikinikwa, or Little Turtle, that inflicted two disastrous defeats on federal armies in 1790 and 1791, bringing settlement there to a halt. Ironically the same anger, now strengthened by victorious fighters from the western alliance, also held up the settlement of Presqu'isle for four critical years. During that time, Washington struggled to impose the authority of the federal government on Mifflin and the state of Pennsylvania. Not until 1794 did he succeed, and the U.S. government begin its long climb to ascendancy from this, the most blatant example of the states' contempt for its authority.

The readiness with which both Pennsylvania and New York ignored instructions from "the general government," as it was called, helps illustrate the basic problem faced by the framers of the Constitution—the fragility of the idea of the United States compared with the robust reality of the states. What drove the least federally committed delegate to want a more perfect union than that created by the Articles of Confederation was the specter of chaos within the states represented by Shays's Rebellion and the fear that warfare between the states might destroy their hard-won independence. But exactly how perfect, whether a compact of states or a consolidated nation, could not be specified without offending the very powers they wished to unite.

During a debate in the Constitutional Convention on the relative strength of the power of the general government compared to that of the states, the wealthy Connecticut lawyer Oliver Ellsworth won general approval for his suggestion that "the U.S. are sovereign on one side of the line dividing the jurisdictions—the States on the other, [and] each ought to have power to defend their respective Sovereignties." But that suggestion that the federal government might even be on a level with the states required the United States to have something more than words to define it.

The power of the states, both north and south, led the framers to back off from confronting the issue that came closer than any other to breaking the Union they created. On both sides, the arguments about the morality of slavery were well understood. The anomaly of fighting to establish a confederation committed to the proposition that all men were born equal while enslaving one sixth of its population had already prompted John Jay, from the largely slave-owning state of New York, to admit, "To contend for liberty, and to deny that blessing to others involves an inconsistency not to be excused." Smarting from defeat on the other side of the Atlantic, Samuel Johnson had put it more acidly: "How is it that we hear the loudest yelps for liberty among the drivers of negroes?"

The contradiction had earlier led Pennsylvania to pass its 1780 law providing for the gradual abolition of slavery. "We conceive that it is our duty," ran the preamble, "and we rejoice that it is in our power to extend a portion of that freedom to others, which hath been extended to us; and a release from that state of thraldom to which we ourselves were tyrannically doomed."

Prompted by similar motives, Massachusetts declared the trade in slaves to be illegal in 1783, followed by all the New England states, and eventually New York and New Jersey. In the most important legislative act of its peacetime life, the Continental Congress made it a provision of the 1787 Ordinance governing the settlement of territory northwest of the Ohio River that "there shall be neither slavery nor involuntary servitude in the said territory, otherwise than in the punishment of crimes whereof the party shall have been duly convicted." The entire free economy of northern states from Ohio to Wisconsin was to grow from that sentence.

Yet not only did the argument of inconsistency fail to carry weight among delegates to the Constitutional Convention, the U.S. Constitution contained three separate provisions condoning slavery—that a slave should count for three fifths of a free man for the purposes of calculating the amount of taxation and representation in Congress allotted to each state;

that the slave trade should continue for twenty years; and most explicitly of all that slaves who escaped and reached a free state should not regain their freedom but be returned to their masters.

James Madison's notes on debates in the Constitutional Convention reveal how clearly the delegates understood the nature of the double standard being applied, especially during the tortuous argument about the three-fifths formula. James Wilson, soon to be an associate justice of the Supreme Court and author of a famous series of lectures on the natural rights of man, asked "on what principle the admission of blacks in the proportion of three fifths could be explained. Are they admitted as Citizens? then why are they not admitted on an equality with White Citizens? are they admitted as property? then why is not other property admitted into the computation?"

When they came to the wording of the Constitution, William Patterson of New Jersey pointed to the hypocrisy that prevented the framers from even using the word *slave*. Instead slaves were referred to as "other Persons" where the three-fifths rule was concerned, and the slave trade became the "Importation of such Persons as any of the States now existing shall think proper to admit." Luther Martin of Maryland, himself a slave owner, admitted that the reason the word could not be used was because "it is inconsistent with the principles of the Revolution, and dishonorable to the American character to have such a feature in the Constitution."

In the end, however, every delegate pulled back from any measure that might endanger even the imperfect Union they already possessed. A proposal to ban the trade in slaves that commanded support from New England and the powerful central states including Virginia and Maryland was stopped in its tracks when Georgia and South Carolina threatened to consider seceding.

"Religion & humanity have nothing to do with this question," John Rutledge of South Carolina said bleakly. "Interest alone is the governing principle with Nations. The true question at present is whether the Southern states shall or shall not be parties to the Union. If the Northern States consult their interests they will not oppose the increase of Slaves which will increase the commodities of which they will become the carriers."

This shrewd reminder that most slaves were carried by northern shippers had the effect of detaching New England from the central states. Under pressure from Boston merchants, an unholy alliance of southern states and

New England was created to keep the slave trade in operation for another twenty years. But another interest kept delegates from questioning the institution of slavery too closely. The right to liberty might be paramount, but it could not be separated from the right to property.

"The moment the idea is admitted into society that property is not as sacred as the laws of God, and that there is not a force of law and public justice to protect it," John Adams declared in his defense of the Constitution, "anarchy and tyranny commence. If 'Thou shalt not covet' and 'Thou shalt not steal' were not commandments of Heaven, they must be made inviolable precepts in every society before it can be civilized or made free."

The right to property was enshrined in almost every state constitution, most placing it as Virginia's did next to life and liberty as one of humanity's inalienable rights. And even Pennsylvania's abolition law did not wholly deny that people could be treated as property—it stipulated, for example, that freed slaves must continue to serve their former owners as indentured servants, and that the state should pay compensation to the owner of a slave executed for murder. Nor was there any objection to the Fugitive Slaves Act of 1793, which accepted that free states had to return runaway slaves to their owners as they did other fugitives from justice, as though by escaping the slaves had stolen themselves from their masters. If a state insisted that behind its borders it should be allowed to include people of African origin as property, the newborn concept of the United States was in no position to challenge it. The outcome left slavery as a matter on which each state made its own policy. Only when the federal government grew sufficiently powerful to challenge the sovereignty of the states would any alternative become politically possible.

The Erie Triangle was still U.S. territory when Andrew Ellicott ran its border in 1790, making it the first specifically federal line to be established. Congress had voted no money to pay for it, but President Washington told Knox it was "a matter of too great importance to the United States to await the organization of the Treasury Department," and he ordered the Indian revenue to be raided to pay Ellicott $1,125 without delay. Consequently when Ellicott returned to Philadelphia that winter with his surveys and his measurements, it was to the president that he reported. With unparalleled pride he wrote from Philadelphia to tell Sally, as she nursed the latest addition to the family, of the reception his maps and his estimates of Niagara's height received. "General Washington has treated me with attention," he boasted, "the Speaker of Congress and the Governor of this State have constantly had me dine with them."

Ellicott's description of Niagara Falls in a letter written to a new friend, Dr. Benjamin Rush, suggests the sort of impact his account must have had when accounts of wild and romantic landscapes served as the cinema of the age: "Down this chasm [below the Falls] the water rushes with a most astonishing velocity, after it makes the great pitch. In going up the road near the chasm, the fancy is constantly engaged in the contemplation of the most romantic and awful prospects imaginable, till at length the eye catches the Falls:—the imagination is instantly arrested, and you admire in silence!" Even Pennsylvania's Senator William Maclay, renowned for his cynicism, responded in astonishment, "Mr. Ellicott's accounts of the Niagara Falls are amazing indeed."

As a land speculator and a general, Washington knew the value of reliable maps and accurate figures better than anyone else. Barely twelve months later, he demonstrated his appreciation of the work in visible fashion. In July 1790 the federal Congress authorized the president to choose a site on the Potomac River for the new capital city of the nation, and soon afterward Virginia and Maryland agreed to cede to the United States the one hundred square miles of territory required. The project was publicly launched by the president on January 24, 1791, but the first step had already been taken. On Washington's instructions, Thomas Jefferson, the secretary of state, had arranged that the boundaries of the new federal district should be surveyed by Andrew Ellicott.

CHAPTER 5

CAPITAL SPECULATIONS

*Speculation, the life of the American, embraced the design
of the new city. Several companies of speculators purchased lots, and began to build handsome streets, with an
ardor that soon promised a large and populous city. Before
they arrived at the attic story, the failure was manifest; and
in that state at this moment are the walls of many scores of
houses begun on a plan of elegance.*

CHARLES W. JANSON, *Stranger in America,* 1806

ON MARCH 12, 1791, the *Georgetown Weekly Ledger* announced the
arrival in town of "Maj. Andrew Ellicott, a gentleman of superior astronomical abilities. He was appointed by the President of the United
States to lay off a tract of land ten miles square on the Potomack for the use
of Congress; [he] is now engaged in this business and hopes soon to accom-
plish the object of his mission."

In this low-key fashion, the birth was announced of what was to become
the most powerful capital city in the world. From the start, its growth was
expected to depend upon the operation of speculators. The role of the federal government would be simply to create the circumstances in which their
activities could flourish. That the government might need to control the
speculators was barely considered, a lapse that would cripple the development of the "Federal district" for years to come. Thus the events that Ellicott was to set in motion contained an important lesson for the nation's
future expansion.

The *Ledger* was late with its news, however. Major Ellicott had been at work for a month, his preliminary inspection of the one-hundred-square-mile federal district was half-complete, and he had begun to miss his wife savagely. On the frontier, he had only been able to write to her, but the site he was now surveying stood just next to Georgetown, a prosperous community of five thousand souls whose stores offered another way of telling her what he felt. With his next letter, he enclosed a pair of black silk mitts and a bottle of perfume, "which I hope you will receive as a small testimony of as pure an affection as ever had a place in a Human Breast." His message ended, "It is now late at night, and my letter carried to a great length, but when I call to mind our happy connection, the consequence of an early attachment, founded in Virtue and in Love, I know not where to conclude; so many objects pleasing to my recollection crowd in upon me—I am my Dear Sally Your Affectionate Husband."

Compared to the hardship of running the Pennsylvania borders, the federal district should not have presented a serious physical challenge. Weekends could be spent in the comfort of Suter's Tavern in Georgetown, and after the jagged landscape of the Alleghenies, the flat woodland on either side of the Potomac made for easy traveling. Nevertheless, Ellicott did not think much of the area chosen for the nation's capital. "The Country thro' which we are now cutting one of the ten-mile lines is very poor," he told her in June, "there is not one House that has any floor except the earth, and what is more strange, it is in the neighbourhood of Alexandria and George-Town . . . As the President is so much attached to this country, I would not be willing that he knew my real sentiments about it. But this country, intended for the Permanent Residence of Congress, bears no more proportion to the Country about Philadelphia than a [scrawny] Crane does to a [fat] stall-fed Ox!"

The Residence Act passed by the First Congress in July 1790 had set aside an area "not exceeding ten miles square" on the Potomac River for the "permanent seat of Government of the United States." The decision to create a capital for the nation on a greenfield site rather than use an existing city such as New York or Philadelphia represented a victory for the Virginians, and especially Washington and Jefferson, over northern interests. Yet the one hundred square miles set aside for it also represented the first indication that the freshly created sovereignty of the United States might become a territorial power to rival the states.

Strategically the site stood at the center of the United States, almost midway between New Hampshire and Georgia. It was easily reached by ship from every major city, and needed only a canal between the Potomac River and the Ohio to connect it directly with the rapidly growing settlements beyond the Appalachians. That George Washington himself was a major shareholder in the Pawtomac Canal company and owned property near the federal district did not present a conflict of interest to contemporary minds. There was no federal cost in creating the capital—Maryland and Virginia agreed to put up seed money of $192,000 for a development clearly in their interests—and the general presumption was that in benefiting himself the president was benefiting the country.

Jefferson and Washington had first discussed locating the capital on the Potomac as early as 1783, but not until 1790 did Jefferson and Alexander Hamilton broker the famous deal that persuaded northern representatives in Congress to accept a southern capital. In return, southern congressmen would support Hamilton's proposal that the federal government should take on the states' debts, including much of the paper money they had issued.

From Ellicott's first measurement on the Virginia side of the river, the complexities created by the site were inescapable. Washington's announced intention was to include the thriving seaport of Alexandria on the Virginia side of the river, and two locations on the Maryland side, Georgetown and the Eastern Branch, a tributary flowing into the Potomac. Ellicott's preliminary calculations led to the exclusion of most of Alexandria because, as he told Jefferson in February 1791, it "would neither produce straight lines, nor contain quite the ten miles square, besides the utmost impropriety of running such lines without tolerable exactness." In the growing chaos of the years ahead, that passion for exactness proved to be both a blessing and a curse.

His starting point was Jones Point, a spit of land on the Virginia bank pushing into the Potomac below Alexandria, where he calculated the meridian, or true north—and the painstaking care he took became the central issue in determining responsibility for the capital's shape. His instruments included both the five-foot Rittenhouse zenith sector and a smaller nineteen-inch version, a transit used for taking equal altitudes that he had constructed the previous year, as well as a circumferentor, or combined compass and telescope, for horizontal measurements, three conventional telescopes, including one made by Dollond of London, and the all-important chronometer that he had built himself. As had become his habit, he cleared a place on high ground, erected an observation tent to protect the intruments, securely attached the clock to the stump of a felled tree to serve as a platform, and began the achingly minute observation of the heavens that would reveal precisely where he stood on earth. His assistant during these first crucial sightings was one of the most notable astronomers of the day, Benjamin Banneker.

Against all odds, Banneker, a fifty-nine-year-old farmer with no education, had taught himself astronomy, helped by advice and the loan of books and instruments from Ellicott's cousin George. What made the feat still more astonishing was that it had been achieved by an African-American living in the slave-owning economy of Maryland.

Benjamin Banneker on the title page of his 1795 Almanac

Although Ellicott would have known him from childhood—Banneker farmed next to the Ellicott Mills—he first learned of his abilities in the summer of 1790 when Banneker wrote asking for help in checking a set of astronomical calculations he had made for an almanac. "I hope that you will be kind enough to view [any errors] with an eye of pitty," ran Banneker's letter, "as the Calculations was made more for the Sake of gratifying the Curiosity of the public, than for any view of profit, as I suppose it to be the first attempt of the kind that ever was made in America by a person of my Complection—"

Unfortunately Banneker's letter took forty-five days to reach the wilds of the Erie Triangle where Ellicott was engaged in the "hardship, trouble and difficulty" of the survey. By then it was too late to correct his calculations in time for the 1791 almanac. Impressed by his achievement, however, Ellicott showed his work to a neighbor and fellow member of the Philosophical Society, James Pemberton, who was also president of the Pennsylvania Society for Promoting the Abolition of Slavery. Pemberton seized upon Banneker's astronomy to rebut the argument made most notably by Thomas Jefferson that slavery was justified on the grounds that black Americans were mentally inferior to whites. Pemberton's pamphlet celebrating Banneker's work provided ammunition for antislavery groups not only in the United States, but across the Atlantic in France and Britain. And when Benjamin Banneker at last produced his almanac, it sealed his fame as the first African-American scientist.

What first brought Banneker public recognition was not his almanac, however, but Ellicott's decision to employ him as his assistant on the survey of the federal district. A month after their arrival, the *Georgetown Weekly Ledger* reported approvingly, "[Mr. Ellicott] is attended by *Benjamin Banniker*, an Ethiopian, whose abilities as a surveyor and an astronomer clearly prove that Mr Jefferson's concluding that race of men were void of mental endowments, was without foundation."

In the next paragraph, the newspaper also told its readers of the recent arrival of "Major *Longfont*, a French gentleman, employed by the President of the United States to survey the lands contiguous to Georgetown, where the federal city is to be built." This was Pierre L'Enfant, whose volubility, energy, and addiction to high drama enchanted and exasperated everyone he encountered.

Ellicott and he had brushed by each other the year before in Pennsylvania senator William Maclay's office, when the senator noted sourly in his journal, "L'Enfant was with us, like most Frenchmen, [he] was so talkative that scarce a word could be said." His face was dominated by dark brows and a heavy forehead, but lightened by quick, black eyes, and a romantic imagination that had in 1777 induced him to cross the Atlantic with the Marquis de Lafayette to fight for American independence.

At the time he was a Paris art student with no military training—a French officer recorded that "he has some talent for drawing figures, but nothing of use for an engineer"—but succeeded in persuading the authorities in France to issue him a temporary commission as lieutenant as a safeguard in case of capture by the British. With characteristic élan, once arrived in America, L'Enfant parlayed the lieutenancy into permanent rank as a captain, then a major in the Corps of Engineers, and with equally impetuous courage volunteered for a doomed assault on Savannah in which he was wounded and taken prisoner.

Apart from that episode, his military experience was limited to providing the illustrations for General von Steuben's military manual and, after his release on parole, sketching fortifications. Once peace came, his artistic ability enabled him to earn his living as an architect in New York, and among several other commissions he was responsible for the restoration of New York's City Hall, where the new federal Congress first met. The magnificence of the hall, and especially the symbol of the United States, a giant eagle clutching thirteen arrows in its talons, immediately caught George Washington's eye. But what convinced the new president of L'Enfant's unique talent was the architect's expansive response when the project for a new capital was published.

"The plan should be drawn on such a scale," L'Enfant wrote Washington, "as to leave room for that aggrandizement and embellishment which the increase of the wealth of the nation will permit it to pursue at any period, however remote." That single insight into the president's unspoken ambitions for the United States and for its capital was what secured him the commission for designing the city. "An eminent French military engineer starts for Georgetown," Washington announced to an associate in March 1791, "to examine and survey the site of the federal city."

In the president's mind, Major L'Enfant always did remain "the Engineer," someone who could plan and build, and his intention was that L'Enfant should not only design the city but construct its public buildings. Major Elli-cott, by contrast, was referred to as "the Surveyor," the person who would lay out the design on the ground. The commissioning letter from Jefferson that L'Enfant carried in his pocket when he left Philadelphia clarified the presi-dent's idea of his duties: "You are desired to proceed to Georgetown where you will find Mr Ellicott employed in making a survey and Map of the Fed-eral Territory. The special object of asking your aid is to have a drawing of the particular grounds most likely to be approved for the site of the Federal town and buildings."

Early in March, the Engineer set out in driving rain to climb to the top of Jenkins Hill, soon to be better known as Capitol Hill. "After coming up on the hill from the Eastern Branch ferry," he reported to Jefferson, "the country

Pierre L'Enfant

is level and, on a space of about two miles each way, present [*sic*] a most elligible position for the first settlement of a grand City." The panorama of flat woodland in front of him was bordered on one side by the Potomac River and extended to the northwest as far as Rock Creek, a stream dividing it off from the bustling streets of Georgetown. Behind him, the southeastern limit was provided by another, wider river known to settlers as the Eastern Branch, but by Native Americans as the Anakostia. L'Enfant is usually given the credit for envisioning the whole grand sweep of the city from the banks of the Eastern Branch to those of Rock Creek. Nevertheless, his initial sketch comprised a capital half that size stretching, as he had been instructed, no farther than Tyber Creek, today's Tidal Basin. The grandiose plan originated with the president himself.

Washington's strategy—and he conducted the creation of the capital like a military campaign—was dictated by the need to purchase at a reasonable price whatever land was needed for the city from the existing owners. He appeared to have in mind two possible sites. "The competition for the location of the town now rests between the mouth of the Eastern Branch, and the lands on the river below and adjacent to Georgetown," he wrote in February 1791. "In favour of the former, Nature has furnished powerful advantages [principally a deepwater harbor]. In favour of the latter is its vicinity to Georgetown." Most of the land around the Eastern Branch belonged to Daniel Carroll of Duddington and his cousin Notley Young. Because they had patented some of the land for a settlement to be called Carrollsburg, Washington used to refer to them as "the Carrollsburg proprietors," and his strategy depended on playing them off against the Georgetown proprietors, so that each group feared that the capital might be located on the other's land.

The order for L'Enfant to begin work at the Eastern Branch was motivated by the reluctance of some Georgetown proprietors to sell at a reasonable price. On March 2, Washington assured his associates that it was only a feint, so that "on seeing this operation begun at the Eastern branch, the proprietors nearer Georgetown who have hitherto refused to accommodate, will let themselves down to reasonable terms."

The same tactics were then applied to the Carrollsburg owners, this time using an outline plan by Jefferson showing streets and buildings on a site nearer to Georgetown. Either site would have produced a capital measuring around fifteen hundred acres, a size that Jefferson advised the president would be "sufficient." But on March 28, when the president appeared in person to negotiate with the holdouts among the proprietors, it became clear that he wanted not one or the other but both, the mouth of the Eastern Branch *and* the lands adjacent to Georgetown, together with territory running inland from the Potomac for more than a mile, an area covering more than six thousand acres.

In a hard-nosed piece of real estate negotiation, he let both groups of proprietors understand that any delay in their agreement to the entire deal might "degear the measure altogether." The threat was effective, and on March 31 Washington observed in his journal, "[They] saw the propriety of my observation . . . and mutually agreed to surrender for public purposes one half of the land they severally possessed . . . This business being thus happily finished and some direction given to the Commissioners, the Surveyor and Engineer with respect to the mode of laying out the district—I left Georgetown, dined in Alexandria and reached Mount Vernon in the evening."

The three commissioners had the task of ensuring that the capital was ready for occupation by the year 1800 and were to play as crucial a role as the Surveyor and the Engineer. Each was Washington's handpicked choice. His personal representative, Dr. David Stuart from Alexandria, Virginia, was an old friend, quiet, well-read, and married to the widow of Washington's stepson. The legal expertise came from Thomas Johnson, a former governor of Maryland and owner of fifteen thousand acres in nearby Anne Arundell County, who had recently been appointed an associate justice of the Supreme Court and was often absent as a result. The real power lay with Daniel Carroll of Rock Creek, a congressman and a member of Maryland's wealthiest and most influential family. He was closely related to both Charles Carroll, generally acknowledged to be the richest man in the United States, and the Carrollsburg proprietors.

This family connection was seen as no more of an obstacle to Carroll's appointment than Washington's own financial interests. "If the commissioners live near the place, they may in some instance be influenced by self interest and partialities," Jefferson acknowledged, "but they will push the work with zeal; if they are from distant and northwardly, they will be more impartial, but may affect delays."

The success of the deal Washington had forced through depended entirely on the boom in land speculation. The proprietors agreed to sell land designated for public buildings and parks to the United States for about $67 an acre; land designated for streets, however, was to be given to the government, while land designated for houses would be split half and half between the government and the owners. The price for public building land yielded the proprietors a fair profit, but the real gain would come from the increase in the value of the house lots as more people flocked to live in the new capital. On its side, the government got the five hundred acres needed for public buildings for about $35,000 and stood to make such large profits on the sale of house lots that the entire operation might be self-financing.

In May, a pamphlet written by an Eastern Branch proprietor, George Walker, was published in London announcing that "the City of Washington [is] now building for the Metropolis of America." Reminding his readers of the "immense fortunes" already made in U.S. real estate, the author predicted this to be "the next field for speculation in America." Apparently no one considered what might happen if the boom came to an end.

Although he had approved L'Enfant's preliminary sketch, the president now wrote telling him to expand his ideas. "It will be of great importance to the public interest to comprehend as much ground (to be ceded by individuals) as there is any tolerable prospect of obtaining," he advised his engineer on April 4. "Although it may not be immediately wanting, it will nevertheless encrease the Revenue." In other words, he wanted as large a city as L'Enfant could imagine, and to L'Enfant's enduring fame, he imagined on a behemoth scale.

He pushed the "President's Palace," as he termed the White House, farther toward Georgetown until it was a full mile northwest of "the Congresshouse"; he created a broad mall running due west to the Potomac from the Capitol; he scattered fifteen great squares across the site to represent the fifteen states that by then made up the Union; he drew vast avenues radiating from the squares like the spokes of a wheel; and since all this was free land, he specified that each avenue should be double the usual breadth of a main street.

The nearest comparison to this gigantism was the new capital of St. Petersburg that another French architect, Jean-Baptiste Le Blond, had laid out across the swampy delta of the Neva River in 1717 for the Russian czar

Peter the Great. But his plans were confined to the land on either bank of the river closest to the island fortress of St. Peter and St. Paul. Not even Czar Peter, an autocrat capable of conscripting a workforce of up to three hundred thousand people, thought of commissioning a design on the scale of that dreamed up by L'Enfant for his democratic patron.

Up to that time, the largest planned city in America was Philadelphia, a plain grid of streets that Thomas Holme had laid out on an arrowhead of land between the Delaware and Schuylkill rivers. Not only was L'Enfant's city approximately three times the size of Holme's, his inspiration was the infinitely more complex design devised by André Le Nôtre in 1663 for the gardens of Versailles, a series of focal points from which radiated paths and vistas connecting the farthest parts of the garden with one another. To complicate matters further, Washington's intricate deal made it of paramount importance to establish accurate plans showing not only streets, avenues, and house lots, but who already owned the land, and where the existing boundaries ran in this enormous construction site.

Even if L'Enfant had been the properly trained engineer Washington supposed him to be, he would have faced difficulties in realizing such an immense concept. But with no scientific training, no technical background, and no experience in drawing up accurate, scale maps, he was lost. His only surviving plan of the city, a sketch delivered to the president in August, consisted simply of ruled lines without compass points, descriptions, or any indication of scale. It is hardly surprising that to translate vision into reality, he should have depended utterly on Andrew Ellicott. What is astonishing, given the American's passion for order and the Frenchman's voluble flamboyance, was the warmth of their partnership. Like many others, Ellicott was charmed by L'Enfant's enthusiasm and imagination, and a warm working friendship quickly developed.

The first essential step was to make up for L'Enfant's lack of expertise. Ellicott had already assembled a team of axmen and four trained surveyors, and he promptly loaned the services of one of them, a professional engineer named Isaac Roberdeau, to help with the survey and act as L'Enfant's lieutenant. During the summer, Ellicott also took time from running the boundary of the federal district to measure the exact longitude and latitude of Jenkins Hill, where L'Enfant proposed to build the Congress-house, or Capitol. And in August, when L'Enfant raced back to Philadelphia to show the president his plan, Sally received a letter from her husband telling her, "I expect my companion Major L'Enfant which is prounounced in English *Longfong* will pay you a visit in my name some time next week. He is a most worthy French Gentleman and though not one of the most handsome of men, he is from good Breeding and native politeness a first rate favourite among the ladies."

Washington had ordered the first housing lots to be ready for sale in October 1791, a deadline that forced both men into a hectic schedule. Shortly after beginning work, Ellicott fell sick with flu, but Isaac Briggs, another of his assistants, reported that not even illness interfered with his early-morning start from Georgetown at the beginning of the week: "He used actually to arrive at our camp on the lines, at no less distance than seven miles from that town, on Monday morning before it was light enough to see distinctly without a candle. It was also his usual custom [during the week] to breakfast by candlelight in the morning; the labors of the day commenced before sunrise."

The rushed timetable took its toll, especially in the woods where a track twenty feet wide had to be cleared along the territory's borders. "I have had a number of men killed this summer," Ellicott reported mournfully, "one of whom was a worthy ingenious and truly valuable character. He has left a wife and three small children to lament his untimely fate." After four months, the fifty-nine-year-old Benjamin Banneker found the pressure too much, and in May when Ellicott's youngest brother, Benjamin, arrived, he took the opportunity to return to the Patapsco.

Banneker already had copious calculations of the ephemerides necessary for an almanac, and during his time in the federal district he had picked up the need for order and accuracy that had become second nature to Ellicott. Before the summer was over, he delivered his figures to the Baltimore printer William Goddard, who was persuaded to publish it with the help of a letter of recommendation signed by no fewer than three Ellicotts, headed by Andrew. The following year, *Benjamin Banneker's Pennsylvania, Delaware, Maryland and Virginia Almanac and Ephemeris for the year of our lord 1792* was published. Presented with this evidence of an African-American's abilities, Jefferson publicly shuffled back from his earlier assertions of black inferiority, allowing the possibility of "respectable intelligence in that race," although privately he insinuated, quite wrongly, that the almanac was produced with "aid from Ellicot[t], who was his neighbor and friend, and never missed an opportunity of puffing him." His equivocations had no effect on the lasting fame that Banneker's almanac secured.

As the summer of 1791 turned to fall and the October deadline approached, Ellicott transferred his brother Benjamin to assist Roberdeau. Eventually he abandoned his own task of running the perimeter of the federal district and put himself, Briggs, and the entire Ellicott team to work on Pierre L'Enfant's survey.

Since the capital consisted of nothing more than surveyor's marks and walkways cut through the woods and undergrowth, potential customers had to have a map showing its proposed shape, otherwise they would, in the president's pithy phrase, be "buying a Pig in a Poke [sack]." In early September the city commissioners ordered an engraving to be made of the master plan in L'Enfant's possession and ten thousand copies printed. It was to be entitled "A Map of the City of Washington in the Territory of Columbia"—the first time that either the capital or the district had been named.

Until that moment, Washington had personally supervised the work, repeatedly visiting the site to talk through problems with both the Engineer and the Surveyor. Now the three commissioners took over. Since Johnson's duties as an associate justice of the Supreme Court frequently took him away from the federal district, Daniel Carroll became the lead figure. Long experience of land speculation, from a 1763 investment in the Mississippi Land Company through postwar deals in confiscated loyalist estates, had conditioned Carroll to regard the business of laying out the city as nothing more than a technical step in preparing the property for sale. It was no way to handle the temperamental L'Enfant.

The flash point came over the map of the city. The very idea of an early sale appalled L'Enfant because it would mean losing control over parts of the city before his masterpiece was complete. Despite the commissioners' peremptory orders, he adamantly refused to provide any kind of map, leaving possible purchasers with no option but to guess the shape of the city from the paths cut through the trees. After a three-day sale that was supposed to finance the rest of the survey, just thirty-five lots were sold for an average of $265 each.

Although disappointed, Washington was more inclined to blame the commissioners than L'Enfant. Gently, he suggested that they try consulting rather than dictating, "because, from a source even less productive than L'Enfant's, may flow ideas that are capable of improvements; and because I have heard that Ellicot, who is also a man of uncommon talents in his way, and of a more placid temper, has intimated that no information had been required either from him, or L'Enfant."

In response to the president's prodding, L'Enfant did finally produce a plan of the nation's capital, which was presented to Congress in December 1791. It was, however, drawn by Andrew Ellicott. Unlike the August sketch, this was an accurate map of the area with longitude and latitude carefully worked out, a specified scale, and a grid of streets running precisely north-south and east-west, and calibrated on the meridian and parallel that Ellicott had measured out from Capitol Hill. The streets were crossed by wide Le Nôtre–inspired avenues reaching to distant hubs—"Philadelphia griddled on Versailles," as Jefferson described it—and the compass bearing of each one was exactly calculated and mapped.

Andrew Ellicott's plan of Washington, D.C.

Accompanying the map was an explanation in Ellicott's handwriting of the symbols and dimensions of the streets and avenues, and in case there was any doubt about its reliability, the map carried a characteristic declaration that began, "In order to execute the above plan, Mr Ellicott drew a true Meridian line by celestial observation," and ended with the usual defensive assertion of the care taken: "He ran all the lines by a Transit Instrument, and determined the Acute Angles by actual measurement, and left nothing to the uncertainty of the Compass."

The latitude of the Capitol was entered as 38° 53′ north, but instead of the correct longitude of 77° 3′ west, it appeared as 0° 0′ west. This was Ellicott's unilateral decision that the prime meridian from which the whole of the United States was to be measured should no longer run through London but through its new capital. Relating the coordinates of meridians and parallels to a point on the mainland rather than overseas allowed exact distances to be measured from the base point, but patriotism was Ellicott's prime motive. The measurement of the United States should, he felt, begin from its capital, and the borders of a dozen states undreamt of in his lifetime would be affected by his innovation.

On a more mundane and practical level, the map also showed that he had begun the vital task of marking out the lots whose sale was supposed to pay for the capital's development. The huge site was divided into more than eleven hundred squares, most of which were subdivided into housing lots, giving over fifteen thousand lots to be pegged out. As each square was marked with marble stones at the corners, its boundaries were entered on the surveyors' plats, then transferred to a large master plan, which symbolically remained in L'Enfant's hands. The success of Washington's plans for the city's development would rest on the use made of this document.

That November, L'Enfant decided to pull down a house being built by Daniel Carroll of Duddington, nephew of Carroll the commissioner, because it was found to project over a line showing where a square was to go. In the city's grand scheme, it was virtually irrelevant, and Ellicott believed the line could be adjusted without harm, but to L'Enfant the intrusion was a deliberate blemish on his masterpiece. He ordered Roberdeau to pull it down and, when the commissioners had Roberdeau arrested, went in person to supervise the destruction of Carroll's building to a pile of rubble.

This violent reaction sprang from L'Enfant's discovery that Carroll the commissioner was actively aiding his relatives to retain strategic lots around the Capitol and the Eastern Branch so that the land could be sold as a package to land speculators in Europe and northern cities. As Washington himself put it, "One of the reasons for L'Enfant's reserve and delay in publishing his mature plan was his conviction that the Commissioners were willing to favor the real estate speculators more than they were willing to cooperate in establishing his plan."

The federal government was less than two years old, and this was the first sale of federal land to individual buyers, but no one except L'Enfant would have been surprised to find such close ties between commissioners and speculators. The government of New York had favored Gorham, just as Pennsylvania acted for Nicholson and Morris. The federal authority could be assumed to do the same, and significantly even Washington did not censure the commissioners on that score. Speculation was the engine intended to drive forward the building of the capital, a fact that L'Enfant refused to accept. He had become an American citizen and changed his first name from Pierre to Peter, but he retained an entirely French belief that Washington was a transatlantic Louis XIV whose commands had to be obeyed. So far from being all-powerful, the chief executive was haunted by the fear that Congress would, if given the chance, strike down the Residence Act, and, as Washington told Stuart in 1792, "the Government will remain where it now is," meaning in Philadelphia. A cultural shift into an American mindset was required to appreciate the consequences of a president who felt too weak even to be confident of retaining his own federal district. It meant that he could not approach Congress for extra funds, and that if his ambitions for his gigantic capital were to be realized, the power of the speculation had to be harnessed rather than opposed.

In December, L'Enfant took down another house, this time belonging to Notley Young. "*He must know* there is a line beyond which he will not be suffered to go," Washington exclaimed in exasperation to Jefferson. "Whether it is zeal—an impetuous temper or other motives that lead him to such blameable conduct I will not take upon me to decide—but be it what it will, it must be checked; or we shall have no Commissioners." Jefferson

sent a final warning that L'Enfant had to respect the commissioners' instructions, but to no effect.

Early in 1792 L'Enfant presented the commissioners with a budget for developments in the coming year of over $1 million. Since their income from
sales was barely $7,000, the commissioners rejected his proposals, but with
magnificent disregard for anything but the beauty of his design, L'Enfant
ordered Roberdeau to begin quarrying stone for the construction of the
President's Palace and the Capitol. This time he had gone too far, and on
February 27 Jefferson wrote to him, "I am instructed by the President to inform you that notwithstanding the desire he has entertained to preserve
your agency in the business, the condition upon which it is done is inadmissable and your services must be at an end."

What snapped Washington's patience was more than L'Enfant's way-
wardness. Sales demanded an accurate illustration of the site, and despite
the existence of the December map, L'Enfant continued to refuse to produce a plan showing the housing lots for would-be customers. "Many weeks
have been lost since you came to Philadelphia in obtaining a Plan for engraving," Washington wrote the day after L'Enfant's dismissal, "notwithstanding the earnestness with which I requested it might be prepared on
your first arrival. Further delay in this business is inadmissable."

Despairing of the Frenchman, Jefferson asked Andrew Ellicott in mid-
February to produce a map, and although L'Enfant refused to let him see the
master plan, Ellicott was able to put a map of the capital in the president's
hands just ten days later. "In this business we met with difficulties of a very
serious nature," Ellicott reported to the commissioners on February 23,
1792. "Major L'Enfant refused us the use of the original! What his motives
were, God knows.—The plan which we have furnished, I believe will be
found to answer the ground better than the large one in the Major's hands."

The authorship of this February map was to prove pivotal in the legends
that rapidly grew about the capital's foundation. It could hardly have been
otherwise, since it became the official plan on which the city was based.
The first of the legends was that Banneker enabled Ellicott to produce the
map by remembering every detail of L'Enfant's master plan, but since the
African-American had left nine months earlier, this tale, however charming, is make-believe. More enduring was the story that Ellicott had stolen
L'Enfant's plan and passed it off as his own. His February map certainly bore

the formula "To execute this plan, Mr Ellicott drew a true Meridian," etc., while L'Enfant's name was omitted, but exactly the same words had first appeared on the map they had jointly produced in December, without any reference to L'Enfant's contribution, and L'Enfant had not objected. The phrase was not a claim to authorship but to accuracy. Finally the legend that the city's shape was dictated by a desire to incorporate into it Freemason symbols is equally fanciful, for although many of those concerned in building the city were Masons, including Washington and Commissioner Stuart, neither of the two people responsible for its design, L'Enfant and Ellicott, was among their number.

The most immediate effect of Ellicott's map was to destroy the men's yearlong partnership. L'Enfant felt himself betrayed and bitterly attacked his former friend for producing a map that "is now most unmercifully spoiled and altered from the original plan to a degree indeed evidently tending to disgrace me and ridicule the very undertaking." For almost a century, the truth of his complaint could not be checked because the December map disappeared, although Washington did confirm that "many alterations have been made from L'Enfant's plan," some of which were suggested by himself and Jefferson. When the map was rediscovered in 1887, however, the similarities appeared more obvious than the differences. There was the same central triangle formed by the Capitol, White House, and Mall, and the same grid of streets overlaid on spokes radiating from hubs scattered across the city.

This resemblance was hardly surprising. Ellicott had drawn the earlier map, he and L'Enfant had collaborated throughout in translating ideas into workable blueprints on the ground and on the page, and because Ellicott's team had primarily been responsible for laying out the city, he had copies of all the survey plats. As Washington expressed it to Congress, "Had it not been for the materials which [Ellicott] happened to possess, it is probable that no engraving from L'Enfant's draughts ever would have been exhibited to the public."

A closer examination, however, reveals the sort of changes that would have infuriated L'Enfant. Massachusetts Avenue was straightened out, South Carolina Avenue was extended, the total number of avenues was reduced and their alignment simplified, the area round the President's House was enlarged, gardens at the center of hubs were omitted, and the general appearance was tightened. But easily the most striking change was that the avenues were named for the first time. Since L'Enfant had never suggested any titles, and Washington and Jefferson would surely have named the capital's chief highway after their own home state, Andrew Ellicott must have the credit for giving the United States' most famous street its name, Pennsylvania Avenue. Nevertheless, in the eyes of the president the innovation that really mattered was that the squares containing the all-important housing lots were at last numbered and laid out ready for sale.

Writing to the commissioners in March 1792, the president suggested there was really only one candidate to take L'Enfant's place: "A better than Mr. Ellicott for all matters, at present, can not be had. No one I presume, can lay out the ground with more accuracy, lay out the squares, and divide them into lots better. He must understand levelling [calculation of heights] also perfectly, and has, I suppose competent skill in the conducting of Water. Beyond these, your opportunities to form an opinion of him must exceed mine. I believe he is obliging, and he would be perfectly Subordinate. What he asks, five dollars a day (if Sundays are included) seems high, but whether a fit character can be had for less I am unable to say."

The hint was enough, and the commissioners duly hired Ellicott in L'Enfant's place. Bearing the title of superintendent, he set about harnessing the engine of speculation with a plan to sell off first the commercially valuable lots closest to Georgetown and the Eastern Branch. To ensure the integrity of the design, the lots in the central area between the Capitol and White House were to be held back until the public buildings were constructed. While the Georgetown and Eastern Branch lots were being measured out, Ellicott returned to defining the last lines of the perimeter. Before the summer was finished, the building of the President's House began, not to L'Enfant's design as originally intended, but following a plan incorporating a pillared façade and graceful symmetry submitted by the architect James Hoban. To preserve the site of Notley Young's house, Ellicott altered L'Enfant's plan again by moving the Capitol two hundred yards farther east, a favor for which the commissioners were duly grateful.

For six months the honeymoon persisted, with each side commending the other—"We have told Majr. Ellicott that we wish an opportunity, to make him a present at the Close of the work for his Expedition in doing it," the commissioners confided to Jefferson in the summer, and Ellicott assured the secretary of state that "in my opinion [the commissioners] have conducted their business with judgment, and firmness."

The harmony did not survive a second disastrous sale of house lots in October 1792. With just fifty-two lots sold, most at the Georgetown end, the simmering jealousy between the two sets of proprietors came to a boil. In a fading market, each side became desperate to obtain any advantage available. Georgetown seemed to be favored by Ellicott because the lots at their end of the site were measured and numbered first, but Carrollsburg held a trump card because, as L'Enfant once confided to Jefferson, "it seemed to be the sole object of the [commissioners] to benefit their interest."

Following the October sale, the commissioners, particularly Carroll and Stuart, began to criticize Ellicott for his slowness in marking out the lots. Loftily Ellicott dismissed their complaints as not having "even the shadow of a phantom for a foundation," but privately he shared L'Enfant's opinion about their real motives. "They never could be taught to distinguish between the President's House, Hotel and Capitol on the plan," he pointed out wearily to William Thornton, the Capitol's designer. "Mr Carroll [the commissioner], however, was enabled to point out Notley Young's and Daniel Carroll's lots which are much less conspicuous!!"

During the summer, a new surveyor and former slave dealer, James Dermott, was hired on the recommendation of David Stuart. An increasing number of slaves were being taken on for construction work, and part of the reason for Dermott's employment was that Ellicott refused to employ slaves himself. A confidential report noted that Dermott "now and then drinks to access [sic], and when enebrated [sic] . . . is unruly and quarrelsome." He was, however, the commissioners' man and, following the failure of the October sale, proved ruthless in favoring the Carrollsburg proprietors at the expense of Georgetown.

Soon after the new surveyor was taken on, Ellicott became convinced that Dermott was tampering with the master plan of the city's lots, and sabotaging the markers that delineated the house lots on the ground. Significantly they all concerned the squares nearest to Georgetown. To prove his suspicions, Ellicott demanded that Dermott hand over his city plans for comparison with the master plan and refused to authorize payment of his wages until he complied. On February 6, 1793, Dermott at last agreed to bring the papers round, but that night Ellicott's offices were broken into, and the master plan together with his astronomical calculations were stolen.

Thereafter matters rapidly descended into chaos. Ellicott bluntly accused Dermott of theft, only to be blamed himself by the commissioners for alterations and inaccuracies. When they ordered Ellicott to hand over all his papers, he refused on the grounds that Dermott had stolen them. The argument culminated with the commissioners demanding that Ellicott withdraw "a severe charge for which he ought to be well grounded before he made it." In a fury, he gave them notice of his intention to quit, and when they fired him anyway, the crew came out on strike in his support. By March 1793 work on the site had come to a complete halt, at which point both Washington and Jefferson intervened to require Ellicott's reinstatement.

The results were apparent from a jubilant letter Ellicott scribbled to Sally on April 10: "My victory was complete, and all my men reinstated in the City, after a suspension of one month. As my reputation depended on the determination, I neglected nothing in my power to defeat the Commissioners, but had to contend very unequally owing to all my papers being seized by their order the day after I returned from Philadelphia. And this day they were all restored to me again!!!"

His return was greeted by cheers from the Georgetown proprietors, but the real victors in the struggle were the Carrollsburg owners. Dermott was kept on the payroll, and with Washington's agreement the commissioners took money from construction of the President's House in the west to begin building the Capitol in the east. In a change of unambiguous symbolism, the Capitol was constructed to face not toward the President's House, but toward the Eastern Branch and the commercial district due to grow up on land owned by the Carrolls and Youngs. Their success appeared to be sealed by the arrival in Washington that summer of one of the United States' richest men, the young Bostonian James Greenleaf. He came with the stated intention of buying no fewer than twenty-five hundred lots, all at the eastern end of the site.

Convinced that his position had become impossible, Ellicott left Isaac Briggs in charge of the survey and returned home. "Where you are is all my happiness," he told his wife, "and if I can manage matters in such a manner as to be able to support you as you deserve without leaving you again, you may rest assured that my arms shall enfold you every night."

In Washington the triumph of the Carrolls seemed complete. The twenty-eight-year-old Greenleaf offered to pay $480,000 over seven years, split roughly half and half between the government and the Carroll and Young families. In addition he promised to build ten houses a year. He kept his word to the point of building twenty houses in the next two years on a knuckle of land pushing into the Potomac now known as Greenleaf's Point. With the President's House rising from its foundations, the Capitol's cornerstone laid, a hotel for congressmen being built, and the Treasury and Mint in the pipeline, the capital was apparently beginning to take tangible form.

Appearances were deceptive. In bleak reality the engine George Washington had relied on to drive the development of his capital had run out of power. Ever since the federal government had taken on the states' debts in 1790, the value of paper money had been growing. Once it became clear that a $100 bill was backed by the federal government, it rose in value from $20 to $90, then to face value. That killed the instant profit speculators were accustomed to make from buying land worth $100 with paper money worth one fifth as much. As demand in the United States slackened, speculators turned to Europe as a market and briefly found Dutch and British financiers ready to invest in American land. But in 1792, European interest started to wane when revolutionary France declared war on Austria. One year later, Britain and Spain were drawn into the conflict, and suddenly there was no more British finance. Frightened by the hostilities, Holland's financiers also drew in their horns. In 1793 when Greenleaf made a fundraising visit to Europe, he was sent away empty-handed.

In desperation Greenleaf brought in the two giants of the land market, Robert Morris and John Nicholson, to finance the capital's development. They persuaded Thomas Law, a wealthy British merchant, to buy five hundred Washington lots for $155,000, but the full deal was never carried through. Nothing could revive the market. When one Georgetown proprietor, Samuel Blodgett, tried to raise money for development by running a lottery with housing lots as prizes, it had to be canceled due to lack of interest. All along the Atlantic coast, land speculators were in retreat. Morris and Nicholson bought one another's stock with promissory notes bearing a face value of $2,000 and a street value of nothing. The shares that Greenleaf received for his Washington investment paid no interest, and the lots

that Andrew Ellicott had marked out so carefully disappeared into the ownership of a web of interweaving companies and trusts whose only assets were
one another's worthless paper.

In 1795 the first set of commissioners were replaced, and soon afterward
Dermott returned to trading slaves. Except for the White House, the Capitol, and a cluster of buildings at either end of Pennsylvania Avenue, development gradually closed down. Almost the last to read the writing on
the wall was Daniel Carroll of Duddington, nephew of the commissioner
and owner of fourteen hundred acres due south of the Capitol. His cousin
Notley Young sold to Greenleaf for what he could get, but Carroll was determined to make a killing and hung on for a higher price. When bankruptcy forced both Morris and Nicholson behind bars in Philadelphia's
plush Prune Street prison—"a hotel with grated doors," to use Morris's non-
chalant phrase—the better part of Washington's eastern end was tied up in
a legal maze that kept lawyers busy for half a century. Carroll died almost
penniless.

Until the tangle was straightened out, Washington remained "the city of
infinite distances," hardly growing beyond the Capitol, President's House,
and a scatter of offices, hotels, houses, and dockyards connected by muddy
paths cut through the scrub. In 1796, a guest of Thomas Law's reported
from the Capitol, "I saw on every side a thick wood pierced with avenues in
a more or less perfect state," but ten years later when the dyspeptic traveler
Charles Janson passed through, the view had deteriorated. "Some half-
starved cattle browsing among the bushes present a melancholy spectacle to
a stranger whose expectation has been wound up by the illusive description
of speculative writers," he noted. "So very thinly is the city peopled, and so
little is it frequented, that quails and other birds are constantly shot within
a hundred yards of the Capitol."

The fate of its first progenitor mirrored that of the city. For years Peter
L'Enfant haunted the doors of Congress, petitioning for compensation,
though nothing would satisfy him. He rejected contemptuously both an offer of $3,000 and a post at the new Military Academy at West Point. Grad-
ually he dwindled into a forlorn, angry vagrant wandering the streets he had
designed. Then toward the end of his life he was rescued and given shelter
by the compassionate William Digges, the son-in-law of L'Enfant's old enemy Notley Young.

The failure of the capital's development was to have a pervasive effect upon the appearance of cities in the United States. In 1811, the New York City commissioners appointed to map Manhattan's growth looked at Washington's street plan, which they sniffily described as "those supposed improvements, by circles, ovals, and stars which certainly embellish a plan, whatever may be their effects as to convenience and utility," and decided that Manhattan should be built "strait-sided and right angled." The ease with which New York expanded and grew rich, compared with the stagnation of Washington during the next three quarters of a century, was enough to convince almost every new American city to construct itself in a neat square grid.

If there was any single individual to blame for the capital's blighted condition, it was the president after whom it was named. Washington's military genius lay in his tactical ability to sense and take instant advantage of any weakness in the disposition of his enemy—whether in the fogbound withdrawal from Brooklyn to Manhattan or the surprise attack at Trenton. However, in making use of the rivalry between the landowners of Georgetown and Carrollsburg to acquire a site for the capital four times as large as originally thought necessary, he bit off more than could be chewed by the tiny government of which he was the chief executive.

By 1790, the short history of the states had shown that land speculation and government were inseparable. Nevertheless, a healthy fear of rebellion and the democratic legacy of 1776 forced the state governments to keep some check on the activities of speculators. The federal district had no western farmers to engender fear and, because Washington was determined to prevent Congress interfering, no democratic supervision to bridle the instinct of the Carrolls to look after family interests. What the federal district needed, paradoxically, was more government.

In its early years, the state of the Union often bore an uncanny resemblance to the state of the capital. To many Americans, the area of the United States seemed impossibly large, and the factions within it impossible to reconcile. What held the Union together were two ingredients missing in the federal district—an increasingly powerful central government and settlers determined that it should be democratic.

CHAPTER 6

MIRRORS OF THE MISSISSIPPI

*I am aware, however, that in the meantime, the attempts
of nefarious men might, for a moment, disturb your re-
pose. Indeed, the anxieties of some amongst you there-
upon have been suggested to me; but fear not; our ability
is proportioned to the occasion, and the arm of the United
States is mighty.*

GOVERNOR WINTHROP SARGENT,
address to the people of the Mississippi Territory, 1798

To ESCAPE THE backbiting in the District of Columbia, Andrew Ellicott took a job as Pennsylvania's commissioner responsible for laying
out the route of a road to connect Presqu'isle with the rest of the state. "We
live here like a parcel of Monks, or Hermits," he wrote happily from upstate
Pennsylvania in 1794, "and have not a woman of any complexion among
us—our linnen is dirty, our faces and hands brown, and to complete the picture our beards are generally long. O sweet Woman, without thee man is a
Brute."

Compared to the intricacies of running a parallel or establishing the exact coordinates of latitude and longitude for the capital of the United
States, this amounted to elementary survey work. It was only necessary to
find a firm surface connecting the few existing settlements that lay between
Pittsburgh and Lake Erie. Compass bearings corrected occasionally by sightings of the Pole Star for true north guided the choice of route, but on this
occasion Ellicott was less valuable for his mastery of the heavens than for

his familiarity with the country and the Native Americans who still lived there.

The road was of vital importance to the Pennsylvania Population Company. Established by John Nicholson and counting Robert Morris as a substantial investor, the company was the principal owner of land within the Erie Triangle, and a direct connection with the rich markets in the south would add enormously to the value of their investment. On the larger scale of history, however, the road was notable for a quite different reason. In 1794, it became the cause of a dispute between Pennsylvania and the United States in which for the first time the federal government won a victory over a state government. The road to Presqu'isle was thus the place where the United States' long struggle for dominance over the states began to take shape.

Having purchased the Triangle from the federal government and persuaded the Senecas through negotiations with Cornplanter to relinquish ownership of their lands, Pennsylvania had good reason to believe that it was entitled to act as it pleased within its own borders. On the ground, conditions were more confused.

An unofficial buffer zone had been created south of the Great Lakes by the British policy of encouraging Native Americans to resist the settlers' advance into their territory. A decade after the Revolution, British troops still patrolled and garrisoned forts south of Lake Erie, and in the Ohio Valley the Western Confederation of Miamis, Delawares, and other nations led by Little Turtle had inflicted a stinging defeat on federal forces under General Arthur St. Clair in 1791. In the Triangle itself, the majority of Senecas furiously contested the area claimed by Pennsylvania under the terms of the agreement with Cornplanter. Their anger suggested they were ready to take up arms in alliance with either the Western Confederation or a revived Six Nations.

Aware of the sensitivities involved, Governor Thomas Mifflin warned the Pennsylvania militia who acted as guards to the road commissioners that they were "to avoid giving any occasion of offence to the Peaceable Indians or to the British Garrisons in that quarter." Ellicott let his teenage son, Andy, join the party, but added his own bleak advice that they could expect "privation and exposure . . . the risk of sickness, and the dangers arising from the revengeful feelings of the Indians."

During 1793 when the route was being explored, their presence was scarcely noticed, but in May 1794 Ellicott and General William Irvine, his fellow commissioner, returned to the Triangle accompanied by seventy militia, who doubled up as axmen to clear a path through the woods. Their arrival provoked immediate hostility, and when a man from the Six Nations was murdered by American settlers, Ellicott's party faced the possibility of war with something like sixteen hundred Senecas. Sensibly they decided to take refuge in a wooden stockade grandly known as Fort Le Boeuf, now Waterford, Pennsylvania, where they were penned up for most of the summer.

Responding to the crisis, Mifflin called up one thousand more militia—an aggressive move that brought Pennsylvania into direct conflict with the interests of the United States. To the west, General Anthony Wayne with a federal army was slowly encircling the Western Confederation, and in London the last details of the Jay Treaty under which the British would withdraw from their forts were being negotiated. All of this would be put at risk by an outbreak of hostilities with the remains of the Six Nations federation.

"The President of the United States, on mature reflection," wrote Henry Knox, secretary of war, to Mifflin, "is of opinion that it is advisable to suspend, for the present, the establishment at Presque Isle . . . [due to] the high probability of an immediate rupture with the Six Nations, if the measure be persisted in." This was an unwarranted interference. The Triangle was certainly within Pennsylvania, and since all Seneca title to it had supposedly been extinguished, the state was entitled to defend its settlers within its own borders. Even his attorney general, William Bradford, deemed that the president was exceeding his authority.

Mifflin, for his part, was outraged. "What power is there," he demanded of the president, "to pass a law which could control the Commonwealth in the legitimate exercise of her territorial jurisdiction?" Nevertheless, the president had in effect declared the situation to be a national emergency, and reluctantly Mifflin decided he had no choice but to give way. The call-up of militia was rescinded, and orders were sent to Ellicott to suspend the road making and settlement of Presqu'isle. In his letter, Mifflin explained that failure to cooperate "in the measures of the General Government, at a crisis deemed by the President to be peculiarly delicate, may be rendered a subject of condemnation."

Mifflin's decision left Ellicott bewildered. "The interference of the General

Government with the internal politics of the State on that occasion appears to me highly improper," he replied to the governor. "The military arrangements of the General Government will leave a valuable portion of our citizens a prey to savage barbarity . . . [The Indians] have nothing to fear from the circuitous route of 300 miles! taken by General Wayne."

His view was shared by most Pennsylvanians, and through the summer of 1794 Washington's influence hung in the balance. In the fort, the militia who planned to settle in Presqu'isle when their tour of duty ended almost mutinied in frustration, and the attempts by state officials, including Ellicott, to find a compromise with Cornplanter and the Senecas all ended in failure. Refusing to back off, however, Washington insisted that a U.S. negotiator, Timothy Pickering, by then his postmaster general, take charge, and Mifflin, thoroughly humiliated, withdrew altogether from the negotiations.

Almost immediately, however, the governor received a second, sharper reminder of the power that his president could exert. In July, farmers in western Pennsylvania saw off at gunpoint a U.S. marshal serving court orders on them for failing to register their whiskey distilleries for taxation, then burned the house of the federal tax collector. Although the Whiskey Rebellion, as it became known, was centered in western Pennsylvania, resistance spread throughout the Appalachians, from Kentucky as far north as New Hampshire, and the list of grievances went beyond the whiskey tax to include the familiar Regulator protests against unresponsive government, unfair fees charged by court officials, and the long distances to be covered to reach the nearest county court.

Having discussed the violence at length, however, Mifflin and senior Pennsylvania officials decided that it did not even merit calling out the militia. President Washington decided otherwise. His decision to call up a huge militia army of almost thirteen thousand men drawn from four states and lead them in person against the rebels was motivated, he said, by "the most solemn conviction, that the essential interests of the Union demand it." These certainly included putting an end to the sort of social unrest, like Shays's Rebellion, that he felt to be a risk to the nation's unity, but the massive response was also designed to impress Mifflin and Pennsylvania too. In a barbed comment in his journal made in late August, Washington noted that he had spent the day overseeing the assembly of the militia, "or rather I ought to have said urging & assisting Genl. Mifflin to do it." Mifflin attempted to duck out of these duties, but he could not miss the wider import of the armed might that the federal government could summon up.

As President Washington led out his troops to overawe the rebels, he received what he called the "official & pleasing accounts of [Wayne's] engagement with the Indians." On August 20, 1794, General Wayne's long encircling maneuver had finally trapped the Western Confederation's army in an opening in the forest, close to modern-day Toledo, Ohio. Firing from behind trees felled by a tornado, his troops annihilated the enemy in a stunning victory that was given the name Fallen Timbers.

The result was a triumph for Washington's use of federal power. For three crucial months during the summer, he had kept Pennsylvania in check and avoided driving the Senecas into alliance with the Western Confederation. In November, his peace policy paid a second dividend when the British signed the Jay Treaty, committing themselves to withdrawal from their forts.

Wayne's victory made it possible for a disgruntled Ellicott to complete the road to Presqu'isle, and to lay out the streets and shape of the city now known as Erie, Pennsylvania. His work brought rewards to both the Population Company and Pennsylvania, but the territory that the United States secured rendered their gains insignificant. The following summer, at the Treaty of Greenville, Wayne would force the defeated members of the Western Confederation to cede most of their territory to the United States. Suddenly the area of federal lands available for settlement stretched far beyond the Ohio River as far west as Wisconsin.

In Pennsylvania, the Whiskey Rebellion quickly disintegrated in the face of Washington's overwhelming force. One of the few rebels to be captured was the elderly Herman Husband, once a spokesman for the North Carolina Regulators, and driven to rebel again because he saw in the federal government "the old form of a beast's head." For seven months he languished in a Philadelphia jail awaiting execution, before being released. Broken in health, he died soon afterward, and his death signaled the end of the latest phase in the backcountry's revolution.

The flood of migrants traveling into the newly opened lands in the west would in time provide the next generation to rebel against the exclusive eastern elite who had always monopolized government in northern America. To that elite, however, the trains of wagons creaking through the Wilderness Road in the Alleghenies and the convoys of flatboats floating down the Ohio River presented the same problem that had earlier faced the states, and before them the colonial proprietors: how could the government retain control of the settlers and banditti moving west beyond their jurisdiction? The solution turned out to be no different from before—like its predecessors, the United States needed to establish a clear-cut boundary marking the area within which its laws held sway. Almost inevitably, it would be run by Andrew Ellicott.

The Treaty of San Lorenzo signed in 1795 with Spain gave the United States its first practical opportunity to demarcate the extent of its power. It provided a salutary reminder of the disparity in power between the young republic and the hemisphere's superpower.

When the American Revolution dismembered Britain's North American empire, Spain was the other great beneficiary. Between 1781 and 1783, it took advantage of the war in the north to seize the provinces of East and West Florida—modern-day Florida and the coastal areas of Alabama and Mississippi—that it had lost to Britain in 1763 after the French and Indian War. In the absence of any opposition, it also gained undisputed control of the entire Mississippi River. With those additions, the grandeur of Spanish America reached its apogee. Its total length stretched from Cape Horn to Canada, and in North America alone, the Floridas with the vast expanses of Louisiana, Texas, New Mexico, and California gave it territory three times that of the United States.

The borders of this gigantic empire were rarely clear. Not until 1771, more than 250 years after it first laid claim to the New World, did Spain find it necessary to try to define its boundaries with Portugal's possessions in South America. Its limits in North America were equally fuzzy. According to the Americans, the Mississippi River served as the unmistakable frontier between the empire and the United States, but Spanish galleys patrolled the waters and its forts commanded strategic points from New Madrid (near Cairo, Illinois) to Natchez. In 1782, John Jay reported that Count d'Arada, the Spanish ambassador to France, had designated the border, as Spain saw it, from a lake "east of the Flint River to the confluence of the Kanawa with the Ohio, thence round the western shores of Lakes Erie and Huron and

thence round Lake Michigan." This included most of Kentucky and Tennessee, and although Jay did not take the claim seriously, there was no doubt
that Spain's influence reached far to the east of the Mississippi.

How far was suggested by a letter sent in 1788 by John Sevier, Revolutionary hero and pioneer settler in Tennessee, to Diego de Gardoqui, the
Spanish envoy to the United States. "The people of this region," Sevier
wrote, "have come to realize truly upon what part of the world and upon
which nation their future happiness and security depend and they immediately infer that their interest and prosperity depend entirely upon the protection and liberality of your government."

The liberality that western settlers sought was permission to ship their
goods down the Mississippi to the great port of New Orleans. Unless the
United States could secure freedom of navigation on the river for its citizens, the transfer of loyalties to Spain seemed an obvious step to take. "There
is nothing which binds one country or one State to another but interest,"
Washington had predicted in 1783. "Without this cement the Western inhabitants can have no predilection for us."

Infuriated by the indifference of the eastern states to their needs, Kentucky's attorney general, Harry Innes, predicted in 1787, "This country will
in a few years Revolt from the Union and endeavor to erect an Independent
Government." That same year, when the territory's constitutional convention met, a powerful group lobbied for Kentucky to secede from the Union
and set itself up as an independent ally of Spain serving as "a permanent
barrier against Great Britain and the United States."

To preserve the Union, it was therefore essential to secure for the western
settlers the right of free navigation down the Mississippi to the great port of
New Orleans. Fuzzy zones of influence had to be replaced by a border that
reached to the middle of the river. All the United States had to offer its
powerful neighbor in return was a guarantee to demarcate an unmistakable
frontier between the Spanish Floridas and its own land-hungry citizens.

By brilliant diplomacy, emphasizing the threat of making an alternative
alliance with Britain against Spain, Thomas Pinckney, the American envoy
in Madrid, persuaded Spain's chief minister, Manuel Godoy, to accept this
lopsided bargain. In exchange for granting American citizens freedom of
navigation on the Mississippi, a clear-cut frontier between Spain and the

United States would be established along the old colonial border between Georgia and the Floridas. As laid down by the British in 1763, this would follow the thirty-first parallel for most of its length. So clearly were the terms of the Treaty of San Lorenzo in the United States' favor that even the president doubted Spain's intention to carry them out.

As the nation's expert on running parallels, Ellicott was Washington's personal choice in 1796 to be the U.S. commissioner responsible for demarcating the southern boundary. At a secret briefing, he warned Ellicott to resist any Spanish attempt to delay putting the treaty into effect. He was also to be wary of influential Americans known to be working for the Spanish government who were trying to detach Kentucky from the Union. "[The president] thought it a business of much importance, both to the honour and safety of the country," Ellicott noted, "and directed me to pay a strict attention to that subject."

The new commissioner moved in a small world. His boss, the secretary of state, was the Teutonic disciplinarian Timothy Pickering, who had made his fortune speculating in Luzerne County, Pennsylvania, while Thomas Freeman, the surveyor appointed to carry out the actual legwork on the frontier, had previously been James Dermott's assistant in Washington. Earlier acquaintance colored Ellicott's judgments. Pickering remained "the excellent Colonel Pickering" who had brought peace to the frontier, while Freeman, an enterprising, hotheaded adventurer, was regarded with dark suspicion. A personal escort of thirty-five soldiers accompanied the commissioner, as well as a small military detachment under the independent command of Lieutenant Percy Pope. The only members of the expedition that Ellicott had personally selected were the assistants required to look after his instruments and records, his son Andy, and two young surveyors, David Gillespie and Peter Walker.

In the absence of her husband and eldest son, Sally Ellicott became the head of a family in which the next five children were all daughters. The girls' lively correspondence showed that they grew up to be opinionated, challenging, and independent, characteristics that must have been fostered by Sally. And since she herself had just become a mother for the eleventh time at the age of forty-five, it is possible that sadness at Ellicott's departure was tinged slightly with relief. Neither could have guessed, however, that it would be almost four years before they met again.

. . .

Although no one could run a parallel like Ellicott, there must have been doubts whether someone so touchy could handle the diplomatic problems that would be involved. In the event, his character rather than his science turned out to be the vital quality on which implementation of the treaty depended. It was clear from the moment the party of surveyors and soldiers assembled in Pittsburgh in the fall of 1796 that he would allow nothing to delay his progress.

In October, falling water levels stopped river traffic on the Ohio, but rather than wait till the spring Ellicott insisted that his team haul their heavy boats over the half-submerged rocks. Below Louisville they came to the infamous Ohio Falls, which normally appeared as a smooth slide of water, but were now reduced to a welter of white horsetails cascading between black rocks. After a brief examination, he "concluded to risk the boats rather than be detained." So his three vessels were steered straight for the lip of the falls, "and a little after noon all the boats were over but not without being considerably damaged, the one that I was in had nine of her timbers broken."

Nowhere in this headlong dash did he forget to note the daily temperature, the flattening of the Alleghenies and gradual appearance of the prairies, the composition of the soil, the salt springs, and the lives of the pioneer farmers. "The people who reside on the Ohio are brave, enterprising and warlike" ran an entry in his journal that offers an early account of the frontier character, "which will generally be found the strongest characteristical marks of the inhabitants of all our new settlements. It arises from their situation: being constantly in danger from the Indians, they are habituated to alarms, and acts of bravery become a duty they owe to themselves and their friends."

On the minus side, they lacked education, science, and the self-restraint required to prevent bravery from degenerating into ferocity, and economically they were in a mess. The Ohio Valley could produce everything people needed for survival—corn, cattle, hogs, apples, whiskey—and any surplus, including the coal that some were mining, could be sent downriver for sale in New Orleans. Anything they couldn't produce themselves, from rifles to saucepans, had to be imported, and "so long as they depend upon the Atlantic states for their supplies of European manufactures, the balance of trade will constantly be against them, and draw off that money which should be applied to the improvement of the country, and the payment of their taxes." As always, he felt that he was carrying civilization with him. Once the treaty was implemented, the Mississippi would be opened, imports would become cheaper, the country would improve, and taxes would be paid.

His goal was Natchez, where Manuel Gayoso de Lemos, governor of the district and the Spanish boundary commissioner, was waiting for him. On the Mississippi, however, Spanish garrison commanders repeatedly tried to prevent them from proceeding, but Ellicott pressed on, claiming diplomatic immunity. In the face of a message from Gayoso demanding that the U.S. party wait for a specific invitation before proceeding farther, Lieutenant Pope decided to remain at Walnut Hills, modern Vicksburg, Mississippi, with the military detachment, but Ellicott was not deterred. An American adventurer named Philip Nolan, whose contract to sell wild mustangs to the Spanish army gave him high-level military contacts, had secretly warned him that Gayoso was under instructions from Madrid to use any means to prevent the treaty from taking effect. Leaving Pope behind, Ellicott hurried on downriver with his assistants and axmen and on February 23, 1797, arrived at Natchez.

The settlement existed on two levels. The older part, a cluster of dwellings and warehouses, stood round the landing stage at the foot of a tall bluff that jutted into the brown, swirling river, but the new city of Natchez itself and its fort were built high up on the hill so that the Spanish cannon could control navigation on the Mississippi. To Gayoso's fury, Ellicott's party ignored all protocol and, having landed without asking permission, simply pitched camp on a level with the fort. The first message from the Spanish was a request that the flag they had hoisted be taken down. "This met with a positive refusal," Ellicott noted, "and the flag wore out upon its staff."

By rights it should not have had time to get even slightly threadbare. According to the celestial observations Ellicott made over the next few nights, the thirty-first parallel, the frontier agreed by Pinckney's treaty, ran thirty-nine miles south of Natchez, and the Spanish therefore had no legal right to remain. But when the two men met, Gayoso offered a plausible reason for not evacuating the fort. Spanish troops had to stay, he explained, to protect the five thousand inhabitants in the area around Natchez from attack by

Chickasaw and Choctaw Indians, and from invasion by Loyalists and British and American freebooters coming south from Canada. The fort could not be evacuated until these dangers passed, and U.S. forces could not take over the fort until it had been evacuated. It was a standoff.

Strategically Natchez commanded both the river upstream and all the hinterland of what is now Mississippi and Alabama down to the Gulf. The city was at the heart of a new Spanish policy toward American immigrants, adopted in 1788 by the then chief minister, José Moñino, Count of Floridablanca. Instead of keeping Americans out of West Florida and Louisiana, Spain would try "to attract to our side the inhabitants of the Ohio and Mississippi." They were to be offered free land, freedom to follow their own religion, and no less enticingly freedom to transport their goods down the Mississippi. Gayoso himself had been chosen to proclaim the new regime, and he had selected the location of the city of Natchez and laid out its streets. Its rapid growth, doubling in population every two years, was testament to the policy's success. Every month of delay brought more immigrants, consolidating the Spanish hold not just on the area round the city but on the vast territory east of the Mississippi that the treaty recognized as part of the United States.

As Bernard Lintot, originally a New Englander, now a Spaniard, and one of Natchez's most respected planters, cynically observed to Ellicott, "I have resided many years [in this district], and have ever found the Spanish Government giving the most liberal encouragement to American and English settlers, and could not perceive that the passing from a land of liberty to a despotic government occasioned any difficulty in the business." Even Daniel Boone, the epitome of American patriotism, would join the throng in 1799, crossing the Mississippi into Spanish Louisiana, where he took an oath of loyalty to the king of Spain.

In the spring of 1797, the river overflowed its banks, astonishing Ellicott by rising fifty-five feet and spreading out across the country to create a slow-flowing ooze that by April was thirty-seven miles across, and it did not completely return to its old course until September. But he also understood why it made the land beside it so attractive to settlers. "The Mississippi is a wonderful river," he told Sally, and the silt it deposited was "uncommonly fertile." Most of the large plantations grew tobacco as their main crop, although others were turning to cotton, and a few specialized in sugar. The owners

raised cattle and hogs, grew their own corn, and could produce with little effort exotic fruits such as peaches, figs, and apricots. From his 250,000-acre
plantation, Anthony Hutchins reckoned on harvesting no fewer than thirty
thousand pounds of tobacco a year as well as four thousand bushels of corn,
with enough pasture left over to feed four hundred head of cattle.

Such wealthy owners had, Ellicott noted, "a natural turn for mechanics,
painting, music and the polite accomplishments," although being the man
he was, he could not help pointing out one major failing. "Their system of
education is so extremely defective that little real science is to be met with
among them." More serious in his eyes was that the plantations depended on
slave labor, and slaves made up about 40 percent of Natchez's population.

The majority of the white inhabitants, however, were either small farmers
with few slaves, or storekeepers, craftsmen, and stevedores in Natchez itself.
Some were on the run from the law or from creditors, such as Ebenezer Dayton, a shoemaker, generally known to Natchez citizens as "Diving" Dayton,
who had faked his own suicide by pretending to drown himself in the Connecticut River after running up huge debts. Two thirds were British or American Tories who had fled the United States because of "their monarchical
principles or treasonable practices." Their unofficial leader was Hutchins,
who had come to Natchez as a British officer in the 1770s, and since he was
the brother of Ellicott's old colleague Thomas Hutchins, the commissioner
was prepared to trust him.

By extraordinary coincidence, Ellicott had a still closer connection to
Gayoso's second-in-command, Captain Esteban Minor. Twenty-six years
earlier his name had been Stephen Minor, and he had grown up close to the
Ellicotts' mills in Maryland. Now a Spanish citizen, Minor owned a plantation in Natchez, and his divided allegiance could have served as a paradigm
for most American-born settlers. As fort commander, he remained loyal to
Spain, but he was ready to see the settlement become American so long as
his ownership of the plantation was not endangered.

There was no guarantee that the hearts and minds of this expatriate,
multinational population would belong to the United States. In 1763, when
the east bank of the Mississippi ceased to be French, the land around
Natchez became British and remained so until Spain acquired it in 1783.
There was no strong desire to become part of the United States. The settlement's only experience of American power, a destructive raid in 1778 led by

James Willing from Pittsburgh, did not encourage friendly feeling. Willing's band of marauders shot and looted their way from Walnut Hills to Baton Rouge—"All was fish that came into their nett," William Dunbar, a prominent cotton planter, recalled. "They took blankets, pieces of cloth, sugar, silver ware, all my waring apparel, bed and table linen: not a shirt was left in the house."

Nevertheless, under U.S. jurisdiction every male landowner would enjoy three freedoms denied to him under Spanish rule: he could vote for his own government, express his opinions openly, and be free of the risk of arbitrary arrest, an important consideration since Governor Hector de Carondelet had recently exiled to Cuba several inhabitants of New Orleans, for no other crime than expressing what he called "diabolical ideas of freedom and equality." The United States also offered a double guarantee against the loss of property. The Bill of Rights declared that property could never be taken except "by due Process of Law," and the Constitution prohibited governments from passing "a Law impairing the Obligation of Contracts." This last was especially attractive to those who feared that the Spanish authorities might find grounds to cancel land grants made simply on the basis of a royal proclamation.

In reports to Pickering, Ellicott estimated that these considerations might persuade most landowners—"seven-eighths," he suggested optimistically—to back the United States. Among the plantation owners, three in particular became his close supporters—two Irishmen, Bryan Bruin and Daniel Clark, and a Scotsman, William Dunbar—while a wealthy shipper, George Cochran, who was awarded the contract for supplying the expedition, mobilized pro-American feeling in town. But against these, at least eighteen influential settlers were militantly pro-Spanish, the influential British majority looked north toward Canada, while others backed the claims of Georgia under the terms of its royal charter that Natchez belonged to the state rather than the United States.

As he began to appreciate the complexities of Mississippi politics, Ellicott concluded that no one's loyalties could be relied upon. "It is therefore necessary," he noted in his journal, "to enquire dispassionately into the situation and probable views of every officious patriot." Paradoxically, the one ally he learned to trust was Esteban Minor, who provided a flow of information about Spanish intentions.

Ellicott was still only the boundary commissioner, but by the time the Mississippi began to subside, his responsibilities had spread more extensively than the river. By international law, Natchez should have been a frontier settlement, the westernmost outpost of the United States, but so long as the true frontier remained undefined, Pinckney's treaty would be a dead letter. And because Natchez and the Mississippi remained Spanish, the secessionist plots in Kentucky continued to smolder. Thus the maneuverings to get Gayoso's troops out of the fort had consequences far beyond Natchez.

In April, Ellicott at last persuaded Gayoso to let Lieutenant Pope and his military detachment join him in the city, a gain that was offset by the sight of Spanish artillery and other reinforcements being carried upstream to strengthen the forts at Walnut Hill and New Madrid. Learning from Minor how thinly the Spanish military was being stretched, Ellicott sent urgent appeals to Pickering for reinforcements to be sent to Natchez to bring pressure to bear on Gayoso.

As the weeks passed, Ellicott discovered to his surprise that he liked his fiery, charming opponent. Since Gayoso was responsible for laying out the street plan of Natchez, they shared an interest other than diplomacy. Thanks to an English education and an American wife, Margaret Watts of Baton Rouge, Gayoso spoke English fluently and, what was always a recommendation in Ellicott's eyes, showed himself to be "a kind father and attentive husband." Their growing friendship did not, however, alter that one was trying to remove the other from a place he had no intention of leaving. While Ellicott could take comfort from the information supplied by Captain Minor, Gayoso trumped that with his American spy, General James Wilkinson, the senior general in the United States army.

The warmth and friendliness of James Wilkinson were qualities that struck everyone at first acquaintance. Though stocky and inclined to fatness, he smiled easily and, as a contemporary noted, had "a pleasing voice and charming manners." Even listing Wilkinson's faults, his severest critic, Humphrey Marshall from Kentucky, succeeded in making him sound attractive: "manners bland, accommodating and popular; and address easy, polite and gracious; invited approach; gave access; assured attention, cordiality and ease. By these fair terms, he conciliated; by these he captivated."

Marshall disliked Wilkinson politically because he advocated Kentucky's secession from the Union, but, like Washington and General Wayne, he also distrusted him as a person. The doubts about Wilkinson had begun when he was a young soldier in the Revolution. He had served closely with Benedict Arnold during the invasion of Canada and had later been involved in the "Conway Cabal," which schemed to replace Washington with General Horatio Gates. A talent for organization saw him promoted to the lucrative post of clothier-general to the army, but in 1781 he was forced to resign amid allegations of corruption.

Having migrated to Kentucky in 1782, Wilkinson quickly joined those calling for independence. Except with Marshall, this stance did not diminish his popularity, and he was widely applauded in 1787 when he took a flatboat loaded with tobacco, pork, and flour down to New Orleans in defiance of the Spanish ban. What was taken to be a unilateral attempt to open up the river, however, masked the beginning of Wilkinson's life of treachery.

General James Wilkinson

The Spanish recorded the declaration he made in New Orleans to the then governor of Louisiana and West Florida, Esteban Miró. It began with an almost unique flash of honesty: "Interest regulates the passions of Nations, as also those of individuals, and he who attributes a different motive to human affairs deceives himself or seeks to deceive others." Following which, he made a formal transfer of "my allegiance from the United States to his Catholic Majesty" because, as he explained, having fought for the welfare of the United States, he was now free to follow his own interests. "Since the circumstances and policy of the United States have rendered it impossible for me to attain this desired object under her government, I am resolved, without wishing them harm, to seek it [with] Spain."

The role he volunteered to fill, and for which Miró was ready to reward him with trading privileges and a salary of $2,000 a year, was to detach Kentucky from the United States. With secessionists in the north, moves for independence in the west, and a widespread apprehension that, as John Jay put it, "our American empire is too big to govern," this goal seemed eminently attainable. On Wilkinson's return from New Orleans, he became the focal point of what was later called "the Spanish conspiracy," involving some of Kentucky's most senior figures, including its first senator, a judge, and a major landowner.

Although popular support for secession began to drain away following ratification of the new federal Constitution in 1789, Wilkinson remained faithful to the cause, and he continued as a spy. As Miró explained to his superior in Cuba, "He is always useful even when he does not achieve his object, since he serves as well to block those enterprises planned against the Province [Spanish Louisiana] as to give notice of others he cannot stop." And his next career move made him more useful than ever.

Despite his Spanish contacts, Wilkinson's export business failed soon after his return from New Orleans, forcing him to rejoin the army. His military experience led to his appointment as General Anthony Wayne's second-in-command in the campaign against the army of the Western Confederation that ended in the battle of Fallen Timbers in 1794. When Wayne died prematurely in December 1796, Wilkinson was left as the army's senior general, a man everyone liked and no one trusted.

Having Wilkinson on his side transformed Gayoso's position. From the Gulf to Illinois, Spanish forces amounted to fewer than one thousand regular troops and slightly more than five thousand militia, scattered by Gayoso's policy in forts along the whole length of the river. Recognizing Spain's military weakness, Ellicott appealed directly to Wilkinson and with increasing urgency for more U.S. forces to be sent to Natchez. The general repeatedly promised to send reinforcements, but none arrived. Blandly and affably, Wilkinson assured Ellicott, "You have a warm place in my heart," and offered his personal support—"I trust in heaven the execution of the treaty may follow to avert consequences painful to contemplate"—yet not a soldier moved south. Gayoso could be confident that with Wilkinson in command there would be no military pressure from the United States.

Unaware of his general's treachery, the new president, John Adams, told Congress in June 1797 that he had reluctantly decided "to leave it to the discretion of the officers of His Catholic Majesty when they withdraw his troops from the forts within the territory of the United States." Congress showed itself still less inclined to act. Ignoring the president's request to create a framework government for the Natchez district in readiness for Spain's eventual withdrawal, the legislature went into recess, leaving Ellicott to cope unsupported. But more than one man's betrayal lay behind the United States' inability to force the Spanish out of Natchez. It was too weak even to keep the states out of federal territory.

The most forceful attempts at seizure were made by Georgia. Alone among the states, it maintained its claims to western lands based upon its royal charter and did not give them up until 1802. In 1789 it created the largest county in American history, Bourbon County, to administer the area between the Appalachians and the Mississippi River, and in 1795 its heavily bribed legislature sold almost forty million acres, most of modern Alabama and Mississippi, to a syndicate of land companies in what became known as the Yazoo Land Fraud. Georgia had some constitutional grounds for its land grab, but the plans of William Blount, once governor and now senator of Tennessee Territory, depended upon pure expediency.

As he foolishly explained in a letter in March 1797, Blount planned to seize Spanish-occupied territory, including the Natchez area, by force, keeping some for himself and leaving the rest to British control. The plot hung on the war in Europe: under pressure from France's citizen armies, Spain had

declared war on her former ally, Britain, in 1794, a development that created the serious possibility of a retaliatory British attack on the Floridas and
New Orleans. Blount needed the land to rescue the Blount Land Company
from bankruptcy, and conspiring with a foreign power to take U.S. territory
was not a crime that weighed heavily with him or, as it transpired, with the
people of Tennessee. "[I] probably shall be at the head of the business," he
boasted to a friend, "on the part of the British."

Unfortunately for Blount, the letter was stolen while its recipient was
drunk, and its contents became public knowledge. Presented with evidence
of his treachery, the Senate voted twenty-five to one for his expulsion and
arrest on the charge of "high misdemeanour inconsistent with public trust
and duty." But, when Blount fled back to Tennessee, the United States
proved powerless to compel his return despite the constitutional obligation
on states to send back fugitives from justice. Tennesseans demonstrated
their own opinion of his offense by electing him to the state legislature,
where he served as speaker until his death.

Left to fend for himself by a government that was too weak to help, either
militarily or politically, Ellicott immediately had to deal with the reverbera-
tions of Blount's conspiracy. Fear of British participation prompted Gayoso
to issue a warning that martial law might have to be imposed. The settlers
reacted with fury, egged on by Blount's chief lieutenant in Natchez, Anthony Hutchins, the silver-haired planter who was the recognized leader of
Natchez's large contingent of British-born settlers. Gayoso should be kidnapped, he told Ellicott, and taken into the prairie on the other side of the
Mississippi to be dealt with by the Chickasaw. By early June the state of
public opinion in Natchez, Ellicott told Pickering, "might be compared to
flammable gaz; it wanted but a spark to produce an explosion!"

In this complex and unstable situation, Ellicott was inexorably drawn
from his role as boundary commissioner to act as the representative of the
United States. An attack by the settlers on the Spanish garrison might trig-
ger a wider conflict with Spain and would certainly kill the already shaky
Treaty of San Lorenzo. Given the hostility of the Spanish government, the
incapacity of the U.S. government, the treachery of its senior general, and
the influence of a British planter over American settlers, Ellicott's actions

over the following weeks entitle him to most of the credit for ensuring that the treaty was finally enacted.

His critical achievement came in late June after Gayoso ordered the arrest of a drunken Baptist preacher named Hannah. This was the spark that produced the explosion. Infuriated by the thought of a Protestant being imprisoned by a Catholic governor, the settlers rioted and threatened to attack the fort. The Spanish artillery, usually trained on the river, was now aimed at the town, except for one cannon sighted on the boundary commissioner's tent. In an attempt to calm the tension, Ellicott issued a proclamation telling American sympathizers to refrain from violence. He urged them instead to sign a petition pledging their support for the United States, and to register with Lieutenant Pope to form a militia in case of Spanish attack. This message was repeated in person at a bellicose meeting in a nearby farmhouse, where Ellicott pleaded with the settlers not to risk their lives by attacking the fort, "but to make a formal declaration of their being, by the late treaty, citizens of the US—that they might have some claim to protection—but to act upon the defensive only."

Using Minor as a go-between, Ellicott maintained contact with Gayoso inside the fort. When the settlers called another conference following an exchange of shots between a Spanish patrol and the newly formed American militia, Ellicott sent the governor an urgent request for a meeting. On June 22, Gayoso stole out of the fort, taking, as Ellicott remembered, "a circuitous route on foot thro' a cornfield to the back of [Minor's] house and entered the parlour undiscovered where I joined him."

There Ellicott offered him a deal—that the settlers would refrain from violence provided the day-to-day running of Natchez was handed over to an elected committee of inhabitants. Gayoso could remain as governor, but Spanish laws should be applied "with mildness and moderation." Facing insurrection as the alternative, Gayoso accepted, although, as Ellicott noted, "the humiliating state to which he was reduced by a people whose affection he had courted made a visible impression upon his mind and countenance."

Hurrying to the settlers' conference, Ellicott found to his surprise that Hutchins, the leader of the war party, was also urging restraint. Exploiting the change of mood, Ellicott begged the meeting to accept the peace plan he had made with Gayoso, adding a pledge that the U.S. government would soon formally include Natchez within the Union—"a free government [would be] extended to them and that without any tumult, or risk of expense." In a fateful gesture, he offered himself as a personal guarantee, promising to help maintain peace and order until Congress had appointed its own official representative. With that offer he ceased to be merely the commissioner for the boundary and became instead the de facto U.S. representative in the territory.

When he sat down, the "large and respectable meeting of gentlemen of property and influence in the country" voted against an attack on the fort, and for the peace plan. Detailed consideration of the deal was left to a group of leading citizens who would also arrange the election of a council, with Ellicott and Pope as ex officio members, to administer the territory until the United States took over. In his report to the secretary of state, Andrew Ellicott ended optimistically with Gayoso's public acceptance of the deal, "which gave general satisfaction and once more restored tranquillity to the district."

Hutchins's unexpected support for peace, however, was merely temporary, an attack on the fort, as Ellicott discovered, "being either premature or not in unison with Mr Blount's plans." What Hutchins wanted was to provoke enough disorder to justify British intervention from Canada. Ellicott's promise to oversee the peaceful transition of the territory into the Union frustrated that outcome, but undeterred, Hutchins set out to undermine the U.S. commissioner.

The most combustible issue in the settlement was the ownership of land. Settlers who had taken advantage of the Spanish promise of free land feared that a U.S. government would make them pay for their farms. Others, who had bought plantations under British or Spanish rule, worried that their title might be overturned by American courts. And everyone wondered how an American regime would dispose of the huge territory that had not yet been settled. The importance of the issue led Bernard Lintot to warn Ellicott that he had to dispel any doubts about "the Distribution of Land" in order "to encourage the settlement of Families attached by principle to the [United] States, and to Grant the Vacant Lands on terms that will prevent their passing to the Spanish side."

Hutchins played on these fears by spreading rumors that the commissioner was in fact both a land speculator himself and the agent for Atlantic coast speculators. If Major Ellicott had his way, Hutchins asserted, the whole region around Natchez would be measured out and administered by the same constitution that Congress had enacted in 1787 for the North-western Territory. This would mean not only dividing up the vacant land in square tracts of 640 acres for sale at $2 an acre, thus restricting it to the wealthiest purchasers, but making slavery illegal.

The suggestion that slavery might be abolished was by itself enough to turn the members of a slave-owning society against the United States and its Quaker commissioner. And Natchez's plantation owners were right to suspect Ellicott of hostility. Before leaving on the expedition, he had paid a visit to his mother in the family-owned mills in slave-owning Maryland, and the sight of the empty, poorly tended fields across the state line jolted him into an expression of his own opinions of slavery.

"That domestic slavery is wrong in a moral point of view is evident from the ordinary principles of justice," he commented in his journal. "And that it is politically wrong may be deduced from the following facts. *First* that a tract of country cultivated by slaves is neither so well improved, rich or populous as it would be if cultivated by the owners of the soil and by freemen. *Secondly* slaves cannot be calculated upon as adding to the strength of the community, but frequently the contrary for reasons too obvious to detail."

He wrote as a Pennsylvanian. The state's border with Maryland and Virginia, first established by Mason and Dixon and extended by Ellicott and the other commissioners, was already defining a difference not just in territory, but in values. On one side, some people were treated almost entirely as property, on the other such people were entitled to most of humanity's rights of freedom and independence. The choice that now faced Ellicott was to repudiate his own values or to alienate the loyalties of the Natchez planters. They made their sentiments apparent in October by electing Hutchins to act as their spokesman to Congress.

By the fall of 1797 Ellicott found that his most vicious critics were Americans orchestrated by a British officer, while his warmest ally was the Spanish governor of Natchez. This was no longer Gayoso. In July he had been elevated to the post of governor-general of Louisiana and West Florida, and his place taken by Esteban Minor, who had been promoted from captain. That he was now Major Minor symbolized the absurdist, upside-down atmosphere in Natchez.

Suddenly wearied by the seeming impossibility of ever running the boundary, Ellicott asked Pickering in October whether he should come home. "I feel a consciousness of having done my duty to the utmost of my power and ability," he wrote plaintively. "I have frequented no places of amusement nor entertainment—I have endeavoured to live like a republican and philosopher. No idle time have I spent in this country—when I have not been engaged in the various correspondence in which I find myself unexpectedly involved, my mind has been occupied by scientific pursuits."

Pickering ignored the special pleading and simply assured him, "The President has judged it expedient that you should remain at the Natchez." Left without support, Ellicott's final decision on slavery was clearly influenced by the friends he had made in Natchez.

In the wealthy Scotsman William Dunbar he found someone with an enthusiasm for astronomy as great as his own. As soon as Ellicott arrived in Natchez, Dunbar had expressed the hope that "you will permit me to look up to you as a Master in Astronomy" and followed his advice by purchasing from a London instrument-maker both a specialized telescope known as an astronomical circle and a new chronometer. In return, Dunbar offered Ellicott a home in a house he had newly built in Natchez, which also served as the headquarters of the Natchez council. Both Dunbar and two close friends on the council, Bryan Bruin and Daniel Clark, counseled Ellicott to ignore Hutchins. In the florid language favored by the planter class, Clark condemned "the Terrorists and Anarchists of Natchez" and urged him to treat with contempt "the machinations of the anarchist, Hutchins." Shrewdly, Bruin pointed to Ellicott's greatest weakness: "You have too much sensibility for your own happiness and suffer the latter to be too much dependent on the opinion of others."

All three men owned large plantations worked by slaves. They could not have failed to make their opinions on the matter known.

That October, Ellicott issued a proclamation dealing with Hutchins's claims that he was engaged in speculation and wanted Natchez to be administered in the same way as the Northwestern Territory: "I now in the most unequivocal manner declare the above reports to be without the least foundation. I have recommended [to the U.S. Congress] that the vacant land be disposed of in such manner as to accommodate settlers of all descriptions, and that the system of slavery be continued upon the same footing that it is in the southern states."

It was a fateful decision. Ellicott still maintained his abhorrence of slavery on every sort of ground, moral, social, and, not least, his knowledge of Banneker's abilities. "I would not by this be understood to advocate the cause of slavery," he explained to Clark, "I am an enemy to it. I am for the abolition of slavery, but I would do it gradually as is now practised by law in the states of Pennsylvania and New York." He had every political reason for his decision—both plantation owners and the floating constituency of small farmers made clear that any proposal for abolition would simply drive them across the Mississippi to the Spanish side or to transfer their loyalties to whatever flag Hutchins cared to fly. Yet the compromise had immeasurable long-term consequences for the entire region.

It gave to landowners such as Dunbar and Clark those particular guarantees of personal liberty and security of property that were embodied in the U.S. Constitution. But by the same token it took from their slaves the protection offered by the Spanish legal code known as the Siete Partidas, which incorporated maxims about the limitations of rights over human beings and the unnaturalness of slavery. Nothing could mitigate the brutality of the institution, and on the plantation a master's or overseer's will was effectively the law, but Spain's colonies allowed slaves certain rights that they could, and sometimes did, enforce through the courts.

These included the right to own property, to be baptized and to marry, and most importantly *coartación*, the right to purchase their freedom. By contrast, American slaves needed their owner's permission to buy their liberty, and in many states, Mississippi among them, the conditions attached made it almost impossible to obtain. In defense of their rights, Spanish slaves could appear in court and give independent testimony, an impossibility within the United States.

Paradoxically, the iron guarantee that the U.S. Constitution gave to property was what denied slaves any legal rights. In a case quoted by the standard textbook, Wheeler's *Laws of Slavery*, a judge declared, "The power of the master must be absolute . . . upon the ground that *this dominion is essential to the value of slaves as property, to the security of the master and the public tranquillity.*" As property, the slaves' humanity became an anomaly, and so in the 1820s, once Mississippi had become a state with control over its internal affairs, it would become illegal to teach slaves to read, or to allow them to be married or baptized. They could not own property. Their only right was not to be murdered.

The status of women would also change when Natchez fell inside the U.S. frontier. Most obviously, they lost their right to own property independently. A striking example was offered by Gayoso's young American wife, Margaret Watts, who had expected to inherit a plantation left to her by her husband. Under Spanish law this would have been an automatic right, because in principle property was regarded as shared by husband and wife. When Gayoso died unexpectedly from yellow fever in 1799, Margaret sold her land, but, after her own death, the sale was challenged by her own son because under U.S. law property belonged first to the husband and then to the son. The widow had use of it, not outright ownership, and that only until the son became an adult.

What happened in Natchez district, in Mississippi, and in the rest of the young United States was that the law guaranteed to an unprecedented degree the fundamental rights of ownership, self-expression, democratic government, and freedom from arbitrary arrest, but it limited them to a minority of the population. A central theme of U.S. history would be the struggle to spread the same rights to every American.

To the vast majority of male landowners in Natchez in the fall of 1797, the assurances given by Andrew Ellicott regarding the ownership of land and of slaves removed all their doubts about becoming American. In practice he was just a frustrated boundary commissioner with no more authority than the reputation created by his thin-skinned, upright character, but it was enough to deal Hutchins's campaign a mortal blow. Once Ellicott had explained that his proposal to allocate land "to accommodate settlers of all descriptions" meant confirming all existing occupancy of land, and measuring out the remainder of the vacant land "in tracts not exceeding 400 acres each," Hutchins's supporters began to ebb away, publicly declaring that he had deceived them.

The members of Natchez's administrative council thanked Ellicott for promoting "the interest and happiness of this country" and condemned "the restless and intriguing disposition of a designing Individual" who had attempted "to injure you in the Public mind and to prejudice you not only in this District but also with the Executive of the U.S."

A critical test of the council's authority occurred soon afterward, when the Spanish government in Madrid announced its intention to replace Major Minor as governor. In response, the Natchez council declared that it would arrest his replacement should he ever appear in the area. Adding to the tension, Hutchins promised a bodyguard of two hundred men to support the new governor. In New Orleans, Gayoso weighed up his options and decided to overrule Madrid, leaving Minor in his post. Even Wilkinson could not mistake the changed reality of the situation. The need to maintain his influence forced his hand, and, as winter approached, he at last sent the long-promised reinforcements.

The arrival of U.S. troops confirmed that the Spanish policy of delay could no longer be sustained. On January 10, 1798, Gayoso sent Ellicott a short message: "By a packet just arrived, I have received orders from court, by which I am authorised and ordered to evacuate the forts of Natchez and [Walnut Hills]."

Early in February, Spanish galleys appeared carrying artillery downriver from Walnut Hills. "My Love," Ellicott scribbled on a scrap of paper to his wife, "I embrace a few minutes at midnight (as the boat is just going off and the night taken up in making out my despatches for the Secretary of State) to assure you that myself and all the party [are] in a good state of health, and that we shall in a few days proceed to business—I have at length worried the Spaniards out."

CHAPTER 7

EVIDENCE OF TREACHERY

Some men are sordid, some vain, some ambitious. To detect the predominant passion, to lay hold of it, is the profound part of political science.

GENERAL JAMES WILKINSON
to Don Diego de Gardoqui, 1783

E VEN TODAY, THE point at which the thirty-first parallel cuts across the east bank of the Mississippi River presents an uninviting prospect. The place where Andrew Ellicott began the U.S. frontier has become the border between Louisiana and Mississippi. To the south, on Louisiana's side, squeezed between a bend in the river and the state line, stand the walls and watch towers of the Angola maximum-security penitentiary, once infamous for its brutality and still chilling in its gigantic, eighteen-thousand-acre scope. Upriver on Mississippi's side, dense woodland and scrubby undergrowth growing above the muddy shore appear almost equally impenetrable. Yet these are puny obstacles compared with the matted barrier of cane more than thirty feet high, attached by a blanket of vines to the branches of an ooze-rooted forest, that confronted the boundary commissioner in April 1798.

That same month, Congress at last created a government for the Mississippi Territory, the immense tract of land that Ellicott had secured for it. Although Georgia only gave up its claim to the northern portion in 1802, it covered an area comprising all of the modern states of Mississippi and Alabama north of the thirty-first parallel. Winthrop Sargent, secretary of the Northwestern Territory, was appointed governor, and as Pickering brusquely informed Ellicott, "The plan [for its administration] is the same as that for the Northwestern Territory with the exception respecting Slaves—that is the inhabitants may keep slaves."

For weeks, Ellicott and the citizens' council had administered the quarrelsome society, solving disputes, and maintaining order between Spaniards and Americans. Worn down by his role as stand-in U.S. representative, Ellicott decided not to wait for Sargent. Fourteen months after his arrival in Natchez, he loaded his men and his baggage on three boats and floated down the Mississippi to begin running the frontier. He landed close to where he thought the line should begin and, with the eagerness of a man returning to what he loves best, recorded in his journal that "on the 11th I set up the clock and small zenith sector, and proceeded to take the zenith distance of [the star] Pollux for five evenings successively, the first three with the plane of the sector to the east, and others with the plane west." No matter that mosquitoes swarmed up from the swamp or that damp clouded his lenses, he reveled in the exactitude of his labors, the intrinsic reliability of his figures, the public usefulness of his calculation, and the absolute indifference of the stars to the shifting, vicious selfishness of people.

Having established that he was still too far north, his team of some forty surveyors, soldiers, and laborers loaded the flatboats again and drifted round the long bend that now houses the Angola penitentiary to Willings Bayou— "eight and a half miles distance but fifty miles on the Mississippi," Ellicott exaggerated. From there everything was transported by hand, boat, and horse through ten miles of swamps and forest to the top of the Tunica Hills, standing almost fourteen hundred feet above the surrounding woodland.

"The situation of our encampment on the top of the hill was both pleasant and beautiful," he purred. "The prospect was very fine, particularly to the southwest which opened to the Mississippi swamp, and gave us an uninterrupted view which was only terminated by the curvature of the earth."

There he was joined by the new Spanish frontier commissioner, his friend Esteban Minor, and the astronomer who would carry out the actual observations on behalf of Spain, William Dunbar. Already in his fifties, Dunbar had, as he told Ellicott, volunteered for the job so "that I might reap all benefit possible from your lessons and instructions." Although they only had a month of collaboration in the field, it was enough to motivate Dunbar to build a late second career in astronomy that led to his election as a member of the American Philosophical Society, and from that to leadership of the first U.S. expedition to explore the Red River.

The sheer quantity of equipment that Ellicott had his team of laborers haul up the mountain testified to his dedication to achieve accuracy at all costs. As well as two zenith sectors, large and small, there were three telescopes plus an equal-altitude instrument he had built himself, three sextants and an apparatus for measuring horizontal angles, a device for creating an artificial horizon for use with the sextants, a chronometer he had made himself and two stopwatches, two copper lanterns, one surveyor's compass, two surveyor's chains, and a variety of mapping equipment. After Dunbar's departure, the Spanish team led by Minor possessed only a sextant, a compass, and a specialized telescope known as an astronomical circle. But the U.S. commissioner's manifest passion for accuracy made anything more redundant. Describing to Gayoso his procedure for establishing the parallel, Ellicott gave way to the delight he took in astronomy.

"It is a pleasing and interesting reflection," he wrote, "that the present state of science is such, that we can extend our views to the Heavens and from them determine with precision the boundaries of the various governments, kingdoms and empires upon our globe: boundaries which when lost by the carelessness or destroyed by the caprice or wickedness of man may be accurately renewed so long as astronomy shall be understood, and the sun, moon and stars continue to shine!"

This was the scientist's credo. Whatever the frailties of human nature, the certainties of science could make them good. And so with an intensity that drove his friends, colleagues, and employer to a fury of irritation, Ellicott dedicated himself to forcing an artificial boundary through the wilderness, guided solely by the stars and undeterred by humidity, mosquitoes, and the hostility of the inhabitants. The feat would take another twelve months, and its scientific significance was only properly acknowledged in France, where the publication of his observations led to his election to the National Institute of France, the nation's premier scientific body.

From the governor-general's office in New Orleans, Gayoso wrote back immediately to assure Ellicott of Spain's faith in his abilities: "The execution of Astronomical observation of such a nature is not to be doubted when performed by such an Eminent character as you." Early in June,

Gayoso came in person to inspect the operation and offer even more direct proof of his support.

"Governor Gayoso paid me a visit a few days ago at my Camp in the woods," Ellicott told Sally, still reeling from the experience. "We met and saluted in the Spanish manner, by kissing! I had not shaved for two days— Men's kissing I think a most abominable custom."

Since this was an international frontier where the most precise measurement was required, Ellicott at first attempted to follow Mason and Dixon's method of tracing a Great Circle to cut the curving parallel. But in the almost impenetrable undergrowth, the party rarely covered more than a quarter of a mile a day. In September, Ellicott reverted to the procedure he had developed for the Pennsylvania–New York boundary, running a guideline taken from a compass bearing and correcting it periodically, usually at each major river-crossing. The true line was then traced back to the previous observation point, and a mound of earth thrown up at each mile.

"This mode tho' less scientific will be much the most expeditious and least expensive," he assured Pickering, "and in my opinion will satisfy the most scrupulous in both nations." Since the added costs of his expedition had already gobbled up the original budget of $30,000 plus an extra $12,000 requested by the State Department, this was a welcome economy in Pickering's view, although it did not stop him from griping at the expense.

Moving more quickly, they pushed the boundary as far as the Pearl River, about one hundred miles east of the Mississippi, by December. They might have arrived sooner but for a mutiny led by the surveyor, Thomas Freeman, who was responsible for cutting the true line. Ellicott regarded him as "utterly useless," while Freeman resented Ellicott's "crusty and unnecessary" interference, and when their quarrel drew in Lieutenant John McCleary, commander of the military detachment, in support of Freeman, work on the line came to a halt.

At the first opportunity Ellicott wrote letters to the governor, Winthrop Sargent, and General James Wilkinson, demanding their recall. A stern, unimaginative New Englander who soon found Natchez's boisterous society intolerable, Sargent had no patience with insubordination and readily

The thirty-first parallel, from the Mississippi River into Florida; the border with Spain then
followed the course of rivers to the Atlantic Ocean

agreed that Freeman should be suspended. But Wilkinson's reply was more
generous. "My friend, you are warranted in drawing upon my confidence
and my friendship at your discretion," he promised Ellicott on September
30. "Your refractory subaltern shall be relieved and his successor shall be
taught how to respect a national Minister."

With the removal of Freeman and McCleary, the work accelerated,
helped by a change in vegetation as they emerged from the thickset forest
into open country. Although numerous creeks meandered southward across
their path, Ellicott's assistants became adept at ranging ahead to lay out the
random line and tracking back to establish the true line. When the team
paused on Novermber 14 at Darling's Creek, the commissioner had every
reason to be grateful to the army's senior general.

Despite Wilkinson's slowness in sending reinforcements, Ellicott had no
firm evidence that he was a traitor. He knew that a spy named Thomas
Power was supposed to have traveled upriver in 1797 with a message from the
Spanish governor, Carondelet, to Wilkinson, but on the Mississippi every-

one, even the upright boundary commissioner, was rumored to be in the pay
of his country's enemies. In the midst of his struggles with Hutchins, Ellicott had passed on to Pickering further allegations that Wilkinson was being paid by Spain, but he had no substantiating proof. Indeed, having
suffered from inaccurate gossip himself, Ellicott readily sympathized with
the general's contemptuous dismissal of such talk. "The rats and mice who
have been gnawing at my reputation have lost their teeth," Wilkinson confided, "and some of them now live upon my bounty." His request to Ellicott
for useful military information about paths, defensible points, and the loyalties of local inhabitants was immediately attended to.

Ellicott was actually at work on a map for the general when a messenger
arrived secretly in his camp with documentary proof supplied by Daniel
Clark Jr., nephew of Ellicott's Natchez friend and newly appointed U.S.
consul in New Orleans, that Wilkinson was indeed a traitor. The critical
item was a letter from Gayoso to Thomas Power revealing the extent of the
conspiracy.

In his accompanying report, Clark described how Power had been sent
upriver in 1797 from New Orleans with a cask of sugar that contained four
dispatches and $20,000 in silver for distribution to Kentucky's leading sepa-
ratists. According to Power's own direct testimony, he had been arrested by
a U.S. patrol but released on Wilkinson's order, then had duly delivered the
money and dispatches to the general. As proof, Clark included Gayoso's letter to Power with his instructions. This revealed that Spain was paying not
only Wilkinson but three other influential Kentuckians, Judge Benjamin
Sebastian, Michael Lackasang, a delegate to the 1787 Constitutional Convention, and Senator John Brown, Kentucky's first U.S. senator. Part of
Gayoso's letter was in the code that Spain used to communicate with its
agents, but Clark showed how it could be deciphered using a popular pocket
dictionary as the key.

"The first object of these plotters is to detach the States of Kentucky and
Tenesee [sic] from the Union," Ellicott wrote in his own ciphered message to
Pickering. "If that could have been effected this season, the Treaty would
never have been carried into effect." This was only part of a larger plan.
Once the secession of the two American states had been achieved, "Genl
Wilkinson is to proceed from Kentucky with a body of troops through the
country into New Mexico which will be a central position." It was the scope

of the plan that made New Mexico central. From Kentucky to Mexico, a new empire would be created.

Whatever Ellicott's inner dismay at this discovery, he immediately went back to work. During the next three days and nights, he studied with a steady eye the distance from the sun's disk to that of the moon and, as a check, from the moon's nearest limb to the meridian of Arcturus and discovered that allowing for magnetic variation the random line was a few inches more than 1,175 yards to the north of the thirty-first parallel and adjusted the course of the true line accordingly.

The State Department, overwhelmed by French attacks on American shipping and the diplomatic crisis known as the XYZ Affair, which saw U.S. protests ignored by France, proved to be less efficient. Ellicott's dispatch detailing the general's treachery was filed without any action being taken. A second message adding what came to be a telling detail—that in 1796 Power had personally delivered the exact sum of $9,640 to Wilkinson on behalf of the Spanish authorities—suffered the same fate.

In a flurry of activity, the line was extended from the Pearl River to the Mobile, and a week before Christmas, Ellicott took time off to report to Gayoso that the first half of the frontier had been put in place. The journey down the Pearl, now Louisiana's eastern boundary with Mississippi, to New Orleans took almost six weeks through pounding rainstorms and waterways choked with fallen trees. As soon as the formalities with Gayoso had been completed, Ellicott hurried to see Clark.

The detailed knowledge that Clark possessed about Wilkinson's treachery came from more than a decade of close intimacy with the general as business associate and confidant. On Ellicott's recommendation, Clark was appointed U.S. consul in New Orleans in 1797, and convinced that the Spanish would shortly be forced to abide by the Treaty of San Lorenzo, he decided to become an American citizen, and to break with Wilkinson. The plan that Clark revealed to Ellicott betrayed an uncanny resemblance to the one hatched by Wilkinson and Aaron Burr eight years later. Clark himself came under suspicion in the aftermath of what became known as the Burr Conspiracy, and only then did he publicly disclose what he knew of the general's treachery in a pamphlet entitled *Proofs of the Corruption of General James Wilkinson and his Connexion with Aaron Burr*. Until its publication, he preferred to have others blow the whistle while his participation was kept under wraps.

"From the manner by which I have obtained the fore-mentioned information (which I am convinced is correct)," Ellicott assured Pickering, "I am unable to make any other use of it than to communicate it to our first magistrate [the president] and the department of state [in order] that the plan so far as it affects the U. S. may be counteracted—it must remain secret."

Under those conditions, Clark produced from a safe a personal letter in Gayoso's handwriting dated June 1796 in which the governor declared "that the court of Madrid has no design of carrying the treaty into effect." But perhaps the most striking part of Clark's information was that Wilkinson had finally abandoned the plan of detaching Kentucky and creating a new empire in the west after the Spaniards evacuated Natchez. What persuaded him was largely Ellicott's doing. Once the Mississippi was open and the needs of the western settlers had been met, Wilkinson had concluded there was no longer any reasonable chance of detaching Kentucky.

By the time Ellicott came to report to the secretary of state in January 1799, Clark had opened his eyes to the full range of forces facing him during his year at Natchez. "When you consider the parties under Spanish influence which were combatted," he boasted to Pickering, "the plans of the officers of his catholic majesty [the king of Spain] which were counteracted, and that contrary to their instructions they were dragged into a cooperation with us in carrying the treaty into effect, I hope you will conclude that my time has not been badly employed."

There was reason for self-congratulation. Before Ellicott's arrival in Natchez, Spain's control of the Mississippi had extended beyond the mouth of the Ohio. Now it was only a few miles north of New Orleans, and the effects of the new frontier were already being felt. U.S. citizens had begun to exercise their right to warehouse goods in New Orleans—Clark's customs records show that he had in store cotton from Natchez and Nashville to be shipped on to Virginia, as well as flour from the Ohio Valley and tobacco from Kentucky in transit to Atlantic ports. Less obvious but in the long term no less significant was the way the line was beginning to separate the old mixture of nationalities. In 1798 Gayoso had issued a proclamation that no one living north of the thirty-first parallel could own land south of it except with his express permission. On the other side of the line, people such as Minor and Dunbar, formerly Spain's most useful citizens, as well as British supporters like Hutchins, now transferred their loyalties to the United States. The nation was taking shape in the south and west.

Ellicott's sense of triumph burst out in full splendor when he wrote his wife late in February. With the letter came gifts—a cask of sugar, fans, pecan nuts, and a miniature portrait painted by a Spanish lady. In it he appears serious and gray-haired with shadows beneath his dark eyes. But the dress is that of a hero: silk stock, ruffled shirt, high-collared broadcloth coat, a man of distinction.

"When you look at the picture," he told Sally, "you will see the face of a person whose life has been devoted to the service of his country, who has ever since he left Philadelphia been up by brake of day and through the encampment. A person who disconcerted all the plans in this country injurious to the interests of the United States, and tho frequently attacked by a set of as complete villains as ever fled from one country to another, he succeeded in every attempt to serve his country, and will without bloodshed have the treaty in a very few months completely carried into effect."

It would have been administratively neat had the frontier continued along the thirty-first parallel right to the Atlantic coast. However, for the last third of its length, it followed the old British line, which was dictated by geography rather than the stars. From the point where it reached the Apalachicola River, the boundary was to descend about twenty miles downstream to its junction with the Flint River—now drowned by the massive, dam-created Lake Seminole—"thence straight to the head of the St Mary's river and thence down the middle thereof to the Atlantic Ocean."

All this was Creek territory. A reputation for ferocity, and the shrewd diplomacy of their half-Scots chief, Alexander McGillivray, who, until his death in 1793, played off Spain against the United States, kept outsiders at bay. Apart from twelve hundred British and Americans living around Fort St. Stephens on the Tombigbee River, there were no settlements between the Pearl River and the Atlantic, and Spain's possessions were situated on the coast. That situation would change once Ellicott's line showed how far U.S. jurisdiction reached. A road connecting the Mississippi with the

Atlantic coast would soon follow, and the knowledge that federal troops offered protection brought an increasing flow of settlers into the area. In the
long run, a boundary would prove as fatal to the Creeks as to the Iroquois.
But for almost twenty years, Benjamin Hawkins, the chief Indian agent for
the south, was responsible more than any other for preventing conflict between the settlers and the Creeks.

A former senator and aide to General Washington, Hawkins was committed to his old chief's program of inclusion. Almost alone in the federal
government, he had developed a coherent policy so that Native Americans
could live alongside incomers. "The plan I pursue is to lead the Indian from
hunting to the pastoral life," he told a Moravian missionary, "to agriculture,
household manufactures, a knowledge of weights and measures, money and
figures, to be honest and true to themselves as well as to their neighbors, to
protect innocence, to punish guilt, to fit them to be useful members of the
planet they inhabit and lastly, letters."

Despite its undertones of cultural superiority, his policy of peaceful assimilation earned him the title *Iste-chatelige-osetat-chemis-te-chango* or The
Beloved of Four Nations—the Cherokee, Chickasaw, Choctaw, and Creek—
a marked contrast to the derisory nickname the Dirt Captain that his predecessor, Blount, had earned for his greed in stealing land. Hawkins's approach
was most effective among the Cherokee, Chickasaw, and Choctaw, earning
them the label of "the civilized nations" in the nineteenth century. But paradoxically, Hawkins felt most at home with the more hostile Creek, among
whom he lived and farmed with his Creek wife.

Ellicott badly needed the help of this legendary figure. He had mishan-
dled the existing policy of the United States, to buy goodwill with gifts and
money, by failing to discuss with the West Florida Choctaws his plans to run
a frontier through their territory. Belatedly he sent them a message in the
summer assuring them, "As soon as the line is marked all our Choctaw
brothers who fall on the north side of it will be remembered with our
Chickasaw brothers and receive good presents."

His lack of diplomacy infuriated the Choctaws, whose suspicions had already been aroused by Gayoso's hints that the Americans intended to take
more of their territory. They expelled the local Indian agent, and word rapidly spread eastward as far as the Creeks in East Florida that the boundary
due to come through their territories was intended to take land from the

American Indians. Before leaving New Orleans, Ellicott sent Hawkins an urgent message to meet him in Pensacola.

Despite Pickering's almost despairing pleas for economy, Ellicott decided to buy a boat in New Orleans for this final part of the frontier and, finding none for sale, had a two-masted schooner built, which he named *The Sally*. It was not an entirely quixotic decision. His precious instruments and rapidly growing stack of official correspondence could be more safely stored aboard ship than hauled across the rough land beyond the Pearl River. The vessel would be sufficiently shallow in draft to sail up the Mobile and Apalachicola rivers to establish exactly where the thirty-first parallel crossed them, and thereafter it would carry most of the team round the tip of Florida and north to St. Marys. Meanwhile the actual line would be marked out by his young surveyors, and especially by an unstoppable northern Irishman named David Gillespie, who ran random and true lines back and forth like a weaver's shuttle.

What was quixotic about Ellicott's choice of transport was his decision to skipper the vessel himself, never having been to sea in his life. Ahead lay shoal waters and privateers in the Caribbean and blue waters in the Atlantic, challenges to make the most experienced mariner pause. When the forty-ton schooner cast off from a New Orleans dockside on March 1, 1799, with the U.S. boundary commissioner as captain, onlookers must have wondered how so sensible a man, one so dedicated to the pure rationality of science, could be so rash.

Surprisingly, the plan worked well initially. The schooner was hauled by teams of laborers thirty miles up the Mobile River to meet the surveyors at a point close to the junction between the Tombigbee and Alabama rivers. After three weeks of painstaking celestial observation, Ellicott established that the thirty-first parallel was precisely 518.55 perches, or 1 mile, 1,189 yards, and 9 feet to the south, a distance that was measured out with chain and compass and checked again. On April 10 a boulder was set in place to mark the boundary's exact position, and this three-foot-high, iron-red marker, despite being half-hidden by trees and blasted by buckshot from drunken hunters, remains intact. On the south side are carved the words "Domino de S M [Kingdom of His Majesty] Carlos IV, Lat.31., 1799," and on the north, "U.S Lat.31., 1799."

A voyage along the coast brought them in July to Pensacola, a larger and more prosperous port than Mobile, whose well-protected bay—"justly considered one of the best on the coast" in Ellicott's opinion—provided quantitites of succulent fish, oysters, and crabs. There, Ellicott encountered the Spanish governor of East Florida, Vicente Folch, who ruled with a harsher discipline than Gayoso used in New Orleans and exercised an active influence over the roughly twenty-thousand-strong Creek population through bribery and political manipulation. To Ellicott's relief, Hawkins was there too, a sparely built man with the contained, almost impassive demeanor that Native Americans often looked for in counselors.

Folch greeted him with the warning that the Upper Creeks, those farthest from the coast, were extremely hostile to the frontier. Hawkins learned, however, that their hostility was being stirred up by Folch himself. Like the Iroquois, the Creek organized their society round a system of checks and balances that divided groups into factions labeled *Italwalgi*, meaning White or peaceful, and *Kipayalgi*, which meant Red or war. The agreement of both sides was necessary before a decision was made.

Far upstream on the Escambia River, *The Sally* was stopped by the Tallassee, the dominant Creek group in the area, under their leader, Mad Dog. In a dramatic encounter, Hawkins persuaded the White majority that the frontier was an international agreement, accepted by both the United States and Spain, and not a device to take their land. Half-convinced, Mad Dog replied that if Hawkins was right, Folch would not appear at the meeting because "his tongue is forked, and as you are here, he will be ashamed to show it."

Folch duly stayed in Pensacola and sent a deputy instead, who was forced to declare publicly that Spain supported the need for a frontier. With that assurance, Mad Dog agreed to accompany Gillespie on the increasingly dangerous task of running the guideline through to the next major river. Two weeks of laborious observations amid clouds of mosquitoes and stinging insects allowed Ellicott to complete his observations on the Escambia. Then *The Sally* slipped back down the river to Pensacola, and out into the Gulf of Mexico once more, rounding the promontory of Cape San Blas that protects the harbor of Apalachicola from westerly storms, and into the port then known as St. Marks.

To Ellicott's dismay, the officer in command of the Spanish fort was Captain Thomas Portell, the man who had physically delivered the sum of

$9,640 to Power for payment to Wilkinson in 1796. The money, he testified, was indeed for the general's services as a Spanish agent. Ellicott's bitterness at this independent confirmation of Wilkinson's treachery found an outlet in his reply in July to yet another of Pickering's dispatches protesting the cost of the expedition. Angrily Ellicott reminded him of the length of the Natchez negotiations, the difficulties of running the line through swamp and forest, and the threat of Indian attack. He ended with a declaration that sounded as though it were addressed not to Pickering but to Wilkinson: "My desire is to support a government I venerate, and my pride to serve faithfully a country which I love, the country in which I was born, and which contains everything I hold dear."

By then he was almost alone in his determination to persist with *The Sally* strategy. Pickering wanted him to cut the expedition short, and Minor, Spain's boundary commissioner, was growing desperate to get back to Natchez. But Ellicott pressed on up the Apalachicola River to meet the survey party. Here the overhanging trees were covered in poison ivy, and a childhood allergy caused blisters from head to foot. "The evaporation from the dew from this plant in the morning falling upon me is sufficient to produce the effect," he observed, and the intensity of the inflammation forced him to plunge into the river, "which was the only relief I could find."

Nevertheless, three weeks were spent taking delicate measurements from the edge of the moon's circumference to the dazzle of the sun and the shimmer of Castor and Pollux at their zenith. On August 21 Ellicott wrote wearily to Thomas Pickering, "I positively am almost worn out by the excessive heat, want of sleep, long, tedious and laborious calculation, in which I have no assistance." He promised himself three hours sleep, then "near three o'clock in the morning, I shall observe an immersion of the first satellite of Jupiter."

On the banks of the Apalachicola they constructed the last observation point marking the thirty-first parallel, loaded the canoes, and while Gillespie returned with his Tallassee escort to run the true line back to the Escambia, Ellicott and the main party paddled down to the junction with the Flint River. There he set himself to another marathon of sky-gazing, but by now his relentless pursuit of exactness had tried everyone too far.

Sixteen months after he had set out with Ellicott from the banks of the Mississippi, the uncomplaining Minor had finally had enough. So long as the Upper Creek inhabited the area, he argued, Europeans would be kept out, and so an exact boundary was irrelevant. They should sail immediately to St. Marys on the Atlantic coast and simply calculate back from there where the boundary should run. Without warning, he dismissed the Spanish military escort and most of the Spanish laborers, telling them they were no longer needed because the line would not be run any farther east. "I suppose you will be angry," he said to Ellicott, "but I must now tell you those men of yours are no longer necessary either."

It was a fruitless protest, and with infuriating persistence, Ellicott once more had an observation hut constructed on the nearest high ground to establish the precise location of the mouth of the Flint River. But the patience of the Upper Creek had also broken. Despite Hawkins's intervention, warriors from the Red factions began to circle the camp threatening to attack. Reluctantly Ellicott packed up his instruments, and under cover of

Esteban (Stephen) Minor

darkness and torrential rain he and his assistant sailed back to Apalachicola while Minor traveled overland with the remainder of the party and the escort to St. Marys.

Ellicott's despair was clear in the report he sent to Pickering. "It is with the most sensible mortification I have ever experienced that I have to inform you of the failure in part of our business," he wrote, seemingly oblivious to Pickering's repeated hints that it was time to abandon running the last part of the line in order to save money.

Waiting for him at Apalachicola was an appeal for rescue that briefly revived his hope. Lieutenant James Woolridge of Britain's Royal Navy had been shipwrecked on a nearby island, and among his passengers was William Augustus Bowles, who claimed to be leader of all the eighteen Creek tribes. "Understanding that you have been driven by the Indians from the country where you were employed," wrote Woolridge, "I beg leave to inform you that General Bowles, the Chief of the Creek Nation expresses his wish to see you much, as he thinks your unfortunate differences may be settled." To Ellicott the message appeared to offer a final opportunity to establish an exact frontier between the Flint and St. Marys.

Loading supplies into an open boat, he sailed with a couple of crew for the sandy strip of land where the British ship was wrecked. There they were stranded for a week by a ferocious storm, in which time Ellicott discovered that Bowles was an adventurer being used by the British against Spain, and that like Cresap and every other adventurer living beyond the reach of formal government, Bowles loathed boundaries. Far from encouraging the Creeks to accept Ellicott's work, he promised to mobilize them to prevent the establishment of any sort of frontier, and to capture the fort at St. Marks, as part of a general uprising to resist any extension of Spanish rule.

With his last hopes dashed, the U.S. commissioner finally did what everyone from the secretary of state, Esteban Minor, and the court at Madrid down to the least important Creek warrior wanted and, in mid-October, set sail for St. Marys. A warning was sent to Hawkins and Pickering of Bowles's plans, but no mention was made of his own folly in aiding them.

Yet the future provided some vindication for Ellicott's obsession. In 1800, Bowles launched his promised attack on St. Marks fort and captured it before embarking on a general campaign of Creek resistance to Spanish rule. The mayhem he created forced Governor Folch to put a reward of $4,500 on his head, but the bounty did nothing to prevent Bowles's influence from spreading in East Florida. It was Ellicott's frontier that proved his nemesis. North of it, Hawkins's influence pervaded everywhere, and when Bowles made the mistake of crossing it to stir up trouble in the United States, Hawkins had him arrested by friendly Creeks. In 1803 he was taken to Pensacola and handed over to Folch, who kept him imprisoned until his death.

Unexpectedly, Ellicott proved a masterly skipper, although he had never been out of sight of land before. The majority of sea captains still relied on dead reckoning—calculating direction from compass measurement and distance from the passage of a float attached to a line thrown overboard—but with a sextant, an equal-altitude instrument, and a chronometer, Ellicott could estimate their location so precisely that when they reached Tampa Bay in October, he could confidently state, "[It] is laid down on our charts too far north by at least 15 minutes [about seventeen miles]."

As they swung eastward through the Keys, the sort of eighteenth-century science practiced by members of the American Philosophical Society allowed him to make himself at home in islands he had never visited before. He ran chemical tests on a specimen from the rocks and "found it to effervesce with the vitriolic acid," showing that it was lime made from dissolved shells. He examined the reefs and concluded, "Coral is not as was formerly supposed a vegetable substance, but a vast collection of small animals which build up those rocky edifices from the bottom of the ocean!" He found freshwater that had been filtrated through the lime and was stored in natural cavities in the rock. He told the crew that it was safe to eat the prickly pears growing wild on the islands, although "my people were not a little surprised the next morning on finding their urine as if it had been highly tinged with cochineal." He identified a score of different kinds of fish pulled from the surrounding sea, ranging from hogfish, grunts, and groupers through snappers, turbot, and stingrays. He fed the crew on three different kinds of turtle and supplied them with meat by shooting deer and plover.

In the Atlantic, The Sally and her crew faced starvation, a long chase from a hostile privateer, and a storm that threatened to capsize them. Their hunger was ended by the gift of a fresh turtle and a barrel of pork from friendly privateers, and having "crowded all our sail," they were able to draw away from their sinister pursuer. And off the coast at Cape Canaveral, "a sudden and violent gale [that] laid the vessel almost on her beams before the sails could be handed" proved that *The Sally* was not only fast but seaworthy. "The appearance of the sea was truly alarming," Ellicott wrote in his journal, "and though our vessel laid to with ease, and laboured but very little, the main deck was constantly covered with water, and the seas broke over us with such rapidity for some hours that I was seriously apprehensive of foundering."

On December 2, the gale blew itself out after forty-eight hours, and the same day they sighted land. Ellicott's noon observation showed that they were just north of St. Marys River, where the frontier began and ended. Waiting impatiently for them were the remaining members of the expedition, Esteban Minor, David Gillespie, and George Cochran, who had walked there from the Flint River. They had arrived in early October and, as an irritated Minor informed Ellicott, "have been in daily expectation of seeing you arrive. This state of suspense and expectation joined to the desire of returning to our families has made these two months go with a leaden step, and increasing tediousness and anxiety. Do for heaven's sake be quick, and let us have done with this disagreeable business."

Being quick was impossible for Andrew Ellicott if it meant skimping on accuracy. Because the treaty stated that the line from the Flint was to run to the source of the St. Marys River, he was determined to find it. Unfortunately it was lost somewhere in the seven-hundred-square-mile expanse of the Okefenokee Swamp. Almost everyone, but especially Gillespie and Minor, was prepared to accept an educated guess at a place just outside the swamp, because no one, not even the Creek Indians, went into it. But Ellicott insisted on hiking right into the waterland until he found a lagoon that fed the stream. From there he ran a traverse line back to the first solid bit of land where an observatory hut could be built and endured two nights of mosquito torture to take his observations.

"The trip was a disagreeable one," he told Hawkins with masterful understatement, but could not help boasting of having gained some unexpected territory for his country. "The United States extends further south than we had any Idea of, and the source of the river is 30 degrees 34' North."

On February 26, 1800, he and Minor marked the spot with "a mound of earth thrown up on the west side of the main outlet, and as near to the edge of the Swamp as we could advance on account of the water." With that the boundary was complete. They descended downriver to St. Marys, drew up their official report, and went their separate ways.

Minor, Ellicott's childhood friend and constant supporter, never spoke to him again, driven as near to outright enmity as someone of his patient nature could be by the torture of the Ellicott passion for exactness. Gillespie too departed in a fury of irritation. But George Cochran, who only had to supply the food, left a testimonial expressing his admiration for Ellicott's "indefatigable zeal and perseverance" and his "gratitude and esteem for the man that so highly contributed to the fortunate issue of affairs at Natchez."

A remnant of the crew helped sail *The Sally* to Savannah, Georgia, where she was unloaded and sent back to the U.S. fort at St. Stephens on the Mobile River for use by the garrison in patrolling the river. Meanwhile a letter dated April 5 was being delivered to Sally Ellicott in Philadelphia: "My Love, I once more have a speedy prospect of returning to you, for whom alone with our dear children, relations and friends, does life appear desirable—I have done my duty to my country to the extent of my abilities, and my ambition is fully gratifyed. I am my dear Sally Your affectionate Husband."

Contrary winds held up the boat from Savannah to Philadelphia, but finally on May 18, 1800, more than than three and a half years after he'd left, he arrived back in his home city. It was dark by the time he stepped inside the door, but once it closed behind him, "all the fatigues, hardships and difficulties I had been exposed to during a long absence were more than compensated by the pleasure I experienced in meeting my family in good health."

CHAPTER 8

THE REACH OF GOVERNMENT

The farther we go northward, the more undecided is the
frontier [of Louisiana] . . . this part of America contains
little more than uninhabited forests or Indian tribes, and
the necessity of fixing a boundary never yet has been felt
there.

DENIS DECRÈS, France's minister of
marine and colonies, 1802

ELLICOTT RETURNED LIKE Rip Van Winkle to a country he barely
recognized. Philadelphia was no longer the capital, Timothy Pickering
no longer the secretary of state, George Washington was dead, so too was
David Rittenhouse. Robert Morris, John Nicholson, and James Greenleaf,
the millionaire land speculators who had dominated the economy, were all
bankrupt. Most astonishingly, a nation that had stretched only raggedly beyond the Appalachians now ran west to the Mississippi, south to the thirty-
first parallel, and was overflowing northwest through the territories of Ohio,
Indiana, and Illinois as far as Michigan. The new republic was growing into
what Andrew Ellicott proudly described as "the American Empire."

The sheer size of the United States that Ellicott had defined—"with
room enough for all our descendants," as Jefferson told Congress in 1801,
"to the thousandth and thousandth generation"—created its own impetus
toward greater freedom. Many moved west to escape the long-established,
hierarchical government of the Atlantic states that always weighed most
heavily on the poorest. Squeezed between subsistence farming and county

courts geared to the demands of banks and creditors, New England and Pennsylvania farmers headed toward the prairies. And in the south, the exhausted soil and the monopolization of good land by politically well-connected planters pushed tobacco and cotton farmers toward the Mississippi Territory.

They were moving away from the Atlantic states psychologically as well as physically. Formed by British colonialism and the Revolution, the instinct of the east coast, typified by Jefferson's recommendation for tight federal control of the territories, was to see itself as the privileged custodian of republican democracy. Until the Spanish were worried out of Natchez, frontier families remained, as Ellicott noted of those in the Ohio Valley, dependent on the eastern states for their markets, their cash, and their protection. With the Mississippi open, however, those ties were immediately weakened. Increasingly the "brave, enterprising and warlike" people to be found on the frontier relied on their own resources, developing an independent outlook at odds with that of the eastern establishment. Had Ellicott retraced his voyage down the Ohio River on his return, he would have found the poverty-stricken past rapidly disappearing. The 1800 census counted in excess of 45,000 settlers on the Ohio side and 220,000 in Kentucky, with more following on their heels faster than ever.

In one important respect, however, settlers still had to look east. So long as they remained within its frontiers, the United States guaranteed their property and liberty. Thus to safeguard those rights, westerners needed influence in Washington.

During his absence, the past had almost disappeared from Ellicott's neat brick house on Market Street. The three eldest children were ready to leave home and begin new lives as married adults. The youngest, born after his departure, had died before his return, to Ellicott's "inexpressible concern"; the two infants had grown to childhood, and the middle three were now adolescents. In his absence, Sally Ellicott had held the household together, paying bills, wheedling allowances from the State Department, and, when her father died, spending her inheritance as she wanted. A miniature painted of her at this time shows someone solid and unaffected, with a determined chin and steady gaze, but missing from it is the quick, teasing humor that her daughters learned from her. In law, wives might be dependent upon their husbands, but by character and necessity Sally Ellicott demonstrated that she possessed a wholly independent spirit.

The demands of modern life were soon brought home to her husband. With a gentlemanly disdain for practicalities, Ellicott had refused to draw his salary while away and expected to receive $8,000 in back pay and expenses on his return. In the dying days of the Adams administration that proved impossible. Pickering had been fired, and his successor would not authorize payment of so large a sum. Twice Ellicott wrote to President Adams, asking for an interview to discuss his work, but was ignored. Then, a few weeks after he had presented his report with its accompanying charts, the Treasury where it was housed caught fire, destroying the only official record of his work. It was as though he had no real existence.

His one political contact was Thomas Jefferson. The first of Ellicott's letters to him was written within weeks of his arriving back in Philadelphia and was concerned almost exclusively with his discovery that lunar observations could give longitude as accurately as Jupiter's moons. On every count, as a scientist, a republican, and a friend, Ellicott regarded himself as a Jeffersonian Republican, and in subsequent letters he expressed increasingly desperate hopes that once his hero was elected, he would be paid. But after the hung election of 1800, three months passed before Congress broke the deadlock by electing Jefferson president over Aaron Burr.

By then Ellicott had his back to the wall. "I have been obliged to sell my valuable library and dispose of my Theodolite to procure money for market to morrow," he burst out, "and for nothing but faithful services, [I] never used a farthing of public money, never lost a single observation by absence or inattention, and never when out on public business was caught in bed by the sun."

Responding to this urgent appeal, Jefferson took up his case, and one of his earliest messages as president promised that Albert Gallatin, the secretary of the treasury, would "receive any application from Mr Ellicott and do justice on it." Not all his expenses were covered by this belated back payment, however. To earn more money Ellicott responded to an offer from a Philadelphia printer and prepared for publication an edited version of the journal he kept during the running of the southern boundary.

The Journal of Andrew Ellicott was published in the summer of 1803. It should have been the great public vindication of almost four years of continuous diplomatic and scientific labor that had defined the western and southern borders of the United States. There was an account of his careful scientific scrutiny of weather and landscape on the descent of the Ohio, the detailed celestial observations at the mouth of the river, and judicious commentary on frontier communities. "That some turbulent persons are to be met with on our frontiers, every person possessed of understanding and reflection must be sensible," he wrote, "but there are few settlements so unfortunate as to merit a general bad character from this class of inhabitant." He argued strongly against the injustice of taxing the whiskey that was their only cash-making activity: it risked stirring up rebellion that might "terminate in the destruction of all order, and regular government, and leave the nation in a state of nature." Ellicott never had any confidence in human nature without a government to keep it in order.

Inevitably his role in keeping the peace in Natchez and maneuvering the Spanish troops out of the fort served as the centerpiece, and he was careful to link Hutchins and Blount as colleagues in the British plot, although Wilkinson and the other participants in the Spanish conspiracy were identified only as "some gentlemen residing in the western part of the US." Despite the immense labor of running the actual frontier, his enjoyment of doing what he was good at was unmistakable, and the last section concerning the voyage home of *The Sally* read so like an adventure story that the detailed maps and long appendix filled with minutely observed and calculated celestial sightings almost seemed out of place. It was, and is, a remarkable record that should have earned him lasting fame.

However, in June 1803 while the book was still in press, the astounding news broke that the United States had agreed to purchase Louisiana from Napoleon Bonaparte, a territory stretching from the Mississippi to the Rockies. Once owned by Spain, it had secretly been transferred to France in 1800 to become the basis of a new French empire in North America, in exchange for a small kingdom in northern Italy. Despite his promise not to let it leave French control, Napoleon had no compunction in selling Louisiana for the $15 million he needed to finance his war with Britain. At a stroke, the western frontier Ellicott had been at such pains to establish had jumped from the banks of the Mississippi to the Rockies.

In a hastily rewritten introduction, Ellicott acknowledged that the

Louisiana Purchase would secure free navigation on the Mississippi, but drew on his Natchez experience to point out that the "sale of the lands west of the Mississippi might have a tendency to scatter our citizens, already too widely extended to experience all the advantages of society, civilization, the arts, sciences, and good government, and to lower the price of our public lands by bringing too great a quantity to market." Far more valuable to the United States, he suggested, would have been the acquisition of the two Floridas with New Orleans, because then superb harbors such as Pensacola and great rivers such as the Mobile would allow not only settlers in the Mississippi Territory but also those in western Georgia to export their produce.

Nothing he could say altered the fact that the immensity of the Louisiana Purchase had utterly overshadowed the first enlargement of the United States through the San Lorenzo Treaty. Yet without the earlier acquisition that brought American territory to within seventy miles of New Orleans, the second might never have taken place. Had the treaty not been implemented, the territory that France received from Spain would have stretched on both sides of the Mississippi as far north as the Ohio River. The strategic pressures that persuaded Napoleon to sell his American empire—the failure of his troops to quell the slave revolt on Haiti and the wish to defeat Britain—would have remained, but the importance of the land he owned, especially with its control of the whole length of the river, would have been immeasurably greater. Had the idea of selling such an asset even arisen, the price would have increased dramatically, perhaps beyond reach of the United States.

In real terms, however, the critical achievement of Ellicott's short-lived western frontier was to be found in its effect on the loyalties of the settlers of Kentucky and Tennessee. Until Ellicott's arrival in Natchez, plans to detach the western states from the United States still seemed feasible. Once the Spaniards had been worried out of their forts, however, General James Wilkinson, the most active conspirator, believed that the opening of the Mississippi had killed any prospect of secession.

Two years after the Louisiana Purchase was arranged, the general had second thoughts. The substance of his earlier plot to create a western empire was resurrected and became the structure of the confused events known as the Burr conspiracy. Since it still depended on enlisting the loyalties of a large number of western settlers against the interests of the United States, it provided a direct check on what changes, if any, had taken place in their allegiance.

The conspiracy began when Aaron Burr, the former vice president and nearly president, shot Alexander Hamilton in July 1804 and thereby killed his own political career. He sought refuge in the Philadelphia house of Charles Biddle, a close relative of James Wilkinson's wife, Ann Biddle. Still ambitious, Burr found a kindred spirit in the general, who was approaching the apogee of both his careers, as Spanish spy and American officer.

Jefferson had publicly demonstrated his confidence in Wilkinson by appointing him military commander of New Orleans in 1803. On the very day that the Stars and Stripes was hoisted in the city, the American general met Governor Folch, recently promoted from East Florida to Louisiana, to complain that his payment as a Spanish agent was $20,000 in arrears. Once that matter was settled, he specified that to protect his cover in future, his handlers were always to communicate in cipher, and never to write his name: "[I] always shall be designated by the number 13."

One of Agent 13's first betrayals after his New Orleans meeting concerned a project that Jefferson deemed vital to the future of the United States, the mission being prepared by Meriwether Lewis and William Clark. Ostensibly, the interests of their expedition were scientific, extending no further than a wish to acquire specimens of soil, vegetation, and fauna, but Wilkinson informed his paymasters that the real purpose of the mission was to discover a route to the Pacific Ocean. The president's close interest was shown when he sent Lewis to Ellicott for three weeks' intensive instruction in mapmaking using an equal-altitudes telescope for star and moon observation (see appendix). Lewis visited other experts such as Robert Patterson and Dr. Benjamin Rush for instruction in navigation, medicine, and botany, but in Jefferson's grand plan for the expedition, the importance of creating an accurate map of their route was second only to the exploration of the land itself.

It was this secret that Wilkinson betrayed. His report enabled the Spanish to send out a series of armed patrols to intercept Lewis and Clark when they set off in May 1804. By luck the Americans evaded the searchers, but subsequent expeditions were less fortunate.

The following year, the president again enlisted Ellicott's aid in finding people to lead further missions to explore the Red River, the Padoucas, and other tributaries of the Mississippi. Candidates' talents had to include "astronomy enough to take the latitude and longitude, the latter by lunar observations indispensable, this being the main object of the enterprise. Bravery, prudence, habits of hardy living, some knowledge of Indian character, a degree of knowledge of the subjects of botany, Nat[ural] history and mineralogy would be useful qualifications." The president asked whether one of Ellicott's former colleagues, William Dunbar or David Gillespie, was available and, with Ellicott's endorsement, chose Dunbar, along with the botanist George Hunter to lead the exploration.

In 1805, the year that he began to conspire with Burr, Wilkinson's fortunes reached a new height of prosperity. On the U.S. side, President Jefferson appointed him governor of Upper Louisiana, while the Spanish, having paid arrears of $12,000 for his past service, arranged a new financial package paying him as much for his work as Agent 13 as he received as a general in the U.S. army. His fortunes were reflected in his face. A contemporary portrait reveals the alert dark eyes sunk to the size of raisins in his swollen pink cheeks, and the jowls inflated until they blur the outline of his jaw and compress his mouth to a pout. But his mind remained sharply attuned to the advantages of playing both sides of the street.

He followed up his treachery over the Lewis and Clark expedition by systematically betraying to the Spanish no fewer than four subsequent exploration teams. Although William Dunbar was lucky enough to escape on his first journey up the Red River, his second mission ended in capture by the enemy, as did Thomas Freeman's and finally Zebulon Pike's. With cold logic, Wilkinson also urged on his paymasters a long-term strategy to hold up the United States' expansion westward by exchanging the two Floridas for the Louisiana Purchase.

The match between Wilkinson and Burr came in their desire for land, the ultimate measure of wealth in the early nineteenth century. The plot they concocted was to seize territory in southern Louisiana, Texas, and Mexico, but the key lay in finding support in Kentucky, Tennessee, and the Mississippi Territory. With a corps of seasoned troops, the conspirators hoped to harness the ambitions of several hundred Americans in New Orleans who had formed themselves into the Mexican Association with the aim of acquiring Mexico's silver mines. Wilkinson undertook to divert U.S. regular troops and militia to Natchitoches near the Red River border with Texas, leaving New Orleans and the southern route into Mexico open to Burr's supporters.

In the course of 1805 Burr sounded out potential allies from Kentucky to New Orleans, including Andrew Jackson and Daniel Clark. The change that had taken place in the new west since 1795 was evident in their response. Jackson's initial friendliness, which extended to providing boats for Burr, evaporated when he discovered that the intended empire included U.S. as well as Spanish territory. "I fear you will meet with an attack from quarters you do not expect," he warned the governor of Orleans Territory, which included New Orleans. "Be upon the alert; *keep a watchful eye on* your general . . . You have enemies within your own city that may try to subvert your government *and separate it from the Union.*" Clark had moved so far from his earlier intrigues with Wilkinson that he was then planning to run for election as territorial delegate to Congress. Long before Burr had completed his preparations, Clark too was warning New Orleans officials to be on alert against the coup.

As information about the conspiracy began to reach both the Spanish and American governments, each turned for confirmation to Wilkinson. Clearly alarmed by so much attention, the general acted true to form by betraying his friend. In the fall of 1806, both Foreign Minister Cevallos and President Jefferson learned of the conspiracy. Early in 1807 Wilkinson arrested two of Burr's advance guard in New Orleans, and with Jefferson publicly proclaiming his guilt as a traitor, Burr himself was taken shortly afterward.

The significance of the Burr conspiracy lies precisely in its failure. Sentiment in Kentucky and Tennessee had changed, and as Jefferson commented, Burr "very early saw that the fidelity of the western country was not to be shaken." The loyalty that Ellicott had struggled to gain from former French, British, and Spanish citizens in the Mississippi Territory had clearly taken root. The U.S. government had kept the Mississippi open for their trade, and the U.S. Constitution guaranteed their freedom and their property. Whatever their previous inclinations, the settlers had become unmistakably Americanized.

. . .

That the first loyalty of settlers in Natchez and the Mississippi Territory should have been to the United States rather than to a particular state illustrated a simple principle: as the territory of the United States expanded so did the power of the federal government. Only Congress could admit a state to the Union, and until its admission, Article Four of the Constitution gave Congress "Power to dispose of and make all needful Rules and Regulations respecting the Territory or other Property belonging to the United States."

Although this draconian power might be limited in practice by local interests, Ellicott's experience in Natchez left no doubt that the federal government possessed the authority to decide the crucial issues of distribution of land and the legitimacy of slavery in a territory. In 1802, when Georgia at last ceded to the United States its claims to western territory, the Natchez demonstration was repeated, this time as the state's gigantic Bourbon County was incorporated under federal law into a larger Mississippi Territory. And what happened on a small scale in Mississippi would occur on a gigantic scale in the Louisiana Purchase.

It was ironic that Jefferson should have arranged the purchase that made this increase in federal power possible. In 1798 he had established the case for states' rights in response to John Adams's Alien and Sedition Acts with their catchall description of sedition as "writing, printing, uttering or publishing any false, scandalous and malicious writing or writings against the government of the United States."

To resist this threat to freedom of self-expression, Jefferson argued in the Kentucky Resolves that individual states need not be bound by federal law because the Union was a "compact" made by "sovereign and independent" states, and they retained all "the powers not delegated to the central government." Consequently the states, not the Supreme Court, had the ultimate right to decide whether federal laws, such as the Sedition Acts, were constitutional or "unauthoritative, void, and of no force."

Although these principles, together with the Virginia Resolves inspired by James Madison, are usually portrayed today as the last-ditch defiance of embattled states in the face of a mighty federal government, the balance of power in the late eighteenth century was the other way round. Adams's administration was only able to enact the sedition laws because they had the approval of the other states. When Kentucky and Virginia appealed for endorsement of their position, they received no support. Four New England states replied that the Supreme Court was the ultimate authority in interpreting the Constitution, three middle states were in favor of the Sedition Acts, with Delaware declaring that the Resolves amounted to "unjustifiable interference with the General Government." The remaining southern states, which should have been the most sympathetic, offered no response at all. Once arrests of critics of the government began, and the dominant states turned against the laws, their opposition quickly rendered Adams's assertion of federal power almost inoperable even before electoral defeat put an end to his administration.

So small was the federal authority that to contemporaries the chief danger presented by the Louisiana Purchase seemed to be that its sheer size might break the frail Union apart. A population dispersed over such a large area was thought to be ungovernable. Alexander Hamilton expressed the common opinion that the political instability would "hasten the dismemberment of a large portion of our country, or a dissolution of the Government." The New England separatist movement that flourished during the Continental Congress instantly revived, fearful that the chief effect of the purchase would be to produce more slave states. "We must form different empires," New Hampshire senator William Plumer told his Senate colleagues in October 1803. "Admit this western world into the union, and you destroy with a single operation the whole weight and importance of the eastern states."

That the chief beneficiary of the new territory would be the puny federal government does not appear to have occurred to anyone, least of all Jefferson. What he expected was the creation of more powerful states, and he appeared ready to accept that their proliferation might lead to a split in the Union and the disappearance of its government. "Whether we remain in one confederacy, or form into Atlantic and Mississippi confederacies," Jefferson told the eminent English chemist Dr. Joseph Priestley, in 1804, "I believe not very important to the happiness of either part . . . It is the elder and the younger son differing. God bless them both, and keep them in union, if it be for their good, but separate them, if it be better."

Yet the reality of the new frontier required decisions that could only be taken at the federal level. By the rules that Jefferson himself had recommended in 1784, every step in the creation of landed property, from the purchase of territory from the Native American owners, through its measurement by federal surveyors, and eventual sale to citizens, could only be undertaken by the U.S. government. As a result, federal intervention at each stage of the process was far more aggressive under Jefferson than under Washington and Adams, the supposed champions of central government, simply because the area of federal territory was so much greater.

In acquiring the land owned by Native Americans, for example, Jefferson was prepared to use the Louisiana Purchase as a gigantic reservation, to be given "to the Indians of the east side of the Mississippi in exchange for their present country." As he implicitly admitted in a letter to Senator John Breckinridge of Kentucky, this would have required federal control of both Americans and Indians on a scale that King George III and the colonial proprietors might have envied. While the Native Americans were moved west of the Mississippi, the settlers would need to be restricted to the east. "When we shall be full on the [east] side," Jefferson explained, "we can lay off a range of states on the western bank from the head to the mouth, and so range after range, advancing compactly as we multiply."

Although such detailed intervention was beyond the scope of the United States in his day, Jefferson's administration was relentless in pressing the original inhabitants to sell their land wherever settlers wished to move. From the Kaskaskias in the north, who sold because they were "reduced by the wars and wants of savage life to a few individuals unable to defend themselves against the neighboring tribes," to the Choctaws in the south, who took the money because they were "indebted to their merchants beyond what could be discharged by the ordinary proceeds of their hunting," Jefferson's administration succeeded in acquiring title to much of the land east of the Mississippi.

But it was at the next stage, through the mechanism of the U.S. Public Land Survey, that the federal government intervened most pervasively in frontier life. Inseparable from Jefferson's achievement in securing the Louisiana Purchase were the steps he took to increase the survey's efficiency in converting the huge territory into property. To the amazement, and envy, of foreign observers, the survey succeeded in chaneling the settlers' insatiable hunger for land into a unifying force strong enough to hold the nation together through six decades of wild expansion.

Since 1785 when Thomas Hutchins had taken two hesitant years to measure out the first thirty-six square-mile townships in the Ohio Valley, the

Public Land Survey had expanded to cover most of the Ohio Territory. Although federal land was measured out in squares formed by lines running north to south and east to west, much of the Ohio Territory had been divided up among nineteen different owners, including states, colleges, churches, companies, and veterans' organizations, each of which used its own methods to survey the ground. Armed only with magnetic compasses, few of the surveyors contracted to do the work at $2 a mile had the time or expertise to work out true north. As a result few squares were actually right-angled, and mistakes in measuring distances with their twenty-two-yard Gunter's chains produced skewed and wavering lines. Explaining his men's shortcomings, especially in the thick woodland, Surveyor General Rufus Putnam observed defensively, "In a covered Country, altho great pains is taken, we must be very fortunate if we don't fall into many errors."

Each township was subdivided into thirty-six sections measuring one square mile, or 640 acres, but in 1800 Congress reduced the minimum parcel of land that could be bought to a half section (320 acres), then cut that again in 1804 to a quarter section (160 acres) with a down payment of only a quarter of the total price, the rest being paid over the next three years. As the demand for land increased, so did the confusion caused by Putnam's rough-and-ready methods. According to a modern surveyor, in the grid of squares measured out under Putnam's supervision, "scarcely two sections could be found of the same shape or of equal contents." With the creation of the Mississippi Territory and then the gigantic addition of Louisiana, it was evident that the system had to be improved.

Jefferson's first choice to replace Putnam was Andrew Ellicott. Unfortunately the offer of the job was made not by the president, but by Jefferson's strongest supporter in the military, James Wilkinson. The post carried a $2,000 salary, almost equal to that of a state governor, together with a clerkship worth $500 a year for his son Andy, but poverty-stricken though he was, Ellicott turned it down. Two years later in 1803, the president appointed Jared Mansfield, a former professor of mathematics at West Point military academy, who was to leave a mark on the land and the society that remains to this day.

The grid of squares between the West Coast and the Appalachians that can be seen from an aircraft window today is Mansfield's work. Its checkerboard regularity grew outward from the crossing points of meticulously surveyed north-south lines, the Principal Meridians, and east-west lines crossing them exactly at right angles, the Principal Baselines. Mansfield himself personally surveyed the Second Principal Meridian running through Indiana, the First being the state line between Ohio and Indiana (see appendix). Others were run as far west as the Willamette Meridian in Oregon, as new areas of land were obtained from the Native Americans and put on the market. In an era when land was the prime source of wealth, and rising land prices made it an irresistible market for speculation, the U.S. Survey allowed anyone to become a settler or a speculator.

Although Ohio was only the test bed for the U.S. Survey's development, it provided an early indication of its effectiveness in putting land into people's hands. In the year 1800, the Ohio land offices sold almost four hundred thousand acres, but by 1820 the figure had reached nearly nine million acres annually, raising more than $17 million for the federal Treasury. From 45,000 inhabitants in 1800, the population surged to 230,760 ten years later, and by 1818 when Andrew Miller wrote his guide *The New States and Territories*, it had passed 400,000, with only 3,000 of its original Native American owners remaining.

This made a striking contrast with the situation on the other side of the Ohio River where Kentucky land titles were thrown into doubt by corruption dating from Robert Morris's day, and by the confusion that resulted from demarcating properties by "metes and bounds"—that is by natural features such as streams and blazed trees. The irregular shapes that this produced were hard to measure accurately, and the complex registration procedure was prone to error and illegal alteration. By 1829, Supreme Court justice Joseph Story surmised that Kentucky's system of land distribution had virtually broken down, forcing settlers to take land wherever they could, "without any previous survey under public authority, and without any such boundaries as were precise, permanent, and unquestionable." The result was that poor Kentucky farmers such as Thomas Lincoln, father of Abraham, could rarely be sure of actually owning their property. When the family moved to Indiana, it was, as Abraham Lincoln explained, "partly on account of slavery, but chiefly on account of the difficulty in land titles in Kentucky."

By 1830, Kentucky's population was only three quarters that of Ohio, and land was selling for 12.5 cents an acre compared with $5 in Ohio. In Tennessee, the chaos was almost as bad, with more than half the households having no title to the land they occupied. Throughout the southern Appalachians, land became a commodity for the wealthy while the poor either squatted illegally or migrated to the thin land in the mountains that no one else wanted. A modern estimate suggests that almost 80 percent of the population occupied just 4 percent of the southern Appalachians, the majority of them being white tenants or sharecroppers, with a scattering of free African-Americans.

Determined to prevent southern land patterns from taking over in the newly organized Mississippi Territory, Jefferson and his clever treasury secretary, Swiss-born Albert Gallatin, appointed the reliable Isaac Briggs in 1803 to be responsible for the Public Land Survey in the south. But even paying surveyors a double rate of $4 a mile, Briggs found it hard to produce a regular grid of squares. Faced with heavily wooded terrain and a complex of existing properties bought through the Yazoo land companies, or by private arrangement with Spain, or by illegal land deals with Cherokee and Choctaw owners, his men turned in plats that looked more like a metes-and-bounds survey than a checkerboard.

Yet the U.S. Survey's difficulties served to show how intensely the federal administration under Jefferson worked to impose a government framework on the wilderness. Impatiently Gallatin urged Briggs to take more vigorous action: "It is true that you will not be able to complete your work in that scientifick manner which was desirable," he wrote in 1805, "[but] it is of primary importance that the land should be surveyed and divided, as well as it can be done." And when Briggs gave up in despair, the same pressure was applied to his successor, Thomas Freeman.

The unexpected consequence of this sustained federal intervention was to give those living on the frontier a compelling interest in the direction of the U.S. government. On the Atlantic coast, by contrast, the states continued to be the focus of citizens' interests and loyalties.

Ellicott had refused to take the job of surveyor general for fear of Wilkinson's influence. To his dismay, the general had written from Washington offering the post to Ellicott in April 1801 shortly after Congress had decided Jefferson's election. Alarmed by this evidence of Wilkinson's intimacy with the president, Ellicott replied by sending Jefferson in June a detailed account of all that he knew about the general's treachery, and in particular of Captain Portell's confirmation that the $9,640 paid to Wilkinson by the Spanish government was for his services as their agent.

The warning was ignored, and instead of federal employment Ellicott chose to take an obscure job as secretary to the Pennsylvania Land Office. The family moved from Philadelphia to Lancaster, the state capital, in October 1801, and Ellicott sank into the routine of administering the sale of Pennsylvania's public lands. It made him unexpectedly happy. At the back of the house, they had a large garden where Sally grew vegetables and he planted fruit trees, and both became passionate about growing things. "To this place," he wrote contentedly, "to my fine garden and young thriving fruit trees and grape vines, all the work of my own hands, I feel more attached than to any other place." The state only paid him $1,500 a year, but it left him time for science, and the clear air of the piedmont made the heavens very visible.

Here he built an international reputation as an astronomer. It was based on the extraordinary series of observations—more than four hundred in all—that he had taken from the mouth of the Ohio River down the Mississippi to New Orleans, across the south to Florida, and ending at the Okefenokee Swamp. When these were published by the American Philosophical Society, they attracted intense interest in France, where the science of earth measurement had been born, and a well-funded scientific establishment understood the value of so much data about the shape of the globe from an area that had hitherto been a blank.

Nothing gave Ellicott more scientific pride than the letter sent to him by the secretary of the National Institute of France, Jean-Baptiste Delambre, "the most able astronomer of any country in the world," according to François de Lalande, concerning "the reception of my printed observations made on our southern boundary." Modestly Ellicott passed on the news to Jefferson that "the work is not only spoken well of [in the institute], but complimented far beyond its real merit, and a correspondence is requested." This was an honor that even Rittenhouse had never known.

In the history of U.S. astronomy, the years between the death of Rittenhouse in 1796 and the opening of the nation's first official observatory at Harvard University in 1844 are generally regarded as a blank. Internationally, the major observational work was being carried out in Britain, principally by William Herschel, discoverer of the planet Uranus, binary stars, and infrared radiation from the sun, and in France with strong theoretical contributions from Pierre-Simon de Laplace about the formation of the solar system, and Delambre on aberrations in the earth's movement. Yet if a single person kept the thread of astronomical research alive in the United States in the first years of the nineteenth century, it was Ellicott.

His observations were regularly published in the American Philosophical Society's journal, inspiring other astronomers such as William Dunbar in Natchez, who credited Andrew for "my resolution of providing myself with a sufficient number of good instruments to enable me to make useful observation." At the same time, Ellicott kept up a detailed correspondence with Delambre, dispatching long tables of observations and calculations for use with his theories on earth perturbations, receiving in exchange news of the latest science from Europe. The value of Ellicott's work was recognized in 1808 by his election to the National Institute of France as one of only eight foreign members, an honor shared with Nevil Maskelyne and Herschel.

In that same year events were set in motion that brought Ellicott's career to an end. First Daniel Clark accused Wilkinson of complicity with Burr, and at a subsequent court of inquiry the general dubbed Clark a traitor himself. Once the mud began to fly, both men turned for confirmation of their charges to the one person whose honesty could not be questioned. Their letters arrived at Ellicott's quiet house in Lancaster within days of each other.

To Wilkinson's request for testimony to his character, Ellicott replied with what was in effect a repetition of the letter he had sent Jefferson in 1801. It began with Washington's warning against Wilkinson as a Spanish sympathizer, continued with the letter intercepted at Darling's Creek showing that Wilkinson had received money from Gayoso, and ended damningly with the evidence of Captain Portell in Apalachicola that he handed over $9,640 for Wilkinson as payment for his services to Spain.

To Clark, Ellicott answered simply that the ciphered dispatch he had sent to Pickering in November 1798 concerned Wilkinson. "This letter places the improper conduct of general Wilkinson, and some others of our citizens, in a point of view not to be mistaken," he declared. "If corruption is criminal, this letter establishes the criminality." And he added, "To my knowledge, the present administration has been minutely informed of the conduct of general Wilkinson, and why he has been supported, and patronized, after this information, is to me an inexplicable paradox."

Jefferson's relationship with Wilkinson remains inexplicable, since any explanation requires the president to be either unbelievably blind or incredibly irresponsible. It is possible that the general dispelled suspicion by claiming to be a double agent, secretly loyal to the United States, and since Jefferson saw no reason to fear Spain's crumbling hold on her empire, he might have decided the claim was credible. Conceivably too there were political considerations. From the first days of the Republican administration, the general had publicly aligned himself with its policies and acted as Jefferson's eyes and ears in a military establishment that the president distrusted as a hotbed of Federalism.

Nevertheless, when the court of inquiry called for all relevant papers to be made available to it, Jefferson's relationship with the general forced the president into an uncharacteristically barefaced lie. In a special message to Congress on January 20, 1808, the president claimed to have turned over all the documents called for except Ellicott's ciphered letter to Pickering, which had been sent on conditions of secrecy. Its contents could be obtained from Ellicott, the president explained, "and directions have been given to summon him to appear as a witness before the court of inquiry."

Ellicott's appearance in court and his testimony of Wilkinson's corruption would surely have ended the career of a man judged by the historian Frederick Jackson Turner to be "the most consummate artist in treason that the nation ever possessed." But Jefferson's message ended with a fatal, final paragraph that rendered any simple response impossible:

"That which has recently been communicated to the House of Representatives, and by them to me, is the first direct testimony ever made known to me, charging General Wilkinson with the corrupt receipt of money."

Knowing this to be untrue, Ellicott found it impossible to appear in court where cross-examination might force him to reveal that the president had lied to Congress. He provided the court with an affidavit covering the material he had sent Clark, but refused to appear in person. Without his presence and manifest integrity in court, his written testimony amounted to no more than hearsay evidence. Although Daniel Clark provided confirmation that Wilkinson had received regular payments from Spain, he was deemed a hostile witness, and Wilkinson's Spanish paymaster testified that the $9,640 was in fact compensation for a spoiled cargo of tobacco. In June 1808 the court found James Wilkinson innocent of treachery.

The consequences of his acquittal reached far. It led to the dismissal of Ellicott from the Pennsylvania Land Office following the election of Thomas Snyder, a supporter and friend of Wilkinson's, as governor of Pennsylvania in 1808. In what amounted to a vendetta, Snyder's administration went on to deny Ellicott the use of a powerful telescope belonging to the state, and to frustrate an attempt by the American Philosophical Society to create an observatory for him in Philadelphia.

On a national level, the damage went deeper, since Wilkinson's long tenure as senior officer continued until the eve of the War of 1812 with a corrosive effect on the capability of the U.S. army. Neither Jefferson nor, from 1809, James Madison questioned his assurances about the state of military preparedness. With an overconfidence chillingly familiar to the present day, Secretary of War William Eustis declared, "We can take the Canadas without soldiers, we have only to send officers into the province and the people . . . will rally round our standard."

The U.S. army that marched into Canada in 1812 was the product of the Wilkinson years, and it was easily turned back by a hastily assembled force of Canadian militia who inflicted heavy losses on the attackers. Only in 1813, and after his promotion to major general, was Wilkinson at last dismissed, and then for inefficiency rather than treachery.

In their contempt for the new boundaries of the United States, Burr and Wilkinson belonged to an earlier era when adventurers like Blount and Sevier, and secessionists like Rufus King and Theodore Sedgwick, barely considered the frontier to be any constraint to their ambitions. The New England shippers who turned smugglers in defiance of Jefferson's 1807 Embargo Act forbidding trade with Britain shared the same outlook, as did Governor Caleb Strong of Massachusetts when he set out to explore the possibility of the state making a separate peace with Britain in 1814. Yet, that the entire nation did go to war in 1812, despite the furious opposition of New England and New York, was itself evidence of the growing sense of oneness.

Out of the conflict came a national anthem, but also a government that, more than any since Washington's, was seen to be national. When the newly elected James Monroe toured the eastern states in 1817, he was acclaimed not just as president but as the representation of the nation, almost an elected king. His arrival in Connecticut, the *New Haven Herald* commented with uppercase pleasure, was the occasion "for a general burst of NATIONAL FEELING," and in Baltimore the welcoming committee "waited upon him and made a speech suitable to the occasion, according to the ancient customs in France, whenever the grand monarch visited different parts of his kingdom."

Nowhere did this deepening sense of loyalty to the Union take firmer hold than in the western states, which had been formed out of U.S. land and had never known a separate existence before the Union. But there national feeling took on a different form. The young generation growing up beyond the Appalachians held independent, egalitarian views at odds with the east coast's instinct for hierarchy. The Atlantic states might have won the Revolution, but as Fielding Bradford, editor of the *Kentucky Gazette*, irreverently put it in 1821, they also "drowned and burned *witches*, and stood with their hats under their arms at the doors of great men." The westerners had their own superstitions, but they did not doff their hats for anyone. They considered themselves to be the very democracy for which the Revolution had been fought.

The incarnation of their values was Andrew Jackson, who was to prove himself the great champion of the U.S. government against the states. He was also the champion of western farmers determined to win land from the Native Americans for their own use. Like no other president before him, he used the formidable power that the federal government possessed within its frontiers to make property available for Americans. And he chose to benefit a class of Americans that had until then been kept away from power by the restrictive voting demands of the eastern states.

So indelibly is Jackson's name and fiery personality associated with the stunning rout of Britain's first-line troops at the battle of New Orleans in 1815, it is easy to forget that he was a lawyer by profession. The traditional picture of him is the archetype of the frontiersman administering his own justice in duels and physical violence, in accordance with the sage advice of his mother: "Andrew, never tell a lie, nor take what is not your own, nor sue anybody for slander, assault and battery. Always settle them cases yourself."

Nevertheless his living came from the law, and in Tennessee's tangled system of land distribution, the majority of legal cases concerned property boundaries and titles. People might fight over personal issues—and for white men the southern code of honor that developed in the antebellum years insisted on this as a mark of masculinity—but where property was concerned, they went to court. There, as a recent historian put it, they would find that the law "treated property offenders much more harshly than those accused of violence."

In fact Jackson's passionate loyalty to the Union and his adherence to a legal system devoted to defending property were two sides of the same coin. Like many of his contemporaries who bore names like Boone, Calhoun, Crockett, and Houston, Jackson traced his family roots to the self-assertive Scots-Irish immigrants who had settled and often squatted in the backcountry of the old Atlantic colonies. Politically he and his colleagues were the heirs of the Regulators, suspicious of eastern elites, hostile to Indians,

Andrew Jackson

insistent on representative government and equal voting rights—at least for white, adult males—and deeply concerned with the efficiency of local administration.

It was not by chance that one of Jackson's earliest exercises in government, as de facto military governor of Florida shortly after its acquisition from Spain in 1819, should have concerned the payment of sheriffs. In a public proclamation creating a structure of administration for the new territory, he stated, "There shall also be a sheriff appointed to each court, to execute the process thereof, whose services shall be compensated by the court to which he is appointed." In other words he was to be paid a salary rather than living off what he could squeeze from poor farmers. Jacksonian democracy began at ground level. But like the Regulators, the need to safeguard their property also drove the Jacksonians to take an interest in Washington. The reason was simple. Only the federal government could take land from the Indians and measure it out as property for its citizens.

From the moment that Ellicott's frontier enclosed the greater part of Creek territory, its inhabitants became vulnerable to the same pressures that had removed the Iroquois from their land. But until the War of 1812, Benjamin Hawkins had acted as a bulwark, fending off white attempts to move into Creek land, and simultaneously enabling the Creeks themselves to learn through practical farming and elementary schooling the skills they needed to adjust to the relentless advance of the new Americans. His efforts had bought both sides fourteen years of peaceful coexistence.

In 1813, Jackson launched his military career when he led the Tennessee militia in a campaign against those Upper Creeks who had supported Tecumseh's war against the United States. Deriving the name from the Reds or *Kipayalgi*, meaning the warrior faction, Americans called them Red Sticks. The *Italwalgi*, or White Stick Creeks, either kept out of the conflict or fought with Jackson's troops at the battle of Horseshoe Bend in 1814 that crushed the Red Stick forces. Yet the treaty that Jackson imposed applied to both hostile and friendly Creeks indiscriminately, forcing them to cede half their territory, more than twenty million acres, to the United States.

It was Hawkins's particular torture to be at Jackson's side as the forced cession was announced. He was thus seen to be associated with the betrayal of those peaceful Creeks who had followed his advice and abandoned traditional ways in favor of those used by property owners. When he died two years later, it was said to be of a broken heart.

But as president, Jackson would have an infinitely larger stage on which to act. The frontiers of the United States were about to expand far beyond the wildest dreams of the most ambitious Tennessee farmer. And one of them would be run by Andrew Ellicott.

CHAPTER 9

AMERICAN TRAGEDY

*. . . the bargain between freedom and slavery contained in
the Constitution of the United States is morally and politically vicious, inconsistent with the principles upon
which alone our Revolution can be justified . . . If the
Union must be dissolved, slavery is precisely the question
upon which it ought to break.*

JOHN QUINCY ADAMS, Journal, 1820

THE FIRST DESIGNATED U.S. frontier, the line separating it from
Canada, was also the most complicated to run. Less than four years
had been needed to establish the southern boundary with Spain, but deciding where on the ground Canada began and the United States ended took
more than six decades after the frontier had first been delineated on a map.

The particular difficulty concerned the most easterly part of the line
from the Bay of Fundy to the St. Lawrence, in other words the strange,
crumpled horn thrusting up into the belly of Quebec and New Brunswick
that is Maine's northern border. On gigantic maps more than six feet tall
and four feet across, the American and British negotiators at the Treaty of
Paris drew thick red lines to indicate where they thought the United States
should extend. Then in 1783 they put in words what they thought they had
indicated.

According to Article II of the Treaty, the frontier would run "from the
northwest angle of Nova Scotia, viz. that angle which is formed by a line
drawn due north from the source of the Saint Croix River to the Highlands;

along the said Highlands which divide those rivers that empty themselves into the St. Lawrence, from those which fall into the Atlantic Ocean, to the northwesternmost head of the Connecticut River; thence down along the middle of that river, to the forty-fifth degree of north latitude."

If ever there was an argument for defining frontiers by Andrew Ellicott's star-based calculations rather than by natural features, it was provided by Article II. Two Saint Croix rivers meandered through the woodlands; instead of a neat row of mountains, "the Highlands" revealed themselves to be a bewildering mess of hills with no clear watershed to make a northwest angle from which a line could be drawn; and anyway nobody was able to find the source of the Connecticut River. Astronomers could locate the forty-fifth parallel, but the rest was confusion. Consequently the frontier remained undefined until after the 1812 war, when it was decided in the Treaty of Ghent that commissioners from each country should be appointed to sort out the muddle.

In 1817 the U.S. boundary commissioner Cornelius Van Ness wrote to the sixty-three-year-old Ellicott asking for his help in running the forty-fifth parallel. His presence was vital, Van Ness said, not only "so that great accuracy should be attained, but . . . so as to gain to both governments entire confidence in its accuracy."

It was a belated tribute to a man who by then had almost been forgotten. His obscurity was partly the consequence of his prickly personality, but mostly because he had blown the whistle on President Thomas Jefferson's favorite general. Denied the chance to earn a living from his science, Ellicott had survived largely on handouts from his wealthy brother Joseph, chief agent for the Holland Land Company, who earned a commission on every acre sold in upstate New York and ended up owning most of Buffalo and assets worth half a million dollars.

Money had never been Andrew Ellicott's priority. What he valued was civilization, by which he meant a proper respect for science. But as though Wilkinson's hostility were a curse, even a contract in 1811 to run the state line between Georgia and North Carolina turned sour. Convinced that the existing line drawn along the thirty-fifth parallel was almost twenty miles too far south, Georgia's governor, David Mitchell, a feisty immigrant from Scotland, employed Ellicott to establish the true line, hoping to gain about eight hundred thousand acres from North Carolina. In his usual, meticulous fashion, Ellicott spent weeks establishing that the existing line was in fact too far north. "All that part of the country [was] erroneously laid down in all the maps of the state," he explained to Joseph. "This discovery embarrassed me extremely as our subsequent operations would have to be performed in the most rugged and mountainous part of the United States." It was far more embarrassing to Governor Mitchell, who learned that instead of gaining land from North Carolina he was about to lose almost 625,000 acres of Georgia. In his frustration, he refused to pay more than $3,000 of Ellicott's bill for $5,000.

Only when Wilkinson was at last relieved of his command did Ellicott's luck turn. Appropriately, the realization that the army needed better-trained commanders was what led to his rehabilitation. In 1813, James Monroe, secretary of war in Madison's administration, wrote asking him "if the appointment of Professor of Mathematics in the Military School at West Point in the State of New York with the pay & emoluments of a Major of Infantry in the Army, equal to One thousand Dollars per annum, with allowance for quarters, fuel & servants, will be acceptable?"

Originally chosen as the site of a fort for its strategic command of the river below, West Point consisted of a scattering of white-walled, red-tiled barracks, schoolrooms, and houses that looked out across a vast parade ground to the Hudson Valley. The military academy had been founded in 1802 with the intention of training officers for the Corps of Engineers and was at first restricted to just twenty cadets, whose selection and education depended largely on the whims of the superintendent. At the outbreak of war, Congress authorized a dramatic increase in its roll to 250 cadets, and the introduction of a more structured curriculum.

"The emoluments it is true are small, but I believe sufficient to support myself and small family," Ellicott acknowledged, "but in point of respectability it is inferior to none in the government, and in the Europe the first scientific characters are attached to their military academies. And there, as well as in this country, the professor of mathematics is considered the principal or president of the institution."

He had always enjoyed passing on knowledge to his "family" of young assistants, and it is clear from their affectionate memories that he was equally good with the cadets. They nicknamed him Old Infinite Series, in reference to his fondness for the circle-squaring sequence, $1 - 1/3 + 1/5 - 1/7 + 1/9 - 1/11$, that Rittenhouse had taught him long ago on the Pennsylvania frontier and that had beguiled the silences of many long Quaker meetings. Cadets would remember how he used to carry a miniature blackboard and sponge attached to his watch chain so that he could work out problems on the move, how his lectures on astronomy began with beguiling ease on the way the sun rose higher in summer than in winter and ended with fearsome equations to work out longitude from the position of Castor and Pollux, and how perfectly he drew geometric shapes on the blackboard with a cord and straight-edge. "There are some," ran one account, "who will recollect Professor Ellicott sitting at his desk at the end of a long room, in the second story of what was called the Mess Hall teaching geometry and algebra, and looking and acting precisely like the old-fashioned school-master, of whom it was written,

" 'And still they gazed, and still the wonder grew

" 'That one small head could carry all he knew.' "

From this comfortable existence he was summoned to help establish the northern frontier as he had the southern. His first summer in 1817 on the line from the St. Lawrence to the Connecticut River was an uneventful exploration of the route. On his return two years later to establish the exact frontier, he had the disturbing experience of being overtaken by history. On the forty-fifth parallel, he was joined by the new generation of boundary-makers, Ferdinand Hassler, the Swiss-born U.S. surveyor, and the British representative, Dr. J. L. Tiark. From August through the end of September, Ellicott followed the old routine of viewing, timing, noting, and calculating that had served him throughout his life. He observed the alpha stars in the constellations of Aquila and Aquarius, the Pole Star, and the beta star in the Little Bear, bodies as familiar as those of his children; he measured their movements and read up his findings, but this time the routine did not quite give him the confidence it always had in the past.

"As to our business I can say nothing at present," he wrote cautiously to Sally, "and candidly confess that I do not yet comprehend the method pursued by the British astronomer and Mr Hastler [sic], it is different from anything I have yet seen or heard of, not more than one observation in ten can possibly be applied to the boundary. Those that can are probably good, but their mode of calculation is laborious in the extreme."

In truth time had caught up with him. Unlike his eighteenth-century predecessors, who had to provide their own instruments, Hassler spent thousands of government dollars on the finest apparatus by the most advanced craftsmen in London—telescopes by George Dollond, lens-maker to King George III, a mechanical dividing engine from Jesse Ramsden capable of machining metal to accuracies of one thousandth of an inch, and the jewel of them all, a thirty-inch repeating theodolite weighing three hundred pounds, created by the Tiffany of instrument manufacturers, Edward Troughton, an object so perfect that Hassler named his next son after its creator. Money bought him time as well. While Ellicott congratulated himself on measuring ninety miles on the Pennsylvania border in ninety days, Hassler spent forty-three days measuring a line less than nine miles long. The difference appeared in their results. The late-nineteenth-century commissioners who checked the Pennsylvania border congratulated Ellicott on making errors of less than one foot in a mile, a ratio of less than 1 in 5,280, but in the 1970s Hassler's work was found to have an error rate of just 1 in 100,000.

Between them, however, the astronomers succeeded in running the forty-fifth parallel from the St. Lawrence 120 miles east to the Connecticut River. Neither they nor anyone else could resolve the confusion created by the nonexistent Highlands and multiple rivers until 1842, when a compromise line was agreed in the Webster-Ashburton Treaty. But sufficient harmony existed in 1819 for the United States and Britain to come to an understanding about the rest of the frontier running west from the Great Lakes. From their shores, it was to follow the forty-ninth parallel as far as the Rockies. Beyond that lay the Oregon Country, the chunk of coast and mountain between the Russian colony of Alaska that stretched as far south as 54 degrees 40 minutes, and Spanish California, which reached a little north of San Francisco. Both Britain's Hudson Bay Company and the United States' John Jacob Astor had fur-trapping bases in Oregon Country, and so in the remarkable Convention of 1819 that settled the rest of the Canadian frontier, the two countries agreed to share control of the area for ten years.

At almost the same time as this agreement was being hammered out in London, the secretary of state, John Quincy Adams, was bringing to an end two years of negotiations with the Spanish foreign minister, Luis de Onís, about the southern frontier. The talks were triggered by Andrew Jackson's ferocious campaign against the Seminoles of Florida to prevent their attacking cotton plantations in southern Georgia and the Mississippi Territory. In 1817 he led a militia force across the boundary with Spanish Florida that Ellicott had so meticulously drawn. He burned Seminole villages, captured Pensacola, hanged two British citizens there, and assured the president, "Let it be signified to me through any channel that the possession of the Floridas would be desirable to the United States, and in sixty days it will be accomplished."

The flamboyant image of Jackson, coughing, cursing, and carrying a bullet in his chest fired during a duel, captured the public imagination and did much to push him toward a political future. Monroe, however, with nearly all his cabinet, disowned the general. Jackson's one defender was the secretary of state, who argued that the Spanish authorities had brought the raid upon themselves by failing to control the Seminoles. To avoid future trouble, Adams proposed that Spain should "cede to the United States a province [Florida] of which she retains nothing but the nominal possession." This argument became the basis of his negotiations with the Spanish foreign minister, backed by huge claims for compensation for the damage suffered by American planters, and by brutal hints that Texas by rights belonged to the United States under the terms of the Louisiana Purchase.

Having set out his negotiating position, Adams then offered to drop the claim to Texas and to find $5 million to pay off the American claimants. In exchange Spain would be required to give up Florida and the Gulf Coast east of New Orleans and agree to establish the western frontier of the Louisiana Purchase. His unremitting hard bargaining coincided with the crumbling of Spain's immense, three-hundred-year-old American empire as revolution spread throughout South America. The outcome was the remarkable 1819 Adams-Onís Treaty.

In it Spain ceded Florida and the Gulf Coast on either side of the Mississippi delta as far west as the Sabine River, marking the border with Texas, but what was chiefly remarkable about the treaty was the new western boundary with the United States that Adams insisted upon. This extended northwest from the Gulf in a series of doglegs until it met the forty-second parallel in the Rockies, then ran due west along the parallel until it reached the Pacific Ocean. Officially, this western frontier simply confirmed the extent of the Louisiana Purchase, but not even Jefferson had supposed that the land bought from Napoleon extended west of the Rockies.

On the day that the agreement with Spain was signed, Adams was exultant. "It was near one in the morning when I closed the day with ejaculations of fervent gratitude to the giver of all good," he wrote in his diary. "It was perhaps the most important day of my life . . . The acknowledgment of a definite boundary to the [Pacific] forms a great epocha in our history. The first proposal of it in this negotiation was mine." Virtually unaided, his diplomacy had parlayed Jackson's illegal raid into a massive acquisition of territory from Florida to Oregon.

For the first time, the United States ran from coast to coast, and a sequence of events had been set in motion that would lead by way of manifest destiny to the Oregon Trail, and the settlement of the far west. Thanks to Adams, wherever the pioneers went, they would always remain within the jurisdiction of the United States, the beneficiaries of its property-owning, freedom-guaranteeing laws. His frontier made the frontier myth possible.

That Adams has never received proper credit for his massive contribution to the nation's growth is due at least in part to his remote and deeply conflicted character. Harvard-educated, first a lawyer, then a diplomat by profession serving in Britain and Russia before being appointed secretary of state, he was deemed too privileged to be in touch with popular opinion, but in 1811, a generation before manifest destiny became the national mantra, he had made it his goal.

"The whole continent of North America appears to be destined by Divine Providence to be peopled by one *nation*," he told his father, "speaking one language, professing one general system of religious and political principles, and accustomed to one general tenor of social usages and customs. For the common happiness of them all, for their peace and prosperity, I believe it is indispensable that they should be associated in one federal Union."

He never lost his passion for U.S. growth, arguing that Canada should become part of the Union, as should Cuba, which he described as a "natural appendage" to the continent. "It is a physical, moral, and political absurdity," he declared, "that such fragments of territory, with sovereigns at fifteen hundred miles beyond sea, worthless and burdensome to their owners, should exist permanently contiguous to a great, powerful, enterprising, and rapidly growing nation."

Yet his astonishing achievements could not prevent Adams from believing his life to have been a failure. For all his cosmopolitan background, he remained a Puritan New Englander, tormented by conscience and convinced that the nation's future greatness depended not on military force, but on its moral virtue. The United States, Adams declared in 1821, "proclaimed to mankind the inextinguishable rights of human nature, and the only lawful foundations of government . . . Her glory is not dominion but liberty."

This was not rhetoric. At the heart of the Monroe Doctrine, the foreign policy strategy that he created for his president, lay his belief in the moral superiority of U.S. democracy to Europe's monarchical governments. Warning Europe to stay out of North and South American affairs, James Monroe told Congress in 1823, "The political system of the [European] powers is essentially different in this respect from that of America . . . We owe it, therefore, to candor and to the amicable relations existing between the United States and those [European] powers to declare that we should consider any attempt on their part to extend their system to any portion of this hemisphere as dangerous to our peace and safety."

It was not his defeat by Jackson in the presidential election of 1828 that made Adams a failure in his own eyes. It was the realization that the expansion of the United States spread slavery as well as freedom, and that the rights of black Americans to life and liberty were being swamped by the right to property guaranteed by the Constitution. The flaw was so deep, he questioned whether the nation deserved to survive. "If the Union must be dissolved," Adams concluded, "slavery is precisely the question upon which it ought to break."

Within the newly enlarged frontiers of the United States, few would have disagreed with Adams's first assessment that Divine Providence had intended the expansion of the United States. Indeed, the association of God with the nation's foundation in freedom and democracy was made explicit in the extraordinary surge of spiritual renewal known as the Second Great Awakening. Like the First Awakening in the 1750s, it was spread by itinerant preachers, and its initial appeal was to western farmers far from centers of organized religion. Ellicott had encountered some of the earliest hot gospelers out in the Alleghenies, and the violence with which they challenged existing beliefs appalled him. "O my God!" he exclaimed. "What mischiefs Arise in this Sublunary World among us small and inconsiderable beings about the forms which will best please thee."

The message preached by wandering ministers in the backwoods was utterly at odds with the unquestioning obedience to God's predestined will that traditional Presbyterian and Puritan churches had always stressed. It was liberty and independence that the mad, unwashed genius of the camp meeting, Lorenzo Dow, used to harp on when he held crowds of thousands electrified during the early 1800s with his theatrical groans, his tortured screams, and shouts of triumph. "But if all men are 'born equal' endowed with unalienable right by their Creator in the blessings of life, liberty, and the pursuit of happiness," he cried out, "then there can be no just reason, as a cause, why he may or should not think, and judge, and act for himself in matters of religion, opinion, and private judgment."

Individual commitment was the first step in the road to salvation mapped out by Dow and other revivalists, followed by good works on behalf of others. To families who had already committed themselves to a life in the unknown far from civilization, and who aimed to get ahead by their own unremitting labor, it was an appealing doctrine. What began as wilderness heresy, however, proved to be in tune with the country's increasingly activist, optimistic mood. Churches once scandalized by the camp preachers' antiauthoritarian message—the Methodist assembly in Britain banned its members from even associating with Dow when he preached there in 1805—adapted their own teachings until by the 1820s the precepts of the Second Awakening had virtually become national orthodoxy. Lyman Beecher, father of Harriet Beecher Stowe and a respected New England minister, prophesied in 1828 that "the West is destined to be the great central power of the nation, and under heaven must Affect powerfully the cause of free institutions and the liberty of the world."

This individualized, democratic form of Christianity was inseparable from the politics that came out of the west at the same time. While most Atlantic states continued to impose high property and wealth qualifications for voting so that the electorate was restricted to less than 10 percent of the white male population, the new western states immediately admitted a much wider selection of voters. One third of Illinois's white males voted in 1820, and an electorate of more than one million sent Andrew Jackson to the White House in 1828. By the middle of the century a majority of states had done what would have been unthinkable to the Founding Fathers and removed voting restrictions for white males altogether.

The east still regarded frontier manners with a mixture of humor and amazement in 1826 when Congressman Davy Crockett came to Washington from Tennessee. Sophisticated journalists invented a coonskin cap for him and wrote a fake frontier biography in which he boasted that he was "fresh from the backwoods, half-horse, half-alligator, a little touched with the snapping-turtle." By the time Jackson stepped down from the presidency a decade later, frontier values had become the norm. Even the campaign managers of William Henry Harrison, the unmistakably aristocratic Whig candidate, found it an advantage to portray him on election posters in 1840 outside a log cabin with a pipe in his mouth and a jug of hard cider at hand.

It had taken a long time, but Jacksonian democracy had demonstrated that eastern government's exclusive democracy could become more inclusive. Its forebears had, in large part, been Scots-Irish squatters—what George Washington and the planter class called banditti—but their sons had succeeded in capturing the nation's capital and colonizing its Anglo-American values. They would not be the last immigrants to attempt the feat.

Yet the most potent agent in distributing power democratically was not the vote but the Public Land Survey, and that too had become a western phenomenon. In 1820 the smallest parcel put up for sale became the half-quarter section (eighty acres), and the minimum price was lowered to only $1.25 an acre. For those who could not afford even this amount, Jackson's government passed the first of several Pre-Emption Acts, allowing squatters under certain conditions to claim up to 160 acres of any land they had improved.

Had John Quincy Adams wanted, he could easily have demonstrated the superiority of the United States to the Old World in this area too. Across mainland Europe, *peasant* was the usual term for someone working the land, meaning that his rights were limited to partial ownership at best or at worst simply to the produce. Even in Britain, where an aggressive program of enclosures in the eighteenth century had created thousands of private holdings from communally owned land, most farms were leased, usually for a term of nineteen years, and the capital value of any improvements the farmer made were retained by the owner.

"Compare this with the situation of the American farmer," the Scottish radical John Melish challenged readers of his *Travels in the United States* in 1818. "He cultivates his own soil, or if he has none, he can procure it in sufficient quantity for 200 or 300 dollars. He can stand erect on the middle of his farm, and say, 'This ground is mine. From the highest canopy of heaven down to the lowest depths, I can claim all that I can get possession of within these bounds; fowls of the air, fish of the seas, and all that pass through the same.' And, having a full share of consequence in the political scale, his equal rights are guaranteed to him. None dare encroach upon him; he can sit under his own vine and under his own fig tree, and none to make him afraid."

Essential to the spread of this form of democracy was the transformation of Jefferson's yeoman farmers into Hamilton's enterprising speculators, or, as they were called with increasing frequency, capitalists. Land was bought and improved only to be sold, and the profit invested farther west. State banks fed the trend by issuing credit with reckless abandon until the markets abruptly collapsed in the fateful year of 1819. But by the time that Alexis de Tocqueville arrived in 1831 to examine the phenomenon of American democracy, the speculative engine was roaring again. "It seldom happens that an American farmer settles for good upon the land which he occupies," he observed in *Democracy in America*. "Especially in the districts of the Far West he brings land into tillage in order to sell it again, and not to farm it."

The dispersal of wealth through the Public Land Survey encouraged the growth of a society unlike any other before it in history. It fostered not only a sense of independence, but also those qualities of resilience, enterprise, and individualism that historians would associate with the frontier. As the influential British economist Edward Gibbon Wakefield wrote in *England and America* in 1833, it was the foundation for a society where "the increase of capital is divided, pretty equally, among a number of capitalists increasing at the same rate as the capital . . . in such a state of things, the independence and self-respect of all begets a love of equality." To the numerous European visitors to the United States in the early nineteenth century, nothing was more astonishing than its egalitarian nature.

"America, then, exhibits in her social state a most extraordinary phenomenon," de Tocqueville concluded. "Men are there seen on a greater equality in point of fortune and intellect, or, in other words, more equal in their strength, than in any other country of the world, or in any age of which history has preserved the remembrance."

. . .

For all their admiration of democracy in the United States and the freedom given to most of its citizens, foreign visitors, especially from Britain, were struck by one glaring exception. "The existence of slavery in its most hideous form," wrote James Stuart of Scotland, in *Three Years in North America*, "in a country of absolute freedom in most respects, is one of those extraordinary anomalies for which it is impossible to account."

In Britain, slavery had been dealt its death blow in 1772 when Lord Mansfield, the chief justice, ruled that an American slave, James Somerset, who had been taken into the country must be released because no British law had been passed to legalize the state of slavery. "The state of slavery is . . . so odious," he declared, "that nothing can be suffered to support it, but positive law [i.e., legislation specifically making slavery legal]."

In the wake of this ruling, the leaders of Britain's own evangelical "awakening"in the early nineteenth century had succeeded in having the slave trade prohibited in Britain in 1807, and to prevent others from taking advantage of her withdrawal from a business she once dominated, Britain's navy assiduously policed the ocean, stopping and searching ships of other nations, including the United States, an irritant that contributed greatly to the outbreak of the 1812 war.

On each of its new frontiers, the United States' neighbors were slave-free. Canada had put a stop to slavery over a twenty-five-year period that ended in 1818, while Mexico's Declaration of Independence in 1812 committed the new nation to abolishing it there as well. Indeed until the 1820s, repugnance in the United States was widespread, even in the South. St. George Tucker, the eminent Virginian lawyer, claimed that slavery was "considered by the great majority of Virginians among its greatest misfortunes," and in 1817 an editorial in Georgia's *Milledgeville Journal* demanded, "Shall we not merit execration, if we fail to provide in time an adequate remedy for this great and growing evil?"

In the North, opinions ranged from the covert support offered by financiers and shippers who had an interest in maintaining the cheap production of cotton to the Quaker view that slavery should be halted—gradually. Until 1831 when William Lloyd Garrison gave them a voice in *The Liberator*, only a few wild extremists called for the immediate emancipation of slaves. Such a policy presented two intractable problems—the need to pay compensation amounting to billions of dollars to former slave owners, and the difficulty of caring for millions of released slaves, other than by resettling them in Africa as proposed by the American Colonization Society. Thus, while few north- erners wanted slavery abolished, most were determined to see that it did not spread.

While opinion in the upper states of the South, Virginia, Maryland, and North Carolina, remained ambivalent about "the peculiar institution," Georgia and South Carolina, always more militant in their defense of slav- ery, received new allies following Jackson's war with the Creeks and the rapid distribution of land from the Louisiana Purchase, both of which made mil- lions of acres available to plantation owners. Northern protests against this increase of slave territory started to grow in 1812 when Louisiana, the first of the states to be carved out of the Louisiana Purchase, was admitted to the Union, to be followed by Ellicott's offspring, Mississippi and Alabama. Al- though they were balanced by Ohio, Indiana, and Illinois, the feeling grew in the north that balance was not enough, slavery should be hemmed in.

In 1819 the first political clash occurred when the rapidly growing popu- lation of the Missouri Territory qualified it for admission to the Union, and leaders such as Thomas Hart Benton, the editor of the St. Louis *Enquirer*, insisted it should be admitted as a slave state. Geographically, the territory was near the northern limits of where cotton could be grown, and only in the center, along the silt-rich banks of the Mississippi and Missouri rivers, was the soil suitable. But almost because of its marginal potential, Missouri symbolized what the north most feared about the capacity of slavery to seep anywhere beyond the Mississippi.

The argument over Missouri's admission to the Union was remarkable because it brought into the open for the first time the extraordinary power that Jefferson had created for the U.S. government. Regardless of the wishes of Missouri's citizens, including Benton's clamorous calls for total indepen- dence from the United States, the issue was decided from start to finish in Washington.

On the basis of Article Four of the Constitution, New York congressman James Tallmadge put forward an amendment linking Missouri's admission to the gradual abolition of slavery in the state. His proposal—no new slaves to be allowed into the state and the children of existing slaves to become free at the age of twenty-five—was taken from New York's experience: a similar

law had put an end to slavery there in 1817 without great difficulty, despite
New York City's having in 1776 the largest population of slaves of any city
outside of Charleston, South Carolina. But the furious response of southern
legislators indicated that Tallmadge had touched a raw nerve.

"You have kindled a fire which all the waters of the ocean cannot put
out," threatened Representative Thomas W. Cobb of Georgia, "which seas
of blood can only extinguish." Despite the savagery of his language, the
continuing embarrassment felt in much of the upper South about slavery
made it possible for the two giants of Congress, John C. Calhoun of South
Carolina and Kentucky's Henry Clay, to broker a compromise. The critical
trade they proposed was to permit slavery in Missouri, but otherwise pro-
hibit it north of the parallel 36 degrees 30 minutes. This was the disputed
frontier that separated Virginia from North Carolina and, after jumping the
Appalachians, Kentucky from Tennessee. West of the Mississippi, it would
now divide Missouri from Arkansas and, following the admission of Texas,
would slice off its northern extremity, the chunk of land that became
known as the Oklahoma Panhandle, before petering out in the mountains
of New Mexico.

For forty years after the Missouri Compromise, the parallel was to serve
as the western equivalent of the Mason-Dixon Line, the frontier between
free and slave states. For the North, it served as the stopper on the spread of
slavery in the territories. But the aged Jefferson, wakened by the argument
over Missouri as by "a firebell in the night," predicted grimly that "a geographical line, coinciding with a marked principle, moral and political,
once conceived and held up to the angry passions of men, will never be
obliterated; and every new irritation will mark it deeper and deeper."

Despite being one of the architects of the compromise, Calhoun was slow to
appreciate its significance as a yardstick of federal strength. During four
years as vice president to John Quincy Adams, he seemed oblivious to the
south's growing resentment against the central government's apparent bias
in favor of the north. The "American System" encouraged by Adams produced federal finance for canals and roads linking western farmers to northern markets rather than to the south, while federal duties on imports
protected northern manufacturers and raised the price of goods that were

needed in the south. Not until 1828, when he was vice president to the newly elected Jackson, did Calhoun at last rebel.

"We cultivate certain great staples for the supply of the general market of the world," he protested in a secretly written pamphlet. "They manufacture almost exclusively for the home market. Their object in the Tariff is to keep down foreign competition, in order to obtain a monopoly of the domestic market. The effect on us is, to compel us to purchase at a higher price, both what we obtain from them and from others."

In his pamphlet, Calhoun tried to develop Jefferson's thesis that the sovereignty of the states who had agreed to the federal compact allowed them to veto laws they deemed unconstitutional. "This very control," he proposed, "is the remedy which the Constitution has provided to prevent the encroachments of the General Government on the reserved rights of the States."

Whatever the validity of Jefferson's original argument, Calhoun's version of it defied the realities of history: that the federal infant had grown to a giant; that a government once small enough to cost by Jefferson's estimate around $68,000 a year now had annual revenues of more than $30 million, almost half of it coming in 1835 from sales of federal land; that the Supreme Court under Chief Justice John Marshall had established beyond doubt its role as sole interpreter of the Constitution; and that after the admission of Missouri, the influence of an individual state in the Union had dwindled from a thirteenth of the total in 1789 to a twenty-fourth in 1828. In short, the nature of the United States was changing.

A sense of what was happening ensured that a Senate discussion in 1831 about the sale of public lands—whether the income should continue to go to the central government or be distributed among the states—would quickly widen into an examination of what the nation had become. The two protagonists were South Carolina's Robert Hayne, supporting Calhoun's argument, and Daniel Webster, who deployed his famous powers of oratory to argue the superiority of U.S. sovereignty over that of the states. "It is to that Union that we owe our safety at home, and our consideration and dignity abroad," Webster asserted in his triumphal peroration. "It is to that Union that we are chiefly indebted for whatever makes us most proud of our country." And his final, bellowed phrase, "Liberty and Union, now and forever, one and inseparable!" was to become the watchword of Unionists for a generation.

John C. Calhoun

This was his answer to the question the framers of the Constitution had dared not address—the United States was a single nation. Two years later Calhoun offered his own interpretation, that the United States was and remained a compact of sovereign states. His bleak Presbyterian advocacy galvanized South Carolina's legislature. In 1833 it decided to nullify federal legislation relating to the level of tariffs and backed its veto with an implicit threat to secede from the Union. Andrew Jackson's response was based on raw power rather than constitutional niceties. Declaring nullification and the threat of secession to be tantamount to "insurrection and treason," the president demolished Calhoun's thesis in a sentence. "To say that any State may at pleasure secede from the Union is to say that the United States is not a nation," he thundered, and let it be known that he would march into Charleston with up to fifteen thousand militia to enforce federal legislation.

The crisis was defused when Henry Clay brokered another deal allowing South Carolina to nullify a different act while accepting the tariff. Thus the issue of sovereignty was left unresolved, but the reality of federal power was not in doubt. Jackson's terrifying display of executive authority in the 1830s, when he created the conditions for the expulsion of the Cherokees from their land in Georgia in direct defiance of the Supreme Court, then demolished the Bank of the United States in the face of ferocious opposition from business and financial interests, demonstrated that none of the checks and balances in the Constitution—neither the legislature, nor the states, nor the judiciary—could prevent a popular president from having his way.

Since Jacksonian democracy randomly benefited state sovereignty, as in its support for Georgia's campaign to expel the Cherokees, as well as limited it, southerners found reasons both to support and oppose it. In the same way, northern opinion was divided about the appeal of the Whigs, who opposed his monarchical power. But on both sides of the slavery argument, one lesson had been learned from Jackson's presidency. There could be no challenge to the power of the United States government in the territories. The goal, therefore, was to gain control of that powerful institution.

The arithmetic was against the south: out of a national population of seventeen million in 1840, nearly ten million lived in the north, in the House of Representatives the north had a majority of fifty, and in the electoral college a majority of fifty-two. Yet by a mixture of intimidation, disarray among their opponents, and skillful use of the two-party system, southerners managed to keep the federal government sympathetic to the institution that underpinned their way of life. Florida and Arkansas followed Missouri into the pro-slavery fold, two presidents attempted to buy Cuba in an effort to bring that slave-owning appendage within the Union, an alliance with western farmers gradually reduced tariffs from their 1830s level, and until some other slave-owning territory could be identified, development of the prairies north of 36 degrees 30 minutes was stalled. So long as the frontier remained at the limits Adams had set, the southern way of life was safe.

The formidable increase of territory made by the Adams-Onís Treaty in the northwest did not satisfy everyone. Some critics immediately condemned the new frontier for not having been extended farther in the southwest to include the gigantic state of Texas, which was widely assumed to have been part of the Louisiana Purchase. The short-term advantage of removing Florida as a sanctuary for runaway slaves stilled these doubts, but they were renewed in 1833 when American settlers in Texas asserted their independence from the republic of Mexico.

Their revolt against the dictatorial rule of General Antonio de Santa Anna was not just about democracy but about slavery. In 1829 the government of Vicente Guerrero had fulfilled the promise made in Mexico's Declaration of Independence and declared all slaves to be free. Mexico's loose confederate structure enabled the slave-owning Americans in Texas to ignore the ban at first. Then Santa Anna reformed the constitution so that power was centralized in Mexico City and in 1833 issued a decree banning further immigration of American settlers to Texas, while requiring slaves there to be set free. Thus the siege of the Alamo and Sam Houston's defeat of Santa Anna in 1836 were triggered by the need to defend not just Texans' liberty but their property in people.

The independent republic of Texas stretched as far north as modern Wyoming, an immense territory two thirds the size of the Louisiana Purchase. When the proposal to include this gigantic, slave-owning state within the frontier of the United States began to be considered seriously in the 1840s, it presented an immediate challenge to the delicate balance of the Missouri Compromise.

The risks might have been thought too great but for the remarkable change in the south's attitude toward slavery as a system. In reaction to the Missouri Compromise, southern leaders began to identify the institution with the south's way of life, while religious figures such as the Reverend Richard Furman of the South Carolina Baptists offered the defense that even the early apostles had deemed slavery "lawful and right." By 1830, the end of the south's lingering embarrassment was signaled by a speech from Calhoun praising slavery as "a great political institution, essential to the peace and existence of one-half this Union."

The change was driven by the sheer scale of the slave economy growing up in the new states of the deep south. It simply defied apology. Although the economic depression caused by Jacksonian economics reduced output briefly, the value of cotton exports bounced back to reach more than $120 million a year by the 1850s—about 54 percent of the total of all exports—creating a financial bonanza that stretched far beyond the deep south. Virginia, Maryland, and North Carolina grew rich supplying slaves for the cotton fields farther south. Philadelphia, New York, and Boston profited from financing the slave economy, and the cotton factories of England earned fortunes for their owners.

The one economic obstacle to the continuation of the "peculiar institution" came from the very success that had driven the price of a slave to $750 in 1845 and would soon send it above $1,000. Yet the rise in value only reinforced slavery's unchallengeable position. The south's three million slaves represented a $2.75 billion investment—more than ten times the total capital invested in northern manufacture. To question the morality of such a gigantic property was, as Mississippi's declaration of secession would later put it, "to strike a blow at commerce and civilization."

Even to an antislavery visitor, the sight of a Louisiana cotton plantation was impressive. "The fields are as level and regular as gardens," wrote Timothy Flint. "They sometimes contain three or four thousand acres in *one* field; and I have seen from *a dozen to twenty* ploughs, all making their straight furrows through a field a mile in depth, with a regularity which, it would be supposed, could be obtained only by a line."

At the dawn of the industrial era, such plantations could easily be compared to large-scale factory production. Southern spokesmen made the comparison with increasing frequency to present their system as one of relative humanity. Unlike the system of hired labor that overworked some and left the old and weak to starve, wrote William J. Grayson in *The Hireling and the Slave*, "Slavery makes all work, and it insures homes, food, and clothing for all. It permits no idleness, and it provides for sickness, infancy and old age . . . There is no such thing with slavery as a laborer for whom nobody cares or provides."

This growing confidence in slavery as an acceptable institution, as well as a source of profits, helped persuade the majority of southern politicians in the 1840s that the frontier of the United States should be extended again to annex the independent republic of Texas. Mexico's announcement that it would regard annexation as a hostile act was positively welcomed as an excuse to enclose still more territory within the American frontier.

Urgency was added to the situation by Britain's decision to recognize Texas as an independent state, and to push for abolition of slavery within its frontiers. According to an alarmist report from Ashbel Smith, Texas's representative to Britain, the plan was to create a free-labor zone in Texas, "a refuge for runaway slaves from the United States, and eventually a negro nation . . . to be more or less, according to circumstances, under the protection of the British Government."

The tipping point came with the popularity of James Polk's expansionist program in the presidential election of 1844, calling for the annexation of Texas and the seizure of the Oregon Country. Deciding that the risk of war with Mexico was worth taking, President John Tyler and his secretary of state, John Calhoun, introduced legislation to annex Texas. To reduce opposition from the north, Texas agreed to relinquish all territory north of 36 degrees 30 minutes. With the addition of this new territory, the U.S. frontier would be pushed almost one thousand miles farther west from the Sabine River to the Rio Grande. This was what Andrew Jackson called "extending the area of freedom."

The tragedy of John Quincy Adams's life was that he lived to see his dream come true. The thin confederation of Atlantic states of his childhood had more than doubled its size while he was still in his prime. He himself then extended it across the continent to the Pacific, and by 1848, the year of his death, the frontier enclosed Oregon and California, Texas and New Mexico, and everything in between. What made this tragic was the gap between his dreams of what the United States stood for and the reality of its power being used to further the ends of slave owners. Freedom had expanded, but slavery had spread with it step by step, and he had connived the deal. In his diary he agonized about his role in which, as his grandson Henry Adams observed in a memoir written toward the end of the century, the great statesman had become "a tool of the slave oligarchy (especially about Florida)."

For almost twenty years following his defeat by Andrew Jackson in 1828, Adams represented Massachusetts in Congress, and there, at least partly to expiate the aid he had given the pro-slavery forces, he became the spokesman, and often sole representative in the House, of the antislavery movement.

"He never rebelled," Henry Adams said disparagingly, "until the slave oligarchy contemptuously cut his throat." Yet when he did rebel, he proved unshakable in the face of overwhelming, bitter hostility and a long campaign even to keep slavery from being mentioned in Congress. He began by presenting petitions that called for the immediate freeing of slaves in

John Quincy Adams in 1847, by Mathew Brady

the District of Columbia, where the Congress had direct responsibility. But when pro-slavery representatives introduced the infamous "gag rules" to ban any discussion of slavery on the grounds that it stirred up insurrectionary ideas among slaves, Adams made stubborn and skillful use of House rules to have the subject talked about on every possible occasion. When his opponents tried to censure him, he used his right of self-defense to filibuster for two weeks about the iniquities of slavery and promised to talk another week until they withdrew the censure motion. Adams, said a Virginia congressman, was "the acutest, the astutest, the archest enemy of southern slavery that ever existed."

What made his stance so unpopular was that by common consent most people who disliked slavery felt it right to censor themselves for fear of agitating the slaves. Southern leaders blamed each of the uprisings, planned or actual, of Gabriel in 1800, Denmark Vesey in 1822, and Nat Turner in 1831 on the resentment stirred up by criticism of the system or the propaganda of abolitionists, as though left to themselves slaves would gladly accept the paternalist care of their owners. To insulate slaves against infection from the north, the states' legislation against teaching them to read was rigorously enforced. By implication, the few outright abolitionists such as William Lloyd Garrison were deemed to be plotting the murder of whites. "Are abolitionists doing the work of God?" demanded South Carolina's James Hammond. "No! God is not there. It is the work of Satan."

The furious hostility of the south to any breath of censure silenced many more. Adams routinely received death threats, Harriet Martineau, a pioneering English sociologist who toured the United States in the late 1830s, was told: "They would hang me: they would cut my tongue out, and cast it on a dunghill; and so forth." Elijah Lovejoy, an antislavery Illinois newspaperman, was in fact lynched, and in St. Louis, Missouri, Francis McIntosh, a free black, was burned alive merely for being suspected of abolitionist sympathies.

The threat of financial loss silenced others. "There are millions upon millions of dollars due from Southerners to the merchants and mechanics of this city," a New York businessman warned one antislaver, "the payment of which would be jeopardized by any rupture between the North and the South." Even to discuss something as upsetting as slavery was regarded as rude. "Every liberty, personal and social," Martineau wrote, "was sacrificed in the attempt to enforce silence on that one sore subject."

Against that background, Adams's solitary courage stood out. His opposition to the annexation of Texas was equally fierce and unforgiving. With freezing accuracy he predicted that the advocates of annexation wanted more than Texas, they wanted war with Mexico.

"What will be your *cause* in such a war?" he demanded harshly in Congress. "Aggression, conquest, and the re-establishment of slavery where it has been abolished. In that war, sir, the banners of *freedom* will be the banners of Mexico; and your banners, I blush to speak the word, will be the banners of slavery."

Annexation did make conflict with Mexico inevitable. As a young lieutenant in the U.S. army, Ulysses S. Grant saw at first hand how a dispute over Texas's border with Mexico was manufactured by American commanders into a skirmish with Mexican forces in which eleven American lives were lost. Looking back at the incident in his sixties, Grant stated squarely, "The occupation, separation and annexation [of Texas] were a conspiracy, to acquire territory out of which slave states might be formed for the American Union."

The brilliant bloodless Tennessean, James Polk, brought about the annexation, created the cause of war, and thereby enclosed almost half of Mexico within the U.S. frontier. In his 1844 presidential campaign he promised to acquire California and Oregon, to reduce tariffs, and create an independent Treasury. His success in achieving all four goals reflects his formidable ability, unmatched by any other antebellum president except Jackson, to weld the southern-dominated arms of federal power, judiciary, and legislature into an instrument of the executive. Polk's administration became, in Adams's acrid phrase, "a military monarchy."

The Mexican-American War ended in the 1848 Treaty of Guadalupe Hidalgo, just before Adams's death. Its cost to the United States, beyond $15 million in compensation for war damage, was the destruction of the Missouri Compromise and the closer approach of Civil War, and, as the twenty-first century has revealed, the creation of a frontier that challenges the values of the United States. The questions posed by Polk's imperial legacy do not go away.

Against Polk's formidable war machine, Adams had found one unexpected ally. The more extreme of Polk's supporters wanted a victorious United States to annex all of Mexico and push its frontiers as far south as the Nicaraguan border. To John Calhoun, the high priest of slavery, this presented an unacceptable risk. "We have never dreamt of incorporating into our Union any but the Caucasian race—the free white race," he told the Senate. "To incorporate Mexico, would be the very first instance of the kind, of incorporating an Indian race; for more than half of the Mexicans are Indians, and the other is composed chiefly of mixed tribes. I protest against such a union as that! Ours, sir, is the Government of a white race."

Like so many of Calhoun's pronouncements, this was an entirely logical deduction, but one based on the premise that the guarantees afforded to property and to individual freedom by the Constitution applied only to white males. So long as that concept of liberty as an exclusive privilege prevailed, it was possible to believe that other races stood at a lower, less free level, and that African-Americans in particular were destined for no better fate than to be the property of free white males. Up to eighty thousand Mexicans were brought within the new frontier—"We didn't cross the border," their descendants would say more than a century later, "the border crossed us"—creating another group somewhere below the whites. "Nothing can be more unfounded and false," Calhoun stated flatly, "than the opinion that all men are born free and equal; inequality is indispensable to progress."

No such problems existed on the northern frontier. By 1845 some twelve thousand mostly white American settlers had moved into the territory on both sides of the Columbia River in what was called Oregon Country. On the basis of the Monroe Doctrine "that no future European colony or dominion shall, with our consent, be planted or established on any part of the North American continent," Polk claimed the area from Britain, as far north as 54 degrees 40 north, the southern border of the old Russian empire and of present Alaska.

Always the New Englander, Adams backed expansion to the northwest because it tilted the United States away from slaves, and toward the great tea and silk markets of China and Japan that were making New England shippers and traders rich. At the age of seventy-nine, he vigorously endorsed the slogan "Fifty-four Forty or Fight," but the Oregon Treaty with Britain was a compromise between the American goal and the British claim for a frontier on the Columbia River. It ensured that the last thousand miles of the longest undefended frontier in the world would run along the forty-nineteenth parallel, excluding British Columbia but bringing Washington, Idaho, and parts of Montana and Wyoming as well as Oregon within the United States.

Yet even this did not provide Adams with consolation for the values that motivated the new, enlarged United States. "Was all this a Utopian daydream?" he exclaimed in despair. "Is the one talent, entrusted to man, to be hidden under a bushel? Is the candle, destined to light the world, to be extinguished by the blasting breath of slavery?" In one of his last public pronouncements, he abrasively denounced the Constitution as "a menstruous rag" stained by the taint of slavery. Soon afterward, he was felled by a stroke that left him incapable of speech.

Two years later, in 1848, a second stroke killed him as he sat at his desk in the Congress. In the range of his dreams and the agony he felt at his failure, his life constituted a genuine American tragedy, a fact usually obscured by celebration of his brief moments of glory as author of the Monroe Doctrine and in his bitter defiance of slavery in Congress. "Americans," said his acerbic grandson Henry, "have always taken their tragedy lightly."

CHAPTER 10

The Values of Government

*We all declare for liberty; but in using the same word we do
not all mean the same thing. With some the word liberty
may mean for each man to do as he pleases with himself,
and the product of his labor; while with others, the same
word may mean for some men to do as they please with
other men, and the product of other men's labor.*

ABRAHAM LINCOLN,
Address at Baltimore, Maryland, 1864

L OOKING BACK FROM the 1890s on the way that Congress had sliced
and diced the immense continent, Woodrow Wilson was astonished
by its insouciance. "States have, indeed, often been whimsically enough
formed," he wrote in the *Atlantic Monthly*. "We have left the matter of boundaries to surveyors rather than to statesmen, and have by no means managed
to construct economic units in the making of States. We have joined mining communities with agricultural, the mountain with the plain, the ranch
with the farm, and have left the making of uniform rules to the sagacity and
practical habit of neighbors ill at ease with one another."

The process ensured that far from being an isolated activity, settlement
of the prairie states was not only enclosed within a framework of law and
government, but directed from Washington in a manner that only partially
reflected the will of the people. In Congress, the Committee on Territories
was the agency responsible, delineating the shapes of new Territories out of
land allocated to Indians or from gigantic counties spawned by older states

by giving them borders that occasionally followed rivers and mountains, but more often simply followed parallels and meridians.

Minnesota, for example, came into existence like a Russian doll, emerging in 1849 from inside the larger Iowa Territory, which until 1838 had been concealed within a greater Wisconsin, originally part of the bigger northern "unorganized territory" that had once been contained within the huge Territory of Missouri, which was hidden inside the enormous District of Louisiana that in 1805 had been carved from the original gigantic Louisiana Purchase.

The impetus for the committee's work came from the spread of population beyond the old state boundaries, but it was a two-way process. The settlers' need to have their claims recognized as legitimately owned property made the wildest and most freedom-loving among them as anxious to bring in government as any politician in Washington. In less than five years, for instance, the process transformed the frontier community of Blodgett's Settlement on the Rock River into Beloit City in Rock County, Wisconsin, with a Board of Commissioners, a school district, a federal postmaster, a delegate to the territorial legislature, and a courthouse.

In 1836 Caleb Blodgett, a forceful Vermonter, accompanied by his sons and some friends, established a squatter's claim to some seven thousand acres of grass-covered bluffs on the border between Illinois and the future Wisconsin by building a log cabin and plowing a hundred acres. The claim overlooked the Rock River, and the following spring Dr. Horace White from Colebrook, New Hampshire, arrived and bought almost one third of it, about two thousand acres, on behalf of the New England Emigrating Society for $2,500. It was not just the location—on the edge of the prairies with woodland and the river at hand—but the chance of planting immediately on the plowed ground that persuaded him to buy, though at that point all he owned was Blodgett's claim to the land. "Purchasers of claims took their chances of being able to hold what they had bargained for," White's son remembered. "What was paid for in such a case was the chance that the government land office would eventually recognize the claim as valid under the pre-emption laws, and give a patent for it." Until then, they relied on the unofficial rules of claimants' associations that based ownership not just on payment but on use and occupancy.

This was the classic squatter's progression, adding layer after layer of ownership from occupancy, possession, and improvement, through purchase

and registration, until with the issue of a patent for the land it became official property. The final layers were added the following summer, when U.S.
surveyors extended the federal Public Land Survey over Blodgett's Settlement, locating it inside Section 35, Township 1 North, Range 12 East, 4th
Principal Meridian.

The system allowed every acre of public land to be given its own individual
identification and put up for sale. So efficient had the survey become that in
the mid-1830s, and again in the early 1840s, the income generated by the
General Land Office, the agency that sold the squared-off land, amounted to
roughly half of all federal revenue. Eventually the grid of squares laid out by
an army of surveyors would transform the continent into more than one billion acres of property. By 1893, the year that Frederick Jackson Turner delivered his speech on the significance of the mythical frontier, the checkerboard
of lines running north-south and east-west had provided the foundation for
about three million farms, more than two thousand counties, and exactly
thirty states and four Territories.

Once the U.S. Survey had noted the claims to preemption of the fourteen settler families squashed into three log cabins, a delegate from the
Blodgett settlement was promptly sent to the General Land Office in Milwaukee to pay the federal government the purchase price for the land. According to a series of Pre-Emption Acts passed since 1831, their receipt
constituted a right of ownership until a formal patent could be issued.

To cope with the hardships of the frontier life required courage and resilience. Horace White recalled that in the roughly constructed cabin he
would wake on winter mornings "under an extra counter-pane of snow
which had sifted through the crevices," and until the first crops were har-
vested, the community had to live on what they could hunt and fish, and on
barrels of flour carted in on almost impassably muddy tracks. Even so, lack
of food forced them in their second year to slaughter an ox used for plowing and send an emergency team to buy a barrel of pork from a settlement
downriver. The married women suffered especially. Worn down by giving
birth and breast-feeding, with no respite from the need to farm and pickle,
preserve and cook, several died in their thirties during the early years.

Looking back over half a century, White could also remember the beauty
of the untouched prairie. "Blackberries, strawberries, wild plums, wild grapes,
hickory nuts, hazel nuts and black walnuts were to be had for the trouble of

gathering them, and as for wild flowers I cannot begin to tell you how the prairies, the woods and the river banks glowed with them," he told a commencement class at Beloit College in the 1880s. And the food shortages began to disappear once the farms were established. "We produced our own vegetables, and poultry, our own pork, and milk and butter. The cows grazed freely on the open prairie round about, and were lured homeward by an enticement of bran at the close of each day. We had a wood lot which supplied our fuel and I cut down the trees."

But what is most noticeable about the story of Blodgett's Settlement, and a thousand frontier communities like it, is the inextricable connection with government. The federal government had provided the state line between Illinois and Wisconsin that put them just inside Wisconsin Territory and also served as the baseline for the Public Land Survey, where their preemption claim was first registered. They looked to the federally appointed governor, Henry Dodge, who nominated the chief justice, judges, and sheriffs, to maintain order, including protection of land records. And they registered with the Territorial census of 1836 to be able to vote for their own legislature, which had the power to legislate for frontier needs. Until then the laws of Michigan, the territory's parent state, remained in force.

On the basis of the census, the Territorial government divided the eastern half of the Territory into four immense counties. This placed the pioneer families of Blodgett's Settlement in Rock County and made them eligible to vote for a board of commissioners with responsibility for law enforcement and administration of the county.

Thus even before the patent was issued confirming the settlers' ownership of their land, and before the water-driven sawmill started turning out boards so that proper houses could be built to replace the log cabins, the settlement had three layers of government—county, Territorial, and federal. Within another three years, it had a federally appointed postmaster, and in 1841 a county courthouse was being constructed where prairie flowers and wild plums had grown a few summers before, in a town that now preferred to call itself Beloit rather than Blodgett's Settlement.

As Woodrow Wilson pointed out, there was nothing organic in the creation of a state like Wisconsin. In 1837 the Committee on Territories sliced away Wisconsin's Upper Peninsula, which divided Lake Superior from Lake Michigan, and gave it to Michigan, when it became a state, as compensation

The First Congregational Church in Beloit, Wisconsin, 1877

for the 468 square miles around Toledo that it had lost to Ohio through a mapping error. The committee also chopped off the territory west of the Mississippi—the future Iowa and Minnesota—because the river had been accepted as a boundary ever since Jefferson had made it the western edge of the imagined states of Michigania and Assenisipia in 1784.

Within the amputated remnant, the inhabitants of Beloit in a southern prairie county had more in common with other New England communities stretching eastward through Illinois and Indiana back to their starting point beyond the Appalachians than with immigrant miners in the north and west or lumber concerns in the forest counties of the center. Like other prairie communities, it soon developed a narrow sense of self based on the shared challenge of farming and building, and through communal institutions such as the churches and Beloit College. An outside influence, however, was to fuse a wider sense of identity and pride in being part of Wisconsin and, more intensely than that, being part of the United States.

Just six years after Horace White decided to settle beside the Rock River, his friend Benjamin Brown started to advocate the "free soil" policies of the Liberty Party. The goal was to keep cheap slave labor out of the Territories, but Free Soil also meant keeping out free African-Americans as well. In 1854 even Abraham Lincoln took this for granted. "The whole nation is interested that the best use shall be made of these territories," he acknowledged. "We want them for the homes of free white people." It was a populist demand, aimed both at the aristocratic planters from the south and at moneyed speculators of the east who might bring in cheap black labor. As the escaped slave Frederick Douglass noted bitterly, "The cry of Free Man was raised, not for the extension of liberty to the black man, but for the protection of the liberty of the white."

Nevertheless, the slogan could be interpreted more broadly, to be against slavery wherever it existed. The way that Brown presented Free Soil policies led him to be dubbed, as his son recalled, "a nigger lover and abolitionist." What had touched the new community of Beloit was the first little tug of a current that would pull it into the mainstream of national events.

By 1848, when Wisconsin was admitted to the Union as a state, Brown was giving shelter to runaway slaves, and the combined influence of a powerful Congregational church and the community's evangelical college ensured that he did so with the approval of Beloit's leading citizens. Then in 1854 came news that Sherman Booth, editor of Milwaukee's leading newspaper, the *Free Democrat*, had been imprisoned by a federal court under the 1850 Fugitive Slave Act for helping to rescue a slave from prison.

At that point, it became impossible for any community in Wisconsin, however remote, to resist the powerful forces that had begun to convulse the rest of the country. No one could be indifferent to the outcome of the battle to control the federal government. The victors would determine the nature of property itself and shape the law that protected personal freedom.

As it happened, the man responsible for the 1850 Fugitive Slave Act had also done more than any other to shape the Territories and states of the United States from Iowa to California. For those reasons alone Senator Stephen A. Douglas of Illinois deserves a greater fame than simply having come second to Abraham Lincoln in the Illinois debates of 1858. Until his encounters with Lincoln, the clout that Douglas wielded made him seem the natural successor in Congress to the great triumvirate of Daniel Webster, Henry Clay, and John C. Calhoun.

He made his mark from the moment he arrived in the House of Representatives in 1843 as a freshman Democrat from Illinois and threw himself into the debate over the annexation of Texas. Standing barely five feet tall, he compensated with a style of oratory that was sweaty, extravagant, loud, and combative. John Quincy Adams, the old Puritan lion, observed "the humunculus Douglas" with distaste. "In the midst of his roaring," he noted, "to save himself from choking, he stripped off and cast away his cravat, unbuttoned his waistcoat and had the air and aspect of a half-naked pugilist."

Nevertheless, Douglas's enthusiasm for annexing Texas, the great cause of the south, led a caucus of southern congressmen to back his election as chairman of the House Committee on Territories. His backers' confidence was quickly justified. Calhoun had written to the British minister telling him that Texas was needed in the Union in order to provide "security to the slave interest," and publication of his correspondence in 1844 so outraged antislavery senators that they threw out the Tyler administration's attempt to annex Texas by treaty. It was Douglas who rescued the south's tattered strategy.

The annexation treaty was needed because Texas was regarded as an independent nation, but such a treaty required a two-thirds majority in the Senate. With characteristic flair, Douglas bypassed the obstacle by persuading Congress that Texas had originally been included within the Louisiana Purchase and thus was territorially part of the United States. On this basis, a simple resolution of Congress, requiring no more than a bare majority, would be sufficient for reannexation, so long as the voters of Texas agreed. Then, in a way that was to become his trademark, Douglas set out to mollify the antislavers with all the roaring energy he had used in upsetting them. He introduced an amendment that severed the long arm of Texas stretching north of the old slave frontier of 36 degrees 30 minutes, ensuring that this land would be free in accordance with the Missouri Compromise. Finally he promised that the rest of Texas, whether it remained one or became several states as some wanted, would be allowed to choose whether to be free or slave. This was to be the basis of the system he would call "popular sovereignty."

A lasting memorial to its inventor's deal-making can still be seen in the Oklahoma Panhandle, the 3.5-million-acre slab of territory separating northern Texas from southwestern Kansas and southeastern Colorado that was lopped off at 36 degrees 30 minutes to soothe the antislavers, then forgotten.

Stephen A. Douglas

For fifty years it remained a no-man's-land, unclaimed by any state, until, almost as an afterthought, it was attached to Oklahoma.

Demonstrating an expansiveness to match that of Adams or Polk, Douglas presented popular sovereignty as the key to a still greater enlargement of the United States. "Our federal system is admirably suited to the whole continent," he thundered to the House of Representatives. "I would exert all legal and honorable means to drive Great Britain and the last vestiges of royal authority from the continent of North America, and extend the limits of the Republic from ocean to ocean. I would make this an oceanbound republic and have no more disputes about boundaries or red lines upon maps."

It was a potent image to which many wavering legislators could subscribe, whatever their reservations about the dangers of conflict with Mexico and about spreading the peculiar institution of slavery. No fewer than sixteen different solutions to the problem of Texas were submitted in the Senate and House of Representatives, but the definitive joint resolution by which Congress annexed the territory and admitted the new state came in January 1845 from Douglas's committee, a symbol of the crucial role he had played.

For the next fifteen years the south and Douglas were to find each other mutually useful. With each new session, the southern caucus, first in the House, then in the Senate, voted him back to his chairmanship, and with each new surge of settlement westward, he and his committee provided Territorial boundaries and a framework of government that allowed a Territory's voters to opt for slavery. The political marriage repeated the pattern of his personal life—born in Vermont, he had married a wealthy southerner, Martha Martin, whose profitable cotton plantations financed his career. Yet tied though he was to the south in both partnerships, he never felt close enough to its spirit to be admitted to the inner circles ruled by Calhoun and Jefferson Davis or to pay more than one brief visit to his wife's Mississippi property.

Douglas's political mastery was already assured when the war with Mexico ended in the Treaty of Guadalupe Hidalgo in 1848, which forced the defeated nation to cede to the United States all its territory from the Rio Grande to San Francisco. By the end of that year, he had steered four new states—Florida, Texas, Iowa, and Wisconsin—into the Union and had three new Territories—California, Minnesota, and Oregon—waiting in line. But nothing that he had done so far compared to the tangle of problems thrown up by the United States' huge acquisition of territory. At every point, sovereignty and slavery were interlocked.

Texas maintained that its slave boundaries included half of nominally free New Mexico; northern Free-Soilers insisted that the Wilmot Proviso banned slavery throughout the newly acquired territory; southerners required the same territory to be opened to slavery; and Mormons, who believed that slavery was, in Brigham Young's words, "of divine institution," laid claim to most of the land between the Rockies and the Pacific, a region that contained California, which, with indeterminate borders and a gold-swollen economy, was applying for admission to the Union as a free state.

The Douglas strategy fell into two distinct stages, shaping the new land into governable units, then selling them to the two rival groups in Congress.

The boundaries of California and the state lines dividing New Mexico from Texas and Utah are all physical memorials to the 1850 deliberations of the Senate Committee on Territories. But it was equally important that the legislation creating Utah and New Mexico as territories should contain the proviso that when they became states, they "shall be received into the Union, with or without slavery, as their constitution may prescribe at the time of their admission."

This was popular sovereignty in action, a democratic solution to the growing conflict over slavery. The new states rather than the federal government would make the decision. The system was based, Douglas said, "on the great and fundamental principle that every people ought to possess the right of forming and regulating their own internal concerns and domestic institutions in their own way." But it also rested on his unparalleled skills as a deal-maker, and the deals that Douglas made were to radicalize the north.

Texas was paid $10 million to drop its claim to New Mexico, while the antislavers, offended by the possibility of Utah becoming a slave state when it lay north of 36 degrees 30 minutes, were bought off with the abolition of slave-trading in the District of Columbia and the assurance that the slave frontier still held good within the Louisiana Purchase. But the admission of a free California would swing the balance in Congress heavily against slavery, and the price exacted by the south was much higher. A new, tougher Fugitive Slave Act was promised and passed in 1850. It made the recovery of escaped slaves a federal responsibility, with fines of $1,000 in a federal court for anyone who hindered a slave's capture, and allowed neither jury trial nor right of habeas corpus for the runaway.

The senior senator, Henry Clay of Kentucky, "the Great Compromiser" of the previous three decades, packaged these proposals into an omnibus bill, but put together they proved too contentious to be accepted. Working his contacts, Douglas had his deals presented again as separate bills and saw them passed into law almost unaltered. Their success sealed his dominance in the Senate. He had eclipsed Clay; Calhoun had died during the debates, and Webster had alienated his following in New England by supporting the legislation on fugitive slaves. Douglas's supporters termed him the Little General, a reference both to his height and to his Napoleonic grasp of strategy.

His one weakness, and ultimately a fatal one, was his inability to understand how passionately ordinary people felt about justice and values—issues that were absent from his deals. Humorously, Douglas remarked that after the Fugitive Slave Act of 1850 had been passed, he could have navigated his way back to Illinois following the line of his effigies that his opponents hung by day and burned by night. But those were only the outward signs of a growing resentment against the south's political power. Just as the south always liked to picture itself as a society distinct from the effete, commercial, corrupted north, so northern states began to pride themselves after 1850 on being unlike the aristocratic, freedom-hating, corrupted society they saw south of the Mason-Dixon Line.

In Wisconsin, the catalyst was the Booth case of 1854. It began when federal marshals acting on behalf of a Missouri slave owner arrested a runaway slave named Joshua Glover under the terms of the Fugitive Slave Act and locked him in Milwaukee's county jail before taking him south. Sherman Booth, the eye-catchingly large and black-bearded editor of the *Free Democrat*, was alleged to have brought out a mob, yelling, "Freemen to the rescue," that broke in and freed Glover when the marshals refused to accept a local judge's writ of habeas corpus.

In the state's newly created Supreme Court, Chief Justice Abram D. Smith dismissed the charges against Booth on the grounds that the Fugitive Slave Act infringed the sovereignty of the new state. The court could not accept, he said, that "an officer of the United States, armed with process to arrest a fugitive from service, is clothed with entire immunity from state authority, to commit whatever crime or outrage against the state." When the United States appealed the case to the U.S. Supreme Court, Booth's supporters pointed to the contradiction of making slavery a matter of state sovereignty beyond the scope of federal law, except where fugitive slaves were concerned and state sovereignty counted for nothing.

The inconsistency was made clearer still in 1855 when the U.S. Supreme Court under Chief Justice Roger Taney, soon to polarize opinion still further with his ruling in the Dred Scott case, overturned Smith's judgment, denying state courts any right to question a federal law. Thus Wisconsin— in common with most other western states created in equally arbitrary fashion—began to discover a sense of identity around the cause of antislavery and in opposition to Washington's laws. Its anger, like that that of other free states, grafted itself onto a deeper-rooted sense of individual liberty growing in New England.

In Massachusetts, Henry David Thoreau, who had already refused to pay taxes for Polk's imperialist war and advocated civil disobedience for those who wanted "to do justice to the slave and to Mexico," pleaded with his fellow citizens in 1850 to remember that "they are to be men first and Americans only at a late and convenient hour." With growing frequency the phrase *the slave power* was applied indiscriminately to the south and to the federal government, which was deemed to be under its control. In a way that eerily resembled Calhoun's definition of the south as an oppressed area at war with Washington, the intellectuals of New England gave voice to the north's feeling that it was in rebellion against an oppressive government.

"The less government we have the better," Ralph Waldo Emerson protested, "—the fewer laws and the less confided power." Long before the Confederates made rebellion their philosophy, Walt Whitman made it his against a slave-supporting government, "My heart is with all you rebels—all of you today, always, wherever; your flag is my flag."

That same mood gave force to the glorious assertion of individual liberty in *Leaves of Grass*, published July 4, 1855:

> *I am for those that have never been master'd,*
> *For men and women whose tempers have never been master'd,*
> *For those whom laws, theories, conventions can never master.*

Twenty years after Calhoun's southern manifesto had declared, "The country is divided and organized into two great parties, the one sovereign and the other subject," Thoreau demanded of the north, "How does it become a man to behave toward this American government today? I answer that he cannot without disgrace be associated with it."

In the end everyone opposed to slavery had to make a similar appeal to a sense of individual integrity and moral principle more powerful than the laws and conventions that supported slavery. Such opposition required a double defiance from women and free blacks, because both were assumed to be subservient to the white males who made the law. Thus a woman brave enough to join the Female Anti-Slavery Sociey not only had to face the real danger of riots and the sort of mob violence that led to the burning of Pennsylvania Hall in Philadelphia in 1837, but to find a personal justification for her behavior. "Whatever is *morally* right for a man to do, it is *morally* right for a woman to do," the South Carolina abolitionist Angelina Grimke asserted in 1837. "I recognize no rights but *human* rights—I know nothing of men's rights and women's rights; for in Christ Jesus, there is neither male nor female."

When the free African-American David Walker published his fiery *Appeal* in 1829, a pamphlet that was circulating among southern slaves within months of its apperance, he too turned to a higher authority than the law that protected property. "Have we any other Master but Jesus Christ alone?" he demanded. "What right then, have we to obey and call any other Master, but Himself? . . . Let no man of us budge one step, and let slave-holders come to beat us from our country. America is more our country, than it is the whites—we have enriched it with our *blood and tears*." The National Black Conventions, which began in the 1830s, and the African churches that started to flourish at the same time, pictured themselves at the other end of the scale, nearer the restrained, middle-class respectability of the black Yankee, but like Walker the identity they envisioned was above all American, and the freedom they looked to lay beyond government.

In the 1850s, abolitionists and the Free-Soilers in the north and west still understood freedom differently. The concept of individual liberty, as expressed by Emerson and practiced by women, free blacks, and abolitionists, was a product of the cities, a rebellion against the stultifying conformity induced by slavery and its supporters. By contrast, the general freedom experienced by pioneers out on the mythical frontier arose from an absence of any restraint, except the need to secure property, and a belief that such freedom was confined to whites.

To fuse these ideas of liberty required the crucible pressure of a civil war and the oratorical grace, political pliability, and unbending morality that constituted Abraham Lincoln's unique genius. Once Lincoln began to interpret the Constitution in the context of the Declaration of Independence, it became evident that individual rights extended to everyone. The critical change began in 1855 when resentment against the tide of Catholic Irish immigrants fleeing the potato famine gave rise to the nativist Know-Nothing party, for a time the most popular party in the Union.

"Our progress in degeneracy appears to me to be pretty rapid," Lincoln wrote despairingly to a friend. "As a nation we began by declaring that 'all men are created equal.' We now practically read it 'all men are created equal except Negroes.' When the Know-Nothings get control it will read 'all men are created equal, except Negroes, *and foreigners, and Catholics*.' When it comes to this I should prefer emigrating to some country where they make no pretense of loving liberty—to Russia for instance where despotism can be taken pure and without the base alloy of hypocrisy.'"

Consequently, the idea of freedom that Lincoln developed in the war possessed one profound difference from what had existed before. It was no longer exclusive. That was the import of the words he delivered on the battleground of Gettysburg, "that this nation, under God, shall have a new birth of freedom and that government of the people, by the people, for the people, shall not perish from the earth."

Every frontier, whether federal or state, had eventually to be marked out on the ground. Without the reality of a physical boundary, disputes over jurisdiction could never be solved. According to the Treaty of Guadalupe Hidalgo, the frontier between Mexico and the United States was to follow the Rio Grande for some twelve hundred miles from the Gulf of Mexico to El Paso, Texas, then cross about seven hundred miles of baking desert and jagged hills to San Diego. The line that border patrols and illegal immigrants now risk lives and fortunes to defend and cross was first demarcated between 1850 and 1855 by Captain William Emory, U.S. Corps of Topographical Engineers, and José Salazar Ylarregui of Mexico's Colegio de Minería.

The Topographical Engineers were in large part Andrew Ellicott's legacy. Despite his fond hopes of becoming the principal figure at West Point when he was appointed professor of mathematics, he had quickly discovered that the academy remained the personal fiefdom of its autocratic senior officer, Captain Alden Partridge, whose other avian characteristics, according to a contemporary account, included "the body of a penguin and the head of hawk." In winter he would capriciously decide that ballistics should be taught not in the classroom but by firing cannonballs down the frozen track of the Hudson, and summer semesters were repeatedly cut short in favor of adventure camps in the forest.

"Some of the men cannot read and write," Ellicott wrote angrily to Monroe in 1815, "much less do they understand English Grammar, Arithmetic &c." He was joined in his protest by the academy's other newly arrived intellectual star, Jared Mansfield, who had returned from setting the Public Land Survey in order. Together they undertook a campaign for reform that lasted for two years. For a time both were put under arrest by an increasingly eccentric Partridge, but their reward was the appointment in 1817 of the great reforming superintendent, Major Sylvanus Thayer, whose rigorous curriculum and discipline were to win him fame as "the Father of West Point."

Undisturbed by these upheavals, Ellicott continued to teach his specialty, celestial navigation, and to the few cadets with sufficient ability, he introduced the different methods of calculating longitude—using the moon's location, the eclipses of Jupiter's satellites, eclipses of the sun, and the occultation of stars by the moon—together with the fiendish math that went with them. The influence of his teaching permeated the discipline of topography (the art of detailed mapping) that began to emerge from West Point in those years.

The need to have accurate records of territory available at short notice persuaded the army to create in 1818 the prototype of what was to become the Corps of Topographical Engineers. Soon afterward, its officers began to be allocated the task of demarcating on the ground the lines of the new Territories that Douglas's committee had selected. Here, Ellicott's legacy could be seen. Many of the earliest topographical engineers had worked under him, such as Isaac Roberdeau and Stephen Long, his assistant at West Point, or came from the generation of cadets he taught, among them James Graham, a founding officer of the corps, who managed to run both the Canadian frontier in the 1840s and the initital stages of the Mexican border in the 1850s. Thus a direct chain of expertise connected Ellicott's Pennsylvania boundaries to the meridians and parallels drawn by his nineteenth-century successors, as well as to the international frontier run by Emory and Salazar.

Not surprisingly, the U.S. team on the Mexican border also used Ellicott's methods of celestial and especially lunar observation to check the line, together with random and true lines for the section of it that followed a parallel. Although the Mexicans relied more on triangulation, they agreed to accept the Americans' figures on the land-based part of the frontier. This was a misjudgment on Salazar's part because he failed to challenge Emory's faulty measurements near Nogales, resulting in the American acquisition of three hundred square miles of Mexican territory.

Nevertheless, the most serious disputes resulted from the constant movement of the Rio Grande. Throughout the nineteenth and twentieth centuries, its repeated meanderings, notably a major alteration at El Chamizal near El Paso in 1864, created disputes that took decades of diplomacy to solve. In 1970, both nations agreed on the unecological solution of channeling the most mobile sections through immobile concrete watercourses. Elsewhere the river remains free, making this the only wandering frontier of the United States.

While Emory and Salazar's teams were still at work on the frontier, its line was abruptly altered. In 1853 the financier James Gadsden made a deal with the seemingly immortal Santa Anna, dictator of Mexico for the third time, to purchase for $10 million almost thirty thousand square miles of territory, the southern strip of today's New Mexico and Arizona, including Tucson, and the most porous stretch of the border with Mexico. Gadsden was planning a railroad to connect the Pacific with Texas, and the flattest route, later followed by the Southern Pacific railroad, lay through country south of the Guadalupe Hidalgo frontier. This new acquisition of territory led directly to Douglas's final disastrous deal that created the states of Kansas and Nebraska.

Even without Gadsden's railroad project, Douglas would eventually have attempted to create a government for the vast tract of land between Missouri and the Rockies stretching north from the slave frontier of 36 degrees 30 minutes to Canada. Although designated part of the Indian Territory to which Native Americans from farther east had been relocated, its dry, short-grass prairies were already being invaded by white ranchers and farmers, who wanted their properties recognized and protected by the federal government. What prompted Douglas to immediate action, however, was his ambition to make Chicago the hub of the nation's railroad system.

He had created the Illinois Central railroad in 1850 by legislating to allow the state to finance it with grants of public land. "If ever a man passed a bill, I did that one," he crowed afterward. "I did the whole work and was devoted to it for two entire years." Links to eastern railroads were easily arranged, but no track existed westward through the dry prairies, and until the region could be organized as a Territory, no federal funds and lands would be available to survey a route to the Pacific.

Four previous attempts to create a Territory in the area had been blocked by the south. Since it lay north of 36 degrees 30 minutes, any Territory would have to be free under the Missouri Compromise, thus tilting the balance even more heavily against slavery. But in a typical deal to buy southern support, Douglas proposed to slice off the southern third of Nebraska to create the Territory of Kansas, reaching west to the Rockies, and to abolish the Missouri Compromise in order to open each Territory for settlement as a slave or free state according to the wishes of the inhabitants. His southern backers accepted on the assumption that Kansas would be a slave state.

It is a testament to Douglas's lack of moral awareness that he never understood how offensive the deal would be to antislavers. While the legislation was still before Congress, Ohio's senators and representatives described it as "a gross violation of a sacred pledge; a criminal betrayal of precious rights . . . an atrocious plot" and promised that the struggle would go on even after the proposal became law: "We shall go home to our constituents, erect anew the standard of Freedom, and call on the People to come to the rescue of the country from the domination of Slavery." In Beloit, college students joined thousands of other northern communities in protesting against the Kansas-Nebraska bill that would allow, as they put it, "the land pledged for freedom [by the Missouri Compromise] to be made into slave states."

The sense of outrage brought together the different interests of Free-Soilers, antislavery Democrats, abolitionists, and Free Labor businesses and became the catalyst that formed them into the new Republican Party. But what really showed how disaffected the north had become was the extra-constitutional reaction.

In New England the Emigrants Aid Society was set up by Eli Thayer and funded by wealthy Amos A. Lawrence to help antislavery settlers find land in Kansas before it was overrun by the "border ruffians" swarming across the border from the slave state of Missouri. When the first settlers left in September, they took with them dozens of Sharps rifles contributed by the congregation of Henry Ward Beecher.

Their warlike preparations produced an equally violent reaction. "Shall we allow such cut-throats and murderers, as the people of Massachusetts are, to settle in the territory adjoining our own State?" demanded the pro-slavery paper *Liberty Platform* of Missouri in June 1854. "No! If popular opinion will not keep them back, we should see what virtue there is in the force of arms." And in the same vein, the *Platte Argus* urged its Missouri readers, "Stake out your claims, and woe be to the abolitionist who shall intrude upon it, or come within reach of your long and true rifles, or within *point blank shot of your revolvers.*"

Yet even as tension grew between the two sets of frontier societies, each obeyed with astonishing formality the rituals of claiming property in land. At Salt Creek, close to the center of Kansas Territory, the first immigrants from Missouri carefully formed themselves into a Squatters Association with a set of twelve rules to "secure safety and fairness in the location and preservation of claims." Common to all squatters clubs was the third rule: "Every person of lawful age who may be at the head of a family, who shall mark out his claim so that it may be apparent how the same lies, and proceed with reasonable diligence to erect thereon a cabin or tent, shall be deemed to have made a proper claim." What made Salt Creek different was rule nine: "That we will afford protection to no Abolitionists as settlers in Kansas Territory."

Three months later, Charles Robinson, a veteran of settling gold-rush claims in Califorha, arrived in northern Kansas with the first New England settlers and stopped at Wakarusa, a high spur of land shortly to be renamed Lawrence that overlooked the Kansas River. Within two days they had set up a city council with a secretary, treasurer, and rules based upon the laws of Maine, meaning that not only would there be no slavery, but no liquor either, and of more immediate importance that the ground would be pre-surveyed before purchase. The same day they appointed a surveyor, A. D. Sean, to lay out the town and surrounding area. At midnight Sean went to the top of the hill with a sextant, compass, and chronometer to find true north from the Pole Star, like Andrew Ellicott and innumerable surveyors before him. The grid of streets and lots running north-south and east-west that he laid out over the following weeks remains at the heart of Lawrence to this day.

For both sets of pioneers, the need to have their unregistered claims recognized made the creation of a Territorial government an urgent necessity. Unlike other prairie states that emerged from an existing Territory, no framework of government existed in Kansas for settlers to build on. The struggle to write a constitution and elect a legislature that would validate claims and draw county boundaries favoring one side or the other was too important to be settled easily. In 1855, the pro-slavers drew up the Lecompton constitution, endorsing slavery in the Territory, and ferrymen on the Missouri River did a roaring trade taking fake settlers into Kansas to vote for it. As the tension grew, threats and intimidating raids led to murder, culminating in John Brown's cold-blooded killing in 1856 of five pro-slavery settlers at Pottawatomie near the Missouri border, and in later years "Bleeding Kansas" was taken to be a portent of the Civil War's carnage. The records show, however, that of 157 documented killings, only one third were certainly political, and at least as many were concerned with land disputes.

Nevertheless, news of the events in Kansas confirmed the north's worst fears about the spread of federally sponsored slavery. In Beloit, Wisconsin, so recently a frontier settlement itself, young men started to volunteer to go down to help the free settlers against the slavers. To the end of a long life that continued into the twentieth century, William Brown, a college student at the time, remembered how at the town meeting before the youths left in early 1856, the most peaceful citizen in Rock County, the "lamblike Deacon Samuel Hinman, got up in front, flourishing his big bowie knife in one hand and a six shooter in the other and calling out his son, presented those weapons to him in succession saying, 'I give you this knife and I give you this revolver so that with them you may help save Kansas for freedom.'"

When unambiguous evidence of fraudulent voting appeared, it seemed that violence would certainly spread. But Douglas's impassioned advocacy persuaded Congress to reject the Lecompton constitution in the face of President James Buchanan's plea to accept it. "No Democrat has ever opposed his party without being crushed," Buchanan warned Douglas grimly, but the senator was not deterred. Popular sovereignty demanded an honest poll, and to the supreme deal-maker some hostility from the south was a useful means of retrieving his reputation in the north.

In the summer of 1858, Stephen Douglas agreed to a series of seven debates with his Republican opponent for the Senate, the almost unknown former Illinois congressman Abraham Lincoln, a stringy beanpole towering over him by more than a foot, but a pygmy by comparison in terms of political influence. "With *me*, the race of ambition has been a failure—a flat failure,"

Lincoln noted privately when comparing himself with Douglas. "With *him*, it has been one of splendid success. His name fills the nation; and is not unknown even in foreign lands."

By the time the debates began, Douglas must have felt that the storm had been weathered. Kansas had adopted a free constitution, property was being registered, and few believed that cotton or slavery could flourish there. "We rely wholly upon numbers now," remarked one relieved Kansas voter, "and not upon Sharps rifles." Despite John Brown's foray across the Missouri border to release slaves and murder another slaveholder, a relative calm had fallen over the north, and the midterm elections offered Douglas a renewed opportunity to persuade voters that popular sovereignty was the only way to reconcile the differences between north, south, and west.

The senator had every reason to suppose that his policy would be overwhelmingly accepted. In little more than a decade, he had made possible the admittance of Texas and California as fully fledged states to the Union, the division of Oregon Territory into Washington and Oregon with the latter about to be admitted as a state, and the separation of Wisconsin, Iowa, and Minnesota so that all three became parts of the Union. From the smoke-filled rooms of the Capitol, he and his committee had cut in half the Mormons' maverick state of Deseret that sprawled from San Diego to Denver and from Wyoming to the Mexican border. He could claim the credit for having delineated California's boundaries, given Utah Territory its southern border, created a Territory of New Mexico containing an embryonic Arizona, and—fatefully—for the double creation of Kansas Territory and a huge Nebraska Territory reaching to the Canadian border. On top of that, he was laying the foundations for the transcontinental railroads that would unify the nation and put Illinois at its heart. No Illinois Democrat could have doubted his quality as senator, and looking ahead to the 1860 presidential election, even Horace Greeley, one of the founders of the Republican Party, was prepared to support Douglas as a "more practical" way of defeating slavery than running their own candidate.

In sultry summer heat and dusty fall winds, before audiences of thousands so that each speaker would begin by asking for silence in order that all could hear him, Douglas and Lincoln hammered at the same old incompatibilities of the slavery question—that the Constitution guaranteed property, that the Declaration of Independence promised liberty. In practical terms, there was not much between them. Both agreed that the Union must be preserved at all costs, that slaveholders could not be deprived of their property by force, and that the federal government ought not to be allowed to impose slavery on territories or states against their wishes. Lincoln did not foresee slavery ending "in less than a hundred years at least," as he admitted in the fourth debate, while Douglas implied that economics might lead it to wither away much sooner. "We in Illinois . . . tried slavery," he reminded his listeners, "kept it up for twelve years, and finding that it was not profitable we abolished it for that reason."

Their first major division was over the impact of the Supreme Court's 1857 ruling in the Dred Scott case. Called on to decide whether the slave Dred Scott had been made free by being taken to live in the free state of Illinois, Chief Justice Roger Taney, writing the majority decision, had determined that

Old lantern slide image of 1858 debate between Abraham Lincoln and Stephen A. Douglas

he remained a slave. His ruling was made on the sweeping grounds that no federal or state laws guaranteeing citizens' liberties could apply to black Americans, whether free or slave, because the Constitution did not recognize them as citizens. Like most people, Lincoln believed that in tandem with the Fugitive Slave Act, the Dred Scott decision would allow slavery to spread into every state because wherever slave owners went, the United States was required to protect their property. Douglas, however, still maintained that where people were opposed to slavery, they could "by unfriendly legislation effectually prevent the introduction of it into their midst." It was to prove a damaging argument when he returned to the south, but in Illinois it did him no harm.

In the fifth debate, however, Lincoln exposed the fundamental chasm dividing them when he pointed to the moral vacuity at the heart of popular sovereignty. "If you will take [Douglas's] speeches, and select the short and pointed sentences expressed by him—as his declaration that he 'don't care whether slavery is voted up or down'—you will see at once that this is perfectly logical, if you do not admit that slavery is wrong," Lincoln pointed out. "If you do admit that it is wrong, he cannot logically say that anybody has a right to do wrong."

Douglas branded this a "base insinuation," claiming that the remark was made during his fight to destroy the Lecompton constitution and promote democracy in Kansas. But Lincoln would not back away. "I object to [popular sovereignty] as a dangerous dalliance for a free people—a sad evidence that, feeling prosperity, we forget right; that liberty, as a principle, we have ceased to revere. I object to it because the fathers of the republic eschewed and rejected it."

When the voting took place, the Democrats won a majority in the Illinois Assembly and, under the rules of the time, reelected Douglas as their senator. But the accumulating alienation of the north had found its champion in Lincoln. Other Republicans, William Seward and Salmon Chase for example, opposed slavery earlier and sometimes more confrontationally than Lincoln, but none could match his ability to cut through the moral emptiness that accepted that one eighth of the people in the United States could be legally owned like horses or hounds.

"If slavery is right, all words, acts, laws, and constitutions against it, are themselves wrong, and should be silenced, and swept away," he told his audience in Cooper Union, New York, in 1859. "If it is right, we cannot justly object to its nationality—its universality; if it is wrong, they cannot justly insist upon its extension—its enlargement." And in two sentences, decades of moral ambiguities were swept away.

When he argued that the Constitution had to be read in the context of the Declaration of Independence, he did so in down-to-earth terms that anyone could understand. "I think the authors of that notable instrument [the Declaration] intended to include *all* men, but they did not intend to declare all men equal *in all respects* . . . They meant to set up a standard maxim for free society which should be familiar to all and revered by all; constantly looked to, constantly labored for, and even though never perfectly attained, constantly approximated, and thereby constantly spreading and deepening its influence and augmenting the happiness and value of life to all people of all colors everywhere." At once the universal significance of the Declaration became apparent, and Chief Justice Taney's ruling that it was intended to apply only to whites could be seen as simply too narrow an interpretation to be valid.

Against this, Douglas could only put forward the dry and untested legalism: "I assert that under the Dred Scott decision you cannot maintain slavery a day in a Territory where there is an unwilling people and unfriendly legislation." It carried no weight with the Republicans, but the southern Democrats were another matter. Unexpectedly deprived of Kansas, they were determined that Dred Scott should be the key to overturning every legal impediment to the extension of slavery.

"The Supreme Court has decided that we have a right to carry our slaves into the Territories and, necessarily, to have them protected after we get there," Senator Albert G. Brown of Mississippi declared in 1858. "We have a right of protection for our slave property in the Territories. The Constitution as expounded by the Supreme Court awards it. We demand it, and we mean to have it."

When the new session of Congress met, the southern senators voted with the Republicans to remove Douglas from his chairmanship of the Committee on Territories, and with the removal of his power base went his policy.

In December 1860, Henry Adams went to Washington to be an assistant to William Seward, Lincoln's intended secretary of state. Ten years had passed since his previous visit, and he was dismayed to find that the capital of the United States still showed no signs of recovery from the collusion between the commissioners and the speculators that had aborted its birth in 1793. "The same rude colony was camped in the same forest, with the same unfinished Greek temples for work rooms, and sloughs for roads," he wrote. "The Government had an air of social instability and incompleteness that went far to support the right of secession in theory as in fact; but right or wrong, secession was likely to be easy where there was so little to secede from. The Union was a sentiment, but not much more, and in December, 1860, the sentiment about the Capitol was chiefly hostile, so far as it made itself felt."

The symbolism was unmistakable. Unity had been George Washington's overriding goal as president, and he had planned his mighty capital in the expectation that it would be achieved. He had relied on self-interest to build it, just as he had relied on self-interest to hold the Union together. But the capital remained half-built, and the Union appeared to be falling apart.

Secession certainly caused no difficulty to South Carolina. Citing a background of persistent northern antagonism to the southern way of life, shown especially by the refusal of northern states to return fugitive slaves, delegates declared at a specially summoned convention in December 1860 that Lincoln's election had finally made the original compact between the states impossible to sustain. "A geographical line has been drawn across the Union," ran the announcement of secession, "and all the States north of that line have united in the election of a man to the high office of President of the United States, whose opinions and purposes are hostile to slavery." As Jefferson had argued in the days when the frontier barely existed, and Calhoun had amplified when Andrew Jackson was at the height of his autocratic power, the declaration asserted that the Union was merely a compact made by the agreement of the states. "The constituted compact has been deliberately broken and disregarded by the non-slaveholding States, and the consequence follows that South Carolina is released from her obligation . . . the Union now subsisting between South Carolina and other states under the name of the 'United States of America' is hereby dissolved."

Within the next two months the geographical line had become a frontier as six other states from the deep south joined South Carolina to form the independent Confederate States of America. After the president called out the militia in response to the shelling of Fort Sumter, the CSA was increased by the addition of Virginia, North Carolina, Tennessee, and Arkansas. The new frontier reached as far north as the Mason-Dixon Line east of the Mississippi, and to the 36-degree-30-minute parallel west of it. The war that followed was in effect a contest about frontiers, and its name depended on which frontier was recognized.

Since Lincoln never accepted the Confederacy's claim to independence, the Union frontier created by Gadsden, Polk, Adams, Jefferson, Ellicott, and Washington still held good, and the war was the Civil War. Because the CSA regarded itself as a confederation of sovereign states extending north to the Pennsylvania border, northwest to Iowa's border, and west to New Mexico, the war was the War Between the States. The difference was not academic.

When General Robert E. Lee surrendered at Appomattox Courthouse on April 9, 1865, the question had to be answered whether the Confederates were American rebels or foreign combatants. True to his Unionist credo, Lincoln saw them as rebels and offered an amnesty to any state in which 10 percent of the voters were prepared to abolish slavery. But the radical Reconstructionists who took power in the Congress after Lincoln's assassination were more in tune with the CSA's claim. To them the south was a conquered enemy power. "I may be asked how we would treat the Confederate States of America?" Congressman Thaddeus Stevens demanded in 1867, and provided his own answer. "Just as Congress chooses. They are our property; their citizens are our subjects. Their lives, their liberties are subject to the supreme will of this body."

The future treatment of the south would depend on where the frontier ran during the war.

CHAPTER II

The Limits of Freedom

*We were told that we needed Hawaii in order to secure
California. What shall we now take in order to secure the
Philippines? . . . We shall need to take China, Japan, and
the East Indies, according to the doctrine, in order to 'secure' what we have. Of course this means that, on the
doctrine, we must take the whole earth in order to be safe
on any part of it.*

WILLIAM GRAHAM SUMNER,
"On Empire and the Philippines," 1898

I N 1867, THE Supreme Court was forced to confront one of the more
mundane consequences of the war of the frontiers. The case concerned
ownership of the $10 million due to Texas under the 1850 Douglas deal for
giving up its claims to New Mexico. The whole sum had not yet been paid,
and the court had to decide whether a new Texas had come into being when
it seceded from the Union, or whether the old state remained in being and
thus continued to be the legitimate recipient of the money. To decide the
matter, the court had first to unravel the constitutional fuzziness at the heart
of the United States of America—was it a compact of separate states or a
consolidated nation?

In his ruling, Taney's successor as chief justice, Salmon Chase, formerly
Lincoln's treasury secretary, held that the Constitution recognized a state to
be made up of three ingredients: "[It] is a political community of free citizens, occupying a territory of defined boundaries, and organized under a

government sanctioned and limited by a written constitution, and established by the consent of the governed." The thirteen original states met those criteria, and as such bound themselves together in the "Articles of Confederation and Perpetual Union." Fourteen years later the preamble to the Constitution showed that the states wanted to take the Articles' purpose a step further by creating "a more perfect Union." The states retained many of their sovereign powers, Chase decided, but a perpetual union made more perfect left the constitutional position unmistakable: "[A state's] admission into the Union was something more than a compact; it was the incorporation of a new member into the political body. And it was final."

This interpretation cleared up many confusions. It meant that the United States was a consolidated nation; that secession was impossible; that Texas had remained the same state despite its brief rebellion and thus kept its $10 million; and that the frontier of the Confederate States of America had never existed. The ruling had the added authority of reflecting Lincoln's stated opinion. "I hold, that in contemplation of universal law, and of the Constitution, the Union of these States is perpetual," he said in his inaugural address in 1861. "I therefore consider that in view of the Constitution and the laws, the Union is unbroken."

Like Washington, Lincoln's prime goal was always unity, and his strategy one of inclusiveness. "My paramount object in this struggle is to save the Union, and is not either to save or to destroy slavery," he told Horace Greeley in 1862. "If I could save the Union without freeing any slave, I would do it, and if I could save it by freeing all the slaves, I would do it; and if I could save it by freeing some and leaving others alone, I would also do that." To achieve that end, he did all he could to bring the Confederate states back home "without deciding, or even considering, whether these States have ever been out of the Union." From 1863 he had proclaimed his readiness to offer an amnesty to the governments of southern states that abolished slavery and took an oath of loyalty to the Union.

In the last years of his life, however, this policy was met by unyielding hostility from Republicans in Congress determined not to allow former Confederates back into power. The confrontation that he would surely have faced did not occur until after John Wilkes Booth's pistol promoted Andrew Johnson to the presidency.

During 1865, conventions in every Confederate state, except Mississippi, withdrew or voided votes for secession, and under federally appointed governors, new legislatures ratified the Thirteenth Amendment abolishing slavery. By the end of the year, all except Texas had reestablished their civil governments and nominated delegates to represent them in Washington. The decision whether to readmit them to the Union was then up to Congress.

With the formal demands met, President Andrew Johnson showed himself ready to restore antebellum relations between Washington and the states by pardoning Confederate leaders. But Congress was less easily satisfied. The new legislatures had all passed "black codes" that effectively prevented black Americans from owning land, restricted their opportunities of employment, and limited their voting rights. "This is a white man's government," said the first postbellum governor of South Carolina, "and intended for white men only." The simmering impatience of Reconstructionists boiled over when one of Georgia's delegates to Congress turned out to be a former vice president of the Confederate States of America. Determined to see fundamental changes made to the old, aristocratic south, Republicans turned to an alternative strategy that had already been mapped out in a speech in 1865 by Thaddeus Stevens, the senior congressman from Pennsylvania. His proposals became the framework of the policy known as "radical Reconstruction."

Stevens's strategy was based on the source of Stephen Douglas's power, Article Four of the Constitution, which stated, "New States may be admitted by the Congress into this Union." This meant that the executive had to take second place, leaving Congress alone to decide whether the Confederate states had seceded, meaning that they were now a defeated enemy outside the Union, or whether they were unsuccessful rebels who were still within the Union. To help his fellow congressmen make up their minds, Stevens referred them to the opinion of Emmerich de Vattel, the supreme authority on international law, that "a civil war breaks the bands of society and government [and] produces in the nation two independent parties, who consider each other as enemies . . . They stand, therefore, in precisely the same predicament as two nations who engage in contest."

Then Stevens pointed his listeners toward South Carolina's declaration in 1861 that in respect to the federal government "their mutual relations are as foreign States." His personal conclusion was that "the late Confederate

Thaddeus Stevens

States are out of the Union to all intents and purposes." Bleak directness was Stevens's preferred style, and he did not attempt to soften the tone of his verdict on the position of the southern states: "The future condition of the conquered power depends on the will of the conqueror. They must come in as new states or remain as conquered provinces."

The influence exercised over his fellow Republicans by the ancient, club-footed Stevens depended partly on his savage tongue and partly on his chairmanship of the powerful Ways and Means Committee, but until his death in 1868 at the age of seventy-five, he dominated the program of radical Reconstruction. In the course of it, the values of the entire United States were redefined. The Fourteenth and Fifteenth Amendments—extending citizenship to everyone born within the national frontier, and prohibiting the states from limiting a voter's rights on the grounds of race or color—were intended to prevent the south from regaining politically what it had lost in war. Their impact was greatest there, but they applied equally to the north, where until the war only five states allowed free black Americans to vote. Thus just as the Revolution had created a momentum for liberty that few had foreseen in 1775, so the Civil War and Reconstruction carried Unionists into guaranteeing an equality of rights that most would have resisted in 1860.

In a democracy that had restricted freedom to white males and allowed the creation of the largest slave economy in the world, the battle for such an inclusive concept of liberty would not easily be won. But resistance was bound to be exceptionally fierce in the racial and social aristocracy of the south. The war had brought about one further change that meant there could be no escape from the battle.

When the Constitution was written, and for twenty years afterward, the national frontier had been so faint that northern senators could discuss secession as an escape from economic strains and a southern vice president could counsel secession as a solution to oppressive laws without any of them being thought disloyal. That Calhoun should have felt able to propose withdrawal in 1830 in protest at the level of federal taxation, and that the CSA's original states should have voted to separate so soon after Lincoln's election, both showed the continuing fragility of the old frontier. More than four years of fighting had changed that.

"Admit the right of the seceding states to break up the Union at pleasure," an anonymous private in the Seventieth Ohio Infantry had written home in 1863, "and how long will it be before the new confederacies created by the first disruption shall be resolved into still smaller fragments and the continent become a vast theater of civil war, military license, anarchy and despotism? Better settle it at whatever the cost and settle it forever."

Whether they had worn gray or blue, none of the survivors could deny that six hundred thousand dead had settled the issue for good. For the first time since the Articles of Confederation had created the United States, the frontier was unbreakable either legally or illegally. Thus Congress confronted the south intent on making it part of a homogeneous nation. This meant imposing upon it a freedom shared by all citizens.

To the Yankee correspondent of the *Atlantic Monthly* who toured the south in 1866, there appeared to be "no homogeneity, but everywhere a rigid spirit of caste . . . the upper classes continually assert their right to rule, and the middle and lower classes have no ability to free themselves. The whole structure of society is full of separating walls." Its sense of hierarchy pitched southern society into head-on conflict with the second phase of Reconstruction, designed to make everyone equal before the law, including people of color. Half a century later, Edward Thomas, a Georgia cotton planter, still felt outraged by the assumption that men who had been freed from slavery could be allowed to vote and be elected alongside whites.

"It is impossible to conceive that the ingenuity of hate could have devised anything which would have so humiliated the white people of the state," he wrote in 1920, "as this cruel and unnecessary act by which the former slave was placed upon a political equality with his master, in many cases superior to his master, for often the slave could vote while the master could not. The people of the north did not understand the character of the negro; to them, or the vast majority, he was a white man with a black skin, while we of the south knew him to be not only an alien race, but so vastly inferior that no fit comparison now occurs to me."

In defense of white supremacy, former Confederate officers turned easily to a strategy of armed resistance. The terrorist and political movements were so closely intertwined that, in Georgia, the Ku Klux Klan's campaign of murder and intimidation against black and white Republicans was directed by General John B. Gordon, the Democrat candidate for governor. As the Virginia diarist Mary Greenhow Lee, a white, wealthy widow, fiercely predicted, "Political reconstruction is inevitable now, but social reconstruction, we have in our hands and we can prevent."

Thus, in the treatment of its conquered provinces, the United States encountered for the first time a conundrum that has frequently baffled it since—how could its values of democracy and freedom be imposed on an unwilling society?

There had been no need for an answer before the war. Within the frontiers of the Union, citizens and government had shared the same understanding that freedom was a universal right among white males, but conditional among other inhabitants. It had to be limited because constitutional liberty was grounded in the guarantees given to property, to which only white males had an absolute right.

Consequently when General William T. Sherman issued Field Order 15 in 1865 allocating approximately eight hundred thousand acres of coastland from South Carolina to Florida to freed slaves, he was taking a potentially revolutionary step. With the distribution of property came the rights that the Constitution so clearly guaranteed to all property owners. The Freedmen's Bureau, which was set up to look after their interests, understood the potential and campaigned vigorously for "forty acres and a mule" for each new freeman. Thaddeus Stevens introduced a bill to redistribute land confiscated from "traitors to the United States," and had he been ten years younger, it might have been carried into law. It was, however, easier to remove land from the Plains Indians in the Nebraska and Kansas Territories than from the white rebels of Georgia and South Carolina. With Stevens's death in 1868, momentum for the colonization of the south dissipated, and within a few years the courts returned the land being farmed by black pioneers to its original owners.

The alternative strategy was to build an infrastructure and forcibly put in place a framework of democracy in the hope that it would take root. This program brought about the construction of eight thousand miles of railroad track, reform of the tax system, the rebuilding of roads, the provision of free education in four thousand new schools, the foundation of black colleges such as Fisk and Howard universities, and above all the participation of African-Americans in government and law. Around twenty thousand northern carpetbaggers came south to take part in these enterprises, and with the assistance of the Freedmen's Bureau, former slaves negotiated labor contracts, established ownership to land, and registered to vote. Together with the establishment of Union Leagues and the activities of scalawags, former Confederates who had switched allegiance, the outline of a political opposition to white supremacy could be seen.

For deep-seated cultural reasons it did not take root, but the most immediate was the resort to force rather than persuasion. In the face of militant resistance to the registration of black voters and the selection of mixed-race legislatures and courts, Congress created five military districts covering the south, commanded by generals exercising martial law. Although the number of troops was small—about eight thousand in total—the power of the military authorities was extensive. An average of about 20 percent of the adult white population were deemed ineligible to vote—up to 45 percent in Louisiana—because of continuing loyalty to the Confederate cause, against about 10 percent of adult African-Americans. In Georgia, General Alfred H. Terry forcibly removed Confederate Democrats from the General Assembly in 1870, an action known as Terry's Purge, and replaced them with Republicans, including black legislators expelled earlier by their white colleagues. In Tennessee and New Orleans federal troops successfully confronted white lynch mobs, and the terrorist campaign of murder and intimidation mounted by the Ku Klux Klan and other white supremacist bodies was broken with the aid of federal agents such as the sinister Hiram C. Whitley, self-proclaimed "head of the secret service," who claimed to have participated in two thousand arrests and to have sweated confessions from suspects with a loaded brass cannon pointed at their faces.

By 1870 these draconian methods had led all the secessionist states to accept the new amendments to the Constitution, allowing them to be readmitted to the Union by Congress. But with state rule restored, national interest waned rapidly, and not even the anguished pleas of Governor Adelbert Ames of Mississippi for federal troops to control armed white mobs in 1875 could persuade President Ulysses S. Grant to send them back. Any lingering enthusiasm in the north for intervention was killed by the economic collapse of 1873, and evidence of the corruption of some carpetbaggers such as Foster Blodgett, who plundered several hundred thousand dollars from Georgia's Western and Atlantic railroad. In the 1875 presidential election, both Republican and Democratic candidates promised to bring an end to Reconstruction, and the high tide of equal rights began to ebb.

It is difficult to fault the goals of Reconstruction, except for one. The desire for revenge was never far from Stevens's rhetoric. It condemned to failure any chance of winning the hearts and minds of those white moderates and pragmatists in the south who understood the need for social and economic change. The imposition of taxes on the South to pay for the war came on top of the estimated $4 billion costs of the abolition of slavery and the massive destruction caused by the fighting and by Sherman's march through Georgia and South Carolina. The burden satisfied the northern impulse to punish the south. It also exaggerated the bitterness of defeat in a society that might have responded to Lincoln's more generous instinct to give it a home in the new consolidated nation.

Without that generosity, Reconstruction appeared to many white southerners not as a matter of democracy but of Yankee imperialism. As late as the

1960s, Senator William Fulbright of Arkansas, a segregationist who also opposed the war in Vietnam, felt able to compare Reconstruction to American
interventions overseas, in Cuba, Haiti, Latin America, and Southeast Asia,
arguing that they all grew out of the same "strand of puritan intolerance."
While the United States saw itself playing "the role of God's avenging angel,
the appointed missionary of freedom in a benighted world," Fulbright wrote,
those on the receiving end felt themselves to be the victims of a power intent on proving "that force is the ultimate proof of superiority."

The reality that crippled the north's efforts to export liberty is that while
the right to freedom may be inalienable, the enjoyment of it by everyone
demands a complexity of cultural experience, social responsibility, and
governmental structure such as only the north possessed. What Lincoln
pointed to as an ideal to be struggled for over generations, Stevens's followers wished to impose at once as a finished article. As Fulbright suggested, it
was not the last time such a mistake would be made.

As the federal government turned an increasingly blind eye to the south,
a series of Jim Crow measures were initiated, bringing about segregation and
the return of the old exclusive freedom that only whites could enjoy. In 1890
Mississippi Democrats under the leadership of Senator James Z. George introduced literacy tests that prevented 90 percent of African-Americans from
voting, and six years later the Supreme Court ruled in *Plessy v. Ferguson* that
the provision of racially divided facilities, disguised as "separate but equal,"
did not conflict with the Fourteenth Amendment, thus ensuring that white
supremacy would continue for another seventy years.

Yet even at that dire moment, a gleam of Lincoln's inclusive freedom
could still be found in the dissenting opinion written by the incomparable
justice John Marshall Harlan. "In the view of the constitution, in the eye of
the law, there is in this country no superior, dominant, ruling class of citizens," he declared. "There is no caste here. Our constitution is color-blind,
and neither knows nor tolerates classes among citizens. In respect of civil
rights, all citizens are equal before the law."

Even as his dissent was delivered, however, the United States was ex-
panding far beyond the borders that Adams, Polk, and Gadsden had drawn.
Whether Lincoln's demanding version of liberty or some more convenient
variant of it would follow the flag outside the frontier was a question on
which the Supreme Court would be bound to deliver its judgment.

. . .

Thomas Jefferson had written loosely of "an empire of liberty" that might one day enclose North and South America, but he did so when the United States was as much an idea as a nation. William H. Seward, the ambitious, outspoken secretary of state to both Lincoln and Andrew Johnson, was the first postwar statesman with the power to put the idea into practice.

In Henry Adams's vivid portrayal, he possessed "a slouching, slender figure; a head like a wise macaw; a beaked nose; shaggy eyebrows; unorderly hair and clothes; hoarse voice; off-hand manner; free talk, and perpetual cigar." His hatred of slavery was only equaled in its intensity by his fierce ambition to see the United States expand beyond its continental borders. In the judgment of his colleague Attorney General Edward Bates, Seward was "an expansionist of hemispheric voracity."

As a young senator before the Civil War, he sketched out his lofty ambitions to an admiring audience in St. Paul's Chapel, New York: "I look off on Prince Rupert's Land and Canada and see there an ingenious, enterprising and ambitious people, occupied with bridging rivers and constructing canals, railroads and telegraphs . . . and I am able to say, 'It is very well, you are building excellent states to be hereafter admitted into the American Union.' I can look southwest and see amid all the convulsions that are breaking the Spanish-American republics, the preparatory stage for their re-organization in free, equal and self-governing members of the United States of America."

In his most expansive mood, Seward could picture the day when American democracy and business would circle the world and bring about "the equalization of the condition of society and the restoration of the unity of the human family." Peace gave him the chance to indulge his ambitions. In 1867, he made no fewer than three attempts to push the United States beyond its landbound frontiers. His first effort, to buy Denmark's Caribbean colonies of St. Thomas and St. John—today's U.S. Virgin Islands—failed, but he bounced back by annexing the Midway islands in the Pacific, and most famously agreed to buy Russia's loss-making colony of Alaska for $7.5 million.

Speaking to a ragged group of non-Russian settlers in Sitka in 1869, Seward predicted that the new land would be settled in the same way as in the lower states. "Emigrants from our own States, from Europe, and from Asia, will not be slow in finding out that fortunes are to be gained by pursuing here the occupations which have so successfully sustained races of untutored men," he assured his frontier audience. That pattern of expansion left no place for the Aleuts, Tlingit, and other Alaskans who "can neither be preserved as a distinct social community, nor incorporated into our society."

His program belonged to the prewar era and so necessarily excluded native peoples from the guarantees of the Constitution. It contrasted poorly with the overtly imperial approach of the Russians, which protected native Alaskans and encouraged the work of Orthodox priests such as Father Ioann Veniaminov, compiler of the first dictionary of the Aleut language. Almost a century later, however, the inclusive democracy that had surprisingly triumphed in the Civil War would extend political power to native Alaskans in a way that would have been impossible for the Czar's officials to contemplate.

William Seward

Seward, however, had his eyes fixed on a larger prize. Ownership of Alaska was intended to squeeze Canada into the Union. This strategy was made clear to his Sitka audience by his repeated reference to the entire west coast of North America as a single unit, and his explicit warning that if British Columbia was not governed in the interests of the United States, "we can all foresee what will happen." The intended annexation of Canada would be "free and spontaneous," he promised, but his audience was left in no doubt about what he expected to happen. Nor were the British. Alarmed by his transparent ambition, and by a spate of terrorist attacks across the border by the Irish Fenian Brotherhood, they sent several thousand troops and a squadron of ships to bolster Canadian defenses.

Their alarm turned to anger when the Massachusetts senator Charles Sumner, as passionate as Seward in his hatred of slavery and no less of an expansionist, tried another tactic in 1867 to lever Canada inside the U.S. frontier. During the war, enormous damage had been caused to Union shipping by the Confederate raider *Alabama*, which had been constructed in Britain and was allowed to escape. Seward claimed $19 million in compensation, but Sumner, chairman of the Foreign Affairs Committee, raised the stakes by demanding $2 billion, half the cost of the war, on the grounds that *Alabama*'s rampage across the oceans had doubled the length of the war. As an alternative, Sumner coolly suggested that the United States would be prepared to accept Canada in recompense.

"If war was his object, and Canada were worth it, Sumner's scheme showed genius," Henry Adams commented drily. "But if he thought he could obtain Canada from England as a voluntary set-off to the Alabama Claims, he drivelled." An international tribunal awarded the United States $15 million, and only then were the claims to Canada dropped.

Nevertheless, the abrasive confidence with which the United States moved to expand its frontier in the far north suggested that its dreams of expansion were not likely to end with Alaska. However, one resemblance with the stiffening resistance to U.S. policies in the south should have given the expansionists pause for thought. North of the frontier, resentment against what were called American "tactics of bully and bluster" produced an outburst of nationalist feeling that led directly to the creation of modern Canada.

The core was formed by the four provinces most directly threatened by

U.S. ambitions: Upper Canada or Ontario, Lower Canada or Quebec, Nova Scotia, and New Brunswick. In 1867 the British Parliament passed the British North America Act, which brought these provinces under a single government and created the Dominion of Canada. Although foreign policy remained under British control, the Canadian Parliament conducted its own domestic affairs, and its westward policy was driven by the same concerns as the United States' had been. Just as the Oregon settlers were encouraged to go west to prevent the British arriving there first, so Canada's Prime Minister John A. Macdonald committed his country to expand across the prairies in response to the American threat. "I would be quite willing, personally, to leave that whole country a wilderness for the next half century," he declared, "but I fear if Englishmen do not go there, Yankees will."

In 1870 Manitoba joined the Dominion, followed a year later by British Columbia. With the earlier purchase of Rupert's Land, comprising the northern expanse of Canada from the Hudson's Bay Company in 1869, the outlines of the modern nation were in place just four years after Alaska's purchase. Seward and Sumner deserve at least some of the credit.

On the U.S. side of the frontier, the new sense of national identity focused on Great Britain. Historically hostile relations with Britain had always served to create a sense of unity within the United States. As Lincoln himself observed, so long as the active memory of the Revolution lasted, "the deep-rooted principles of *hate*, and the powerful motive of *revenge*, instead of being turned against each other, were directed exclusively against the British nation." Anglophobia had been integral to the formulation of the Monroe Doctrine, with its agenda of reaching the Pacific before the British, and remained powerful enough to generate national outrage at any kind of accommodation with an empire whose monarchical, aristocratic society represented everything the United States was not. "It is not in the nature of things that she can be our friend," Stephen Douglas declared, denouncing the 1850 Clayton-Bulwer treaty with Britain, which guaranteed Nicaragua's neutrality. "Sir, we have wounded her vanity and humbled her pride. She can never forgive us."

The hostility existed alongside an equally fierce attachment to the liberties and culture that the United States had inherited from Britain, so that in

1842 Congressman Henry Wise of Virginia could in a single speech boast of having "derived every drop of the blood in his veins" from Britain and admit that he "honored her; loved her arts; loved her learning," yet also declare that "he hated English arrogance; he hated English selfishness; he hated English ambition." In the aftermath of the Civil War, the ambivalence gave rise to a curiously intense sense of rivalry, not just for economic superiority but for cultural dominance.

Throughout most of the nineteenth century the power of the second British empire grew, boosted by patented technology, by profits from the ever-increasing American market, and by the moral certainties of an abolitionist foreign policy. Its most visible aspect could be found at sea, where the Royal Navy policed the world's shipping routes in the interests of Britain's policy of free trade.

Yet inexorably the statistics reflected the rise of U.S. power. By the 1880s the population of fifty million was almost double that of Great Britain, and at last factory production was matching the leap forward its great competitor had made half a century earlier. In 1890, coal mining, the basic source of energy, was still 20 million tons behind at 160 million tons a year, but the number of patents issued, a critical indicator of innovation, was almost level at approximately sixteen thousand, and the building blocks of industry, iron and steel production, were creeping ahead at around nine million tons each. "One held one's breath at the nearness of what one had never expected to see," wrote Henry Adams as the twentieth century approached, "the crossing of courses and the lead of American energies."

Yet still Great Britain's overwhelming naval power dominated the oceans, and even the Anglophile Theodore Roosevelt had no doubt about the threat that posed to the United States. "The British Navy," he wrote his friend Rudyard Kipling, "when, as was ordinarily the case, the British Government was more or less hostile to us, was our greatest danger." A start was made to develop a rival U.S. navy in the 1880s, but not until Captain Alfred Thayer Mahan published his 1890 study, *The Influence of Seapower upon History*, did it become a priority.

"The nation neither has nor cares to have its sea frontier defended," Mahan scolded his readers. "Not only has Great Britain a mighty navy and we a long, defenseless seacoast, but it is a great commercial and political advantage to her that her larger colonies, and above all Canada, should feel that the power of the mother country is something which they need, and upon which they can count . . . What harm can we do Canada proportionate to the injury we should suffer by the interruption of our coasting trade, and by a blockade of Boston, New York, the Delaware, and the Chesapeake? Such a blockade Great Britain certainly could make technically efficient, under the somewhat loose definitions of international law."

Other empires offered a challenge. Germany was moving into the Pacific, and the Meiji regime in Japan was creating a new modern power, but still Britain was the rival to be surpassed. To defend the sea frontiers that suddenly seemed to be so vulnerable, Mahan recommended a navy of modern, steel-hulled, steam-powered warships and, since they needed to take on coal after four thousand miles or two weeks at sea, the seizure of Hawaii and other islands in the Pacific for use as coaling stations. To buttress his argument, he introduced the newly fashionable Darwinian concept of the survival of the fittest, reminding his audience that they were engaged in "the race of life" in which "nation is arrayed against nation." In the last decade of the century it was a compelling thought.

Around the world, the last spasm in a century of land seizure by Europe was taking place. In fifty years France had expanded south from its Algerian base, taken by force in 1830, to the banks of the Congo River and, by the 1880s, was acquiring most of Southeast Asia, including Vietnam, Cambodia, and Laos. Germany was balancing its acquisition of Pacific islands with chunks of southern Africa. Russia had used the $7.5 million Seward had paid for Alaska to consolidate its hold on Central Asia and in the 1880s was developing Vladivostok as the center of its Far East empire. And the British were adding to their control of nearly one quarter of the world's landmass by establishing an East African empire from Kenya to Cape Town, a process that in 1898 pitted them against the resistance of Boer farmers in the Transvaal. Not to make use of superior technology to acquire strategic territory and valuable raw materials was unthinkable. Indeed, possession of the Gatling gun and the steam turbine engine virtually made it a moral duty to spread the civilization that made such inventions possible.

"I went down on my knees and prayed Almighty God for light and guidance more than one night," President William McKinley reported of his decision to take over the Philippines in 1898. "And one night late it came to me this way . . . that there was nothing left for us to do but to take them all."

Other, more materialist reasons existed for this lurch into empire building. Business was only just recovering from a sharp economic crash in 1893, and as Republican senator John M. Thurston, formerly chief counsel for the Union Pacific Railroad, put it to his fellow senators, "War with Spain would increase the business and earnings of every American railroad; it would increase the output of every American factory, it would stimulate every branch of industry and domestic commerce."

The hunger of the railroad and steel industries for new international markets meshed with Mahan's argument for the United States to join the imperial contest. The naval program accelerated until two new fleets could be put to sea, in the Pacific and the Atlantic. In 1898 President McKinley's Republican administration, backed by an impressive array of Wall Street, railroad, and newspaper interests, took advantage of Cuba's rebellion against Spain to push the frontiers of the United States far overseas. By the time the Spanish-American War was concluded, the new American navy had destroyed Spanish fleets in the Philippines as well as Cuba, and American power had colonized the Philippines, Guam, and the other Mariana islands, made protectorates of Cuba and Puerto Rico, and annexed Hawaii and Wake Island.

What Secretary of State John Hay called "a splendid little war" commanded wide support in the United States, but it appealed especially to the executive branch of government. For a forceful president anxious to overturn the supremacy established by the legislature during Reconstruction, imperialism possessed one great quality—constitutional checks on the president's power inside the frontier of the United States ceased to apply outside it or at worst were brought to bear too late. The perfect example was provided by President Theodore Roosevelt's preemptive decision in 1903 to recognize the creation of the state of Panama following an American-inspired revolt against Colombian rule, and to commit funds to begin construction of a canal.

The proper response, as Roosevelt gleefully recalled in a speech at Berkeley, California, in 1911, would have been to submit "an admirable state paper occupying a couple of hundred pages detailing all of the facts to Congress and asking Congress' consideration of it. In that case there would have been a number of excellent speeches made on the subject in Congress; the debate would be proceeding at this moment with great spirit and the beginning of work on the canal would be fifty years in the future. [Laughter and applause.] Fortunately the crisis came at a period when I could act unhampered. Accordingly I took the Isthmus, started the Canal and then left Congress not to debate the canal, but to debate me. [Laughter and applause.]"

In his desire to sell the imperial adventure to the people, however, Teddy Roosevelt argued that its roots were deeper than that and grew from the very history of the United States. In the introduction he wrote in 1900 to *The Winning of the West*, he declared that in occupying the Philippines the United States had simply "finished the work begun over a century before by the backwoodsman, and [driven] the Spaniard outright from the western world . . . At bottom the question of expansion in 1898 was but a variant of the problem we had to solve at every stage of the great western movement."

The United States would pay a heavy price for Roosevelt's interpretation of history.

A congressional amendment to the declaration of the Spanish-American War prevented full annexation of Cuba, although treaties with the fledgling nation effectively made it an American protectorate. In 1904, under pressure from its protector, Cuba granted the United States an unlimited lease of the naval base at Guantánamo Bay. But technically the island remained independent. It was, therefore, the long campaign in the Philippines against a popular guerrilla movement led by Emilio Aguilnaldo that brought the United States face-to-face with its possession of an empire. Not only did the death toll account for some 250,000 Filipinos and more than 4,000 Americans, but the tactics used, including the use of fortified camps to enclose the civilian population, were as brutal as those used by other empires.

In a way that astonished many, appalled some, and brought pleasure to a few, American imperialism seemed almost indistinguishable from the British variety. Mahan himself pointed to the similarities each faced and argued, "The annexation of the Boer republics was a measure forced upon Great Britain as the annexation of the Philippines has been upon ourselves." The once Anglophobic *Chicago Tribune* proclaimed its belief that "the two great branches of the Anglo-Saxon race are drawing nearer and nearer together for cooperation in peace, and, in logical sequence, in war as well."

In the early 1900s the crossing point in coal production was reached, and superiority over the British empire was no longer in doubt. But instead of arriving at an independent identity, it seemed as though the republic's face had simply merged with the imperial image on the other side of the frontier.

Attacking U.S. policy, the anti-imperialist commentator J. W. Martin condemned the way that "England has suddenly become a guiding star to many of the American people." In 1902 a committee of inquiry set up by Secretary of War Elihu Root turned up the sort of evidence that is inseparable from military occupation and armed resistance.

"Our men have been relentless, have killed to exterminate men, women, and children, prisoners and captives, active insurgents and suspected people, from lads of ten up, an idea prevailing that the Filipino was little better than a dog, a noisome reptile in some instances, whose best disposition was the rubbish heap," the wife of an officer sickened by the killings wrote to the *Philadelphia Ledger* in November 1901. "Our soldiers have pumped salt water into men 'to make them talk,' have taken prisoners of people who had held up their hands and peacefully surrendered, and, an hour later, without an atom of evidence to show that they were even insurrectos, stood them up on a bridge, and shot them down one by one to drop into the water below and float down as examples to those who found their bullet-loaded corpses."

Another officer argued that such cruelty was inescapable: "We exterminated the American Indians, and I guess most of us are proud of it, or at least believe that the end justified the means; and we must have no scruples about exterminating this other race standing in the way of progress and enlightenment, if it is necessary."

One critical difference existed between imperialism and westward expansion—the frontier. Right up to that line, the settlers had colonized the land, and the need to have it confirmed as property had given them an incentive to bring government with them. Because the territories carved out by Stephen Douglas's committee lay within the United States, immediate responsibility for devising the regulations that governed their lives, liberties, and property rested with Congress, and the template that it had to use was the U.S. Constitution. Most of the American empire, however, was not being colonized by settlers anxious for U.S. government, and Congress had no intention of admitting it into the Union.

In 1904 the Supreme Court had to deal with the dilemma that this posed. It came in the unlikely form of an appeal by Fred Dorr, editor of the *Manila Freedom*, who had headlined a juicy story about the private activities of a member of the Philippine governing commission with the eye-catching but unfortunately libelous words TRAITOR, SEDUCER AND PERJURER. Dorr argued that since the Philippines lay under U.S. control, he should have had the protection of the Constitution and been tried by a jury rather than by a judge under the civil code inherited from Spain.

The majority decision of the Supreme Court, written by Justice Edward D. White, dismissed his appeal on the grounds that Congress could devise its own regulations in any form not directly prohibited by the Constitution. It was a matter of being realistic. "If the United States, impelled by its duty or advantage, shall acquire territory peopled by savages," White pointed out, the Constitution would require it to set up courts, empanel juries, and follow due process, but "to state such a proposition demonstrates the impossibility of carrying it into practice." In other words, outside its frontier the United States could adapt and adjust its democratic procedures as it saw fit. Dorr, therefore, was not entitled to trial by jury despite living in an American colony.

This was the rational choice. Other nations faced by the conflict between democratic values and the command structure of empire had made similar decisions. What makes the case stand out, however, was the minority opinion of the "Great Dissenter," Justice John M. Harlan. "Neither the life, nor the liberty, nor the property of any person, within any territory or country over which the United States is sovereign, can be taken," Harlan declared, "under the sanction of any civil tribunal, acting under its authority, by any form of procedure inconsistent with the Constitution of the United States."

This was what Lincoln's Constitution required: the guarantee of individual rights on a basis of absolute equality, as promised by the Declaration of Independence. There could be no adjustment to different races or different places—"the Constitution," Harlan maintained, "is the supreme law in every territory, as soon as it comes under the sovereign dominion of the United States for purposes of civil administration."

On one fundamental point, however, White and Harlan were in agreement—democratic values as practiced inside the frontier of the United States were not compatible with imperial rule. That was why the line that marked the limits of the nation was so important. The freedom that had been won at such cost and defined the very nature of the United States could not be exported.

Even Roosevelt, the standard-bearer of imperialism, accepted that a fundamental error had been made and admitted in 1907 that he would be "glad to see the [Philippines] made independent." When it was suggested that the Dominican Republic should be made an American colony, he exclaimed, "I have about the same desire to annex it as a gorged boa constrictor might have to swallow a porcupine wrong-end-to."

CHAPTER 12

The American Frontier

*A man has a right to be employed, to be trusted, to be
loved, to be revered. The power of love, as the basis of a
State, has never been tried.*

RALPH WALDO EMERSON, "Politics," 1844

W HEN FREDERICK JACKSON Turner delivered his speech entitled
"The Significance of the Frontier in American History" to the
American Historical Association in Chicago in 1893, he did so as a young
Wisconsin professor with no reputation. His thesis, that the frontier deserved serious study by historians, could hardly have been more far-fetched.
History was concerned with the study of constitutional and military events,
while the frontier was the stuff of dime novels and Buffalo Bill Cody's traveling circus. Worst of all, Turner was offering a deliberate challenge to the
University of Chicago's head of history, Professor Hermann von Holst, the
supreme authority on the events leading to the Civil War. The seventh and
final volume of von Holst's magisterial *Constitutional and Political History of
the United States* had been published the year before, delineating with Teutonic thoroughness—it was originally written in German—the divisions,
and especially the conflict across state lines, that slavery had triggered between federal and state constitutions.

What Turner's audience heard was an aggressive demolition of von Holst's
analysis. "It is believed that many phases of our political history have been
obscured by the attention paid to State boundaries and to the sectional lines
of North and South," Turner stated. ". . . But, from the point of view of the

rise and growth of sectionalism and nationalism, it is much more important to note the existence of great social and economic areas, independent of state lines, which have acted as units in political history." The emphasis on states' rights and slavery was, he concluded simply, "a wrong perspective." To say this in Chicago was equivalent to giving a middle-fingered salute to von Holst.

In place of the forces that divided the United States, Turner proposed that the most important element was the unifying experience of the settlers' expansion across the continent. "Up to our own day American history has been in a large degree the history of the colonization of the Great West," he declared in his opening paragraph. It was important because, from the moment the first English colonists arrived, the infinite opportunities and extraordinary challenges presented by the wilderness had transformed

Frederick Jackson Turner

the outlook of generations of immigrants pushing westward and "promoted the formation of a composite nationality for the American people." Sweeping away arcane discussion about the significance of dusty paragraphs in half-forgotten constitutional conventions, Turner presented the influence of wide horizons and immense forests on living people with hopes and dreams. It was an exhilarating, easily understood picture. "The demand for land and the love of wilderness freedom drew the frontier ever onward," and from the physical and psychological demands of building a cabin, breaking the virgin soil, and holding off hostile attacks emerged the distinctive characteristic that made Americans different—"that coarseness and strength combined with acuteness and inquisitiveness; that practical, inventive turn of mind, quick to find expedients; that masterful grasp of material things, lacking in the artistic but powerful to effect great ends; that restless, nervous energy; that dominant individualism, working for good and for evil, and withal that buoyancy and exuberance which comes with freedom."

His speech began and ended with the report of the superintendent of the 1890 census that the empty places were now filled, and the "frontier line" no longer existed. But the elegiac tone was tempered in a defiant final paragraph: "America has [always] been another name for opportunity, and the people of the United States have taken their tone from the incessant expansion which has not only been open but has even been forced upon them. He would be a rash prophet who should assert that the expansive character of American life has now entirely ceased."

Despite his eloquence, little suggested that his ideas, indeed the very phrases, would remain in currency more than a century after they were delivered. Lacking analytical detail, the speech failed to inspire enthusiasm among his audience of constitutional historians. Even the influential endorsement of Professor Woodrow Wilson of Princeton University missed the point about the frontier's continuing influence. What Wilson welcomed was the idea of the frontier as "a stage of development," and he concluded that it must lead to the west becoming increasingly civilized and "eastern," rather than that the western experience should leave a permanent imprint on the American character. This was an understandable mistake, because as Turner himself admitted the frontier had ceased to exist, making it difficult to explain how its influence could continue to affect future generations.

Yet the myth of the frontier captured the popular imagination because it seemed to offer a historical explanation for the extraordinary phenomenon of westward expansion. Not only had the United States spread across the continent in little more than two generations, but it had created a society so homogeneous, despite its diversity, that to say *American* was to describe a set of characteristics that referred only to the citizens and society of the USA and specifically excluded all the other Americans in South, Central, and North America.

Turner's theory seemed the more credible because the myth of the frontier was already lodged in every American's imagination. History was in fact the last discipline to appreciate its power. Visually, the land of the frontier had provided the raw material for artists since Thomas Cole had depicted the upper Hudson Valley in the 1820s, when old-timers could still remember the Mohawks living there. In 1859 Albert Bierstadt traveled to the Rockies with a U.S. Public Land Survey party, then displayed its spectacular scenery to eastern eyes for the first time through a series of immense canvases. Most spectacularly of all, Thomas Moran's gigantic landscape *Grand Canyon of the Yellowstone*, painted after a visit to Yellowstone in 1871, had helped persuade Congress to set the area aside as the first national park in the country.

While painters dealt with the scenery of the frontier, writers concentrated on the people. Eighteenth-century Andrew Ellicott, recoiling from the fleas and squalor of Beeson Town, had allowed himself to be amused by the skewed language of the innkeeper there who solemnly predicted "there would be a great conjunction of Rain or Snow for there was a large Circumstance round the Moon." But the nineteenth century took frontier struggles and sayings more seriously.

The style was set by James Fenimore Cooper's iconic character Natty Bumppo or Leatherstocking, who first appeared in *The Pioneers* in 1823. Raised by Delaware Indians, and conditioned by a life spent in the wilderness, Natty stood for simple virtues and the vast freedom of the unclaimed land. When he leveled his rifle at an intruder, saying, "If you come a foot nigher you shall have frontier punishment," the reader knew he was not bluffing.

Cooper placed his stories in the past when the frontier lay no farther off than upstate New York, but the conflict between the liberty of the wilderness and the privileges of property was timeless. "There's two rights to all the land on 'arth," another frontier character, the squatter Thousandacres, said to a surveyor who was the symbol of the law in *The Chainbearer*. "One of these rights is what I call a king's right, or that which depends on writin's, and laws, and sich like contrivances; and the other depends on possession. It stands to reason, that fact is better than writin' about it can be."

But as the settlers moved out of the forest and into the prairie, the fictional frontiersman became less of a junction between Anglo- and Native-American cultures. A work of nonfiction, Timothy Flint's hugely influential 1826 memoir of missionary work among the newly arrived settlers in Missouri, *Recollections of the Last Ten Years*, created the template for the enduring image of the white frontiersman at war with the bloodthirsty Indian. "The antipathy between the two races seems fixed and unalterable," Flint declared. "Peace there often is between them when they are cast in the same vicinity, but any affectionate intercourse, never."

Unfortunately, Flint arrived in Missouri at the end of a long period of cultural harmony between natives and newcomers. What he saw were the last Shawnee being driven from their lands by the torrent of settlers who poured across the Mississippi—almost one hundred thousand had come by 1824—and laid the foundations for an exclusive property-owning democracy. Nevertheless, this was the frontier that provided the staple of the western adventure novels published in the 1840s. Unlike Cooper's forest-bound fiction, these placed their heroes in the wide-open spaces of the prairie, and while Natty Bumppo was half-Indian in his ways and outlook, the frontiersman of the westerns was the implacable enemy of the Indians.

Their defining hero was the real-life Kit Carson, guide and adviser on all matters Indian to John C. Frémont on his trail-finding expeditions to California. As a trapper, hunter, and soldier, Carson's adventures among Apache, Cheyenne, and Ute became so legendary that in later life he could not visit San Francisco without attracting crowds of celebrity hunters, who were usually disappointed to discover that their hero stood a scrawny, pockmarked five feet and a few inches. On one surreal occasion in 1849 while pursuing a company of Apache who had kidnapped and subsequently killed a white woman, Carson found among her scattered possessions one of the books about him, "the first of the kind I had ever seen," he reported, "in which I was represented as a great hero, slaying Indians by the hundreds." He imagined her reading it and praying, fruitlessly as it happened, that the real Kit Carson would ride up in time to rescue her.

So much of his early life was actually spent hunting and trapping in the company of Indians that Carson might have been portrayed as part of the original inclusive frontier, but that was not what the market wanted. In the 1860s, the New York publisher Erastus Beadle began to churn out his orange-covered dime novels on new steam-powered rotary presses. Sixty thousand copies was the average run, but *Seth Jones; or the Captives of the Frontier* sold four hundred thousand copies, and Beadle retailed no fewer than five million books in his first five years in business. The appeal of Seth Jones and his buckskin-clad successor, Deadwood Dick, was that single-handedly they kept savagery at bay, by slaughtering huge numbers of Indians, so that they could rescue delicate, civilized, and very white damsels in distress.

The dime novels were escapist, but their theme belonged to a larger yearning. To an audience trapped in the complexities of urban and industrial life, the idea of the frontier in its largeness and simplicity and absence of boundaries stood for all that their own everyday existence was not. "Eastward I go only by force; but westward I go free," Thoreau wrote in his posthumously published "Walking." "I must walk toward Oregon, and not toward Europe. And that way the nation is moving, and I may say that mankind progresses from east to west."

The first suggestion that the frontier might hold the key to the American character was made a generation before Turner. It came in 1865 from a sophisticated New Yorker, Edwin Godkin, founder of the literary weekly *The Nation*, whose interest was sociological rather than historical. In the dying days of the Civil War he wrote an article for the *North American Review* proposing, "If we enquire what are those phenomena which distinguish [the American spirit] from that of older countries, we shall find that by far the larger number of them may be attributed to what we shall call 'the frontier life' led by a large proportion of the inhabitants, and to the influence of this portion on manners and legislation rather than to political institutions or even to the equality of conditions."

What interested Godkin was the classless, egalitarian nature of American society, so different from the strict hierarchy of his native England. His choice of the frontier as the source of those values might have surprised his urban, eastern readership, for whom the quintessentially American characteristics were those derived from the Puritan ethos of the *Mayflower's* passengers—freedom of belief, an egalitarian society, and reliance on individual conscience. Even de Tocqueville, whose phrase "the equality of conditions"

Godkin quoted, had found the most vibrant examples of democracy in the township meetings of New England. But four years of civil war had revealed those to be sectional values, while the aristocratic freedom of the white south was equally unacceptable. The west, by contrast, offered a glimpse of the United States untainted by slavery.

Turner's frontier theory fitted neatly into this background. History, it seemed, could confirm what sociology, literature, and art had long suspected. That Turner himself never satisfactorily developed his original hypothesis should raise doubts, however. In later accounts, he tended to recapitulate the argument rather than provide detail to confirm or refine it, and he entirely failed to follow up his own suggestion of comparing the American frontier experience with that of other frontiers. Significantly, his most interesting work in later life focused instead on the sectional interests of the south and west that he had dismissed in his Chicago speech.

Modern historians of the west such as John Mack Faragher and Patricia Nelson Limerick largely treat Turner's frontier theory as irrelevant or "fraught with error." The frontier experience that Turner took to be unique to the United States is now increasingly seen as a struggle between the migrants' economic muscle and strategies of resistance by aboriginal owners, comparable to other colonizing movements around the world, and his male-dominated battle with the wilderness has been replaced by a mosaic of struggles involving ecological forces, women's activities, and cultural expectations.

Many of these criticisms are what might be expected of a different age with different priorities, and the popular appeal of Turner's misreading of history has not been appreciably diminished. The idea of the frontier as a uniquely American experience offering fresh and unlimited opportunities particularly suited to exploitation by American enterprise and adaptability continues to be attached to such boundless areas as space, the Internet, or intellectual property.

"We stand today on the edge of a New Frontier," John F. Kennedy told the Democratic National Convention in 1960, "the frontier of the 1960s—a frontier of unknown opportunities and perils, a frontier of unfulfilled hopes and threats." Thirty years later, Mitch Kapor and John Perry Barlow, founders of the Electronic Frontier Foundation, boldly outlined the future of the Internet as "a frontier region, populated by the few hardy technologists who can tolerate the austerity of its savage computer interfaces." Indeed, if an instant explanation is needed to describe how the American outlook, the American character, the American way, came into being, the default version remains Turner's romantic vision of the lone individual fighting against nature, Indians, and government.

"The frontier is productive of individualism," wrote Turner. "The tendency is anti-social. It produces antipathy to control, and particularly to any direct control. The tax-gatherer is viewed as a representative of oppression."

Appealing though it is, this image of libertarian self-expression bears no relation to reality. What made the settlement of the West such an iconic American experience was precisely that it took place under the umbrella of the U.S. government. At every level, from the toughest gold miners panning gold in 1849 California to financially sophisticated land speculators, the first impulse of anyone working a square yard of land was to register its use and a claim to ownership—first unofficially with others in the claim group, then officially with government. The tax-gatherer might not have been liked, but payment of taxes then as now has the compensating benefit of guaranteeing legal possession.

The basic flaw in Turner's argument was there at its starting point. What made the American frontier experience unique was not the freedom of the wilderness but the lines drawn in previously uncharted ground—around claims, properties, states, and the republic itself. So far from from being hostile to the individual, government made it possible for the individual to gain due reward for his or her enterprise.

By the same token, what made the new frontiers of space, the Internet, and intellectual property potentially rewarding for pioneers was that there too claims could be registered under the umbrella of the U.S. government. Through the World Bank, the World Trade Organization, and the International Monetary Fund, through the Web-controlling Internet Corporation for Assigned Names and Numbers (ICANN), and through the patent enforcement Agreement on Trade-Related Aspects of Intellectual Property Rights (TRIPS), the influence of the United States reaches worldwide, enforcing concepts of property backed by American law. As the economics commentator John Gray noted, the fabric of globalization itself "is largely an artifact of American power, which was constructed in the belief that it would serve American interests."

. . .

No one suffered more from the artificial boundaries drawn in the ground than the Native Americans. With the buffalo gone, their hunting grounds signed away, and their reserves under threat, Massachusetts senator Henry L. Dawes made a last attempt in 1887 to bring them the benefits of the system that had overpowered them. As he frankly confessed to the Senate, a conversation with the paramount chief of the Cherokee had revealed that there was no poverty in the nation, and yet "the defect of [their] system was apparent. They have got as far as they can go, because they own their land in common . . . There is no enterprise to make your home any better than that of your neighbor's. There is no selfishness, which is at the bottom of civilization. Until this people consent to give up their lands and divide them among their citizens so that each can own the land he cultivates, they will not make much progress."

As a piece of social engineering, Dawes's General Allotment Act, assigning community land to each individual Native American, turned out to be a mockery. The fail-safe provisions designed to protect the new owners from unscrupulous buyers were immediately swept aside. By 1900, more than half the remaining reservations had been bought up by white settlers, while the nominal owners saw little of the money since payments were held in trust by the Bureau of Indian Affairs. There they were so mismanaged that a lawsuit conducted by the Blackfeet lawyer Elouise Cobell on behalf of Native Americans today claims a total of $176 billion in unpaid royalties from the U.S. government.

Yet there was a fundamental truth in Dawes's analysis. Individual land ownership was the key to the uniquely American system that evolved from the nation's expansion westward. It made capitalists out of squatters, settlers, and speculators, it rewarded individual enterprise, and in the years following the Civil War it subsidized the profits and corporate structure of railroads, banks, manufacturing, and a dozen other peripheral businesses.

The central importance of property made the maintenance of law and order vital in the west. It also made the violence so beloved by pulp fiction deeply unpopular in reality.

The legend of Wild Bill Hickok, city marshal of Abilene, Kansas, in 1871, which declared him to have "contributed *more than any other man* to making the West a place for decent men and women to live in," demonstrated how far myth could escape from history. Not only was the real James Butler

Hickok assisted by three deputies—unkind gossip said it was they who patrolled the streets when the range cowboys came to town leaving Hickok to concentrate on gambling—but his dismissal after just eight months in the job was for excessive violence in shooting a man rather than arresting him. "He acted only too ready to shoot down, to kill out-right, instead of avoiding assassination when possible as the higher duty of a marshal," Abilene's Mayor Theodore C. Henry commented reprovingly. "Such a policy of taking justice into his own hands exemplified, of course, but a form of lawlessness."

In the actual world, even the trail cowboys—whose lives as pictured by Hollywood epitomized the free life, riding the wide, open range under big skies and creating hell in any town they arrived in—were caught in the network of city, state, and federal government and could hardly have existed without it. When the cattle drives began out of Texas in the 1860s, many did not follow the Chisholm Trail to the railhead in Abilene but went straight to the Indian reservations in Oklahoma, where federal officials from the Bureau of Indian Affairs needed to buy regular supplies of meat to feed the inhabitants after the buffalo herds had been wiped out. It was a shorter, less romantic drive than a three months' trail to the railhead, but the compensations appealed powerfully to a Texas rancher. Not only did the government pay a higher price than the meat companies' agents, the herds did not have to be quarantined against "Texas fever," as was required by law after crossing state lines into Kansas, Colorado, or Missouri. Nor did a trail boss run the same risk of being fined and having his cattle impounded by a county sheriff when the animals strayed into a wheat field.

When the herd did travel all the way to Dodge, Abilene, or some other railhead, the rancher and trail hands benefited from another piece of government intervention. The railroad network that served the markets in Chicago and the east coast had been financed by grants of federal and state land measured out by Public Land surveyors. Without the government and its laws, there would have been no Chisholm Trail, and no legends big enough to fit John Wayne.

The harshest indictment against Frederick Jackson Turner's frontier myth, however, is not just that its roots were planted in a romantic escape from reality, but that the thesis itself represented a deliberate turning away from the chief anxiety of the day. What most disturbed Americans about the 1890 census was not the end of the frontier of settlement, but the information that more than eight million of the country's sixty-three million citizens had been born abroad in no fewer than thirty-seven different countries, from Africa and Austria through Turkey and Wales. Already made anxious by the rising level of immigration—in a decade it had increased by 50 percent to an average of five hundred thousand a year, equivalent to five million today in relation to the existing population—Turner's contemporaries were especially alarmed by the racial mix.

The British, Irish, Germans, and others from northern Europe who had in the past provided the bulk of the settlers became a minority. In some years, up to 70 percent of immigrants came from southern and eastern Europe, including the first great surge of Jewish immigration. The newcomers tended to cluster in urban centers, speaking their own languages—Italian, Yiddish, Polish, Russian—and creating their own cultural ghettos. For the first time since the Know-Nothings, anti-immigrant feeling reached the point of becoming a serious political force. Calls were made for restrictions on the number of entrants through the use of literacy tests, and for the total "exclusion of elements undesirable for citizenship or injurious to our national character."

To contemplate the courage and resourcefulness of the Anglo-American pioneers who colonized the wide-open spaces of the west was a welcome antidote to such problems. But Turner might have found a more useful key to the American character by studying the people who had crossed the national frontier into the United States.

CHAPTER 13

CROSSING THE FRONTIER

*Will the United States remain a country with a single na-
tional language and a core Anglo-Protestant culture? By
ignoring this question, Americans acquiesce to their eventual transformation into two peoples with two cultures
(Anglo and Hispanic) and two languages (English and
Spanish).*

SAMUEL P. HUNTINGTON,
"The Clash of Civilizations?" 1993

IMMIGRATION HAS ALWAYS challenged the values of American society. The conflict is inherent in the democratic structure and the guarantees of freedom that enable those already inside the frontier to mold their
society. Because U.S. democracy affords the same opportunities to each new
wave of migrants, it is inevitable that existing citizens should resent the
new arrivals who come with their own values and priorities, knowing that
they will alter what is already in place.

The pattern began with the edicts of the Puritans that guaranteed coreli-
gionists in their "city built on a hill" unprecedented political liberty, but
banned the practice of any other religions or even variant forms of Protes-
tantism. As late as the 1700s, the first appearance of Catholic settlers in Massachusetts provoked an order for the arrest of "any Popish Priest and other
Papists."

In Pennsylvania, famous for its protection of religious liberty, the stream
of German immigrants in the eighteenth century provoked even Benjamin

Franklin to an outburst of xenophobia. "Why should Pennsylvania, founded by the English," he demanded in a pamphlet in 1751, "become a Colony of Aliens, who will shortly be so numerous as to Germanize us instead of our Anglifying them, and will never adopt our Languages or Customs, any more than they can acquire our Complexion."

Such tensions between incomers and residents grew sharply as immigration increased in the nineteenth century, erupting into violence in New York and Boston in the 1850s following the arrival of close to one million Irish Catholics. On the west coast, similar resentment broke out into attacks on Chinese immigrants brought in as cheap labor by the railroad companies in the 1860s. Immigration had always been regarded as the responsibility of the states, but in 1882 Congress stepped in with the Chinese Exclusion Act, restricting entry to male workers with guaranteed employment. Eighteen months before Turner's frontier speech, the federal government took over full control with the passage of the Immigration Act, barring the entry of polygamists and those suffering "loathsome or contagious" diseases, or guilty of crimes of "moral turpitude." Almost two hundred inspectors were recruited to enforce these rules at the principal ports of entry, more than half being assigned to the main processing center at Ellis Island, New York.

On January 2, 1892, a twenty-one-year-old Irishwoman, Ellie King, en route to Nebraska, disembarked from the steamship *Nevada* and became the first immigrant to walk through the long hallway on Ellis Island and into the United States. Unfortunately for her place in the footnotes of history, she was followed by fifteen-year-old Annie Moore, arriving with two younger brothers in tow to join relations in New York, a much more attractive proposition for the city newspapers, which promoted her to the head of the queue and won her an award of a gold $10 piece from the chief immigration officer.

For the twelve million people who followed them through the hall before the facility closed in 1954, the first and great Americanizing experience was walking through the door at the end of the hall marked PUSH—TO NEW YORK and stepping across the U.S. frontier. On the far side of it lay a seemingly arbitrary confusion of languages and customs. The two Irishwomen at least spoke English, but in Nebraska Ellie King would have known scores of German farmers who had arrived there directly from Bremen, courtesy of an all-in-one purchase from the Atchison, Topeka and Santa Fe railroad that included a through ticket to Lincoln, Nebraska, and a 160-acre quarter-

section of prairie. In New York, Annie Moore might have found herself lis-
tening to a Latin mass alongside Italian seamstresses whose only other contact with Americans came from their compatriots in a Bowery sweatshop.
But all of them became American precisely because the confusion was not
arbitrary.

What they had entered was a series of areas of freedom—properties,
places of work and entertainment, wards, counties, and states—delineated
by legally recognized boundaries. Each was subject to regulation by laws and
democratic procedures in which, nominally at least, anyone could partici-
pate. "It is not by the consolidation or concentration of powers, but by their
distribution, that good government is effected," Jefferson, the great molder of
their new country, had written in his autobiography. ". . . Every State is again
divided into counties, each to take care of what lies within its local bounds;
each county again into townships or wards, to manage minuter details; and
every ward into farms, to be governed each by its individual proprietor."

In the accounts of immigrants, the emotion that emerges more often than
any other is the mixture of fear and hope as they realize what freedom
means—the old social structures that looked after them and kept them in
their place had gone, and all that prevented them from starving or living in
a mansion was their capacity to make money. Yet, according to the economic
theories of The Wealth of Nations and the eighteenth-century Scottish belief
in human sociability, that was the best guarantee of social well-being. "Were
we directed from Washington when to sow, and when to reap," Jefferson had
explained, "we should soon want bread. It is by this partition of cares, de-
scending in gradation from general to particular, that the mass of human affairs may be best managed, for the good and prosperity of all."

Reality did not always accord with theory, and in the early 1900s the
left-wing New York Independent began printing the stories of what it called
"undistinguished Americans," newly arrived immigrants as well as farmers'
wives and released slaves, and their experiences offered a glimpse of the
freedoms and dangers contained in Jefferson's structure.

The 1890s immigrants arrived in a world where $5 a week was a living
wage only because rent, clothes, and basic meals amounted to $4.50. As
garment-maker, slaughterhouse worker, or homesteader, the work was un-
remittingly hard and life a gamble dependent on the whim of bosses and the
fluctuations of fashion and a ruthless market. "I lay down on the floor with

three other men and . . . did not go to sleep for a long time," Antanas Kaz-
tauskis, a Lithuanian meat-worker, confessed after his first day looking for
work in Chicago's stockyards. "My money was almost gone and I thought
that I would soon die unless I got a job, for this was not like home. Here
money was everything and a man without money must die."

Although work was what they needed to live and get ahead, it was
through their leisure that the immigrants took the second step toward becoming American. They still joined Lithuanian concertina bands, read Italian and Yiddish newspapers, attended fund-raisers for Polish churches, but
inevitably more and more of the raw material in the stories that they told,
the music that they performed, the dramas that they acted out, and the
sports that they played came from the new land. In the 1880s three quarters
of a million Americans still spoke German as their first language, but as one
parent admitted, "Although our children all speak German and learn to
read and write German at school, they are more familiar with English since
it is, after all, the language of the country." As local loyalties and affections
became alloyed with the traditional, the children produced literature, music, theater, and above all movies that fused the different allegiances into a
new form that was distinctively American. It was, nevertheless, forged in
the face of deep suspicion about its un-American roots.

When Emma Lazarus wrote her tribute poem for the Statue of Liberty in
1883, its now much parodied lines "Give me your tired, your poor, Your
huddled masses yearning to breathe free, The wretched refuse of your teem-
ing shore" could not have run more clearly against public opinion. What
had given rise to Ellis Island was the rising anger against immigration, and
the poem itself was rooted in Lazarus's own efforts to help Russian migrants
find work and housing in New York in the face of the city's hostility. Few
people other than business interests and the children of earlier immigrants
supported their arrival. They were the ones who bought most enthusiasti-
cally into the ideals of Israel Zangwill's schmaltzy play The Melting Pot, first
performed in 1908. Zangwill's story, however, has a sharp edge that is usually
overlooked today.

Ostensibly, the plot concerns a brilliant young Jewish composer, David
Quixano, who falls in love with the daughter of an anti-Semitic Russian
baron and wins her over with his sizzling new symphony and his vision of
Europeans becoming American in the crucible of the United States. "A fig

for your feuds and vendettas!" David exclaims. "Germans and Frenchmen, Irishmen and Englishmen, Jews and Russians—into the Crucible with you all! God is making the American."

Inside the upbeat message about losing their European prejudices, however, was a darker one about overcoming American prejudice against their presence in the country. As an appendix to the play put it on behalf of the migrant, "I am the great American problem. When I pour out my blood on your altar of labour, and lay down my life as a sacrifice to your god of toil, men make no more comment than at the fall of a sparrow. But my brawn is woven into the warp and woof of the fabric of your national being. My children shall be your children and your land shall be my land because my sweat and my blood will cement the foundations of the America of To-Morrow."

To the accuracy of this forecast, an estimated one hundred million Americans descended from Ellis Island migrants, as well as the quintessentially American movies of Ellis Island alumni such as Sam Goldwyn and Frank Capra, provide eloquent support. Nevertheless, an underlying prejudice remained against the arrival of so many immigrants who spoke no English, were neither Protestant nor Christian, and frequently had an olive-skinned, Mediterranean color.

As president, Woodrow Wilson, whose admiration for the Ku Klux Klan was never concealed, swiftly responded to the widespread sense that the new arrivals were undermining the true Anglo-American spirit of the United States. Under his administration literacy tests were brought in before the First World War to reduce immigration, a lead followed by the governments of Warren Harding and Calvin Coolidge after the war with the introduction of quotas for immigration and the restriction of entry to those with passports and the necessary visas.

Nevertheless, one of the central patterns within the history of the independent United States is the way in which its sense of freedom, once Anglo-centric and exclusive, has been shared with and shaped by successive waves of immigrants. Jacksonian democracy levered the western farming Scots-Irish into power at every level from county to federal. A generation later the city-based Catholic Irish took control of wards and city halls behind political leaders such as Tammany Hall's New York assemblyman George Washington Plunkitt in the 1870s and Boston mayor Hugh O'Brien in the 1880s. As one of O'Brien's successors, the legendary James Michael Curley, put it when boasting of the transfer of power, "The Massachusetts of the Puritans is as dead as Caesar, but there is no need to mourn the fact . . . It took the Irish to make Massachusetts a fit place to live in."

Despite the suspicions they aroused, the new Americans acted remarkably like their predecessors. In other words, they acquired property, by the early twentieth century predominantly urban, commercial, and manufacturing, then took steps to safeguard it by acquiring influence in the existing structures of government and law. In addition, they swayed new centers of authority, like the movies, Wall Street, and organized labor.

Politically, the most dramatic sign of their clout came in the 1933 election of Fiorello La Guardia, son of Jewish and Italian immigrants, as mayor of New York, which broke the corrupt stranglehold exerted by the Irish-dominated Tammany Hall. In the long run, however, the economic success in California of Italian-American Amedeo Giannini, whose network of savings and loan associations enabled him to take over the Bank of America in 1928, was more significant, demonstrating as it did the financial heft that the new Americans could exercise, however poor. In Hollywood, Schmuel Gelbfisz, later Samuel Goldwyn, and Eliezir Meir, soon to be Louis Mayer, achieved a similar feat, using the movies to make storytelling democratic.

Nevertheless from the perspective of the twenty-first century, the nineteenth-century Anglo-Americans had good reason for their hostility. Those crossing the frontier were not just immigrants but, like their predecessors, colonists who changed the society they settled in. That the United States in the first half of the twentieth century possessed a recognizably more vibrant culture, a more liberal outlook, and a more diverse economy than in the last half of the nineteenth was due in large part to the influence of its new Americans.

Against that more variegated background the great revolution of the twentieth-century United States took place. Race and the long history of slavery made the black-American fight to win equality of opportunity exceptional in its intensity and its challenge to the core values of the United States. But African-Americans were also the longest-established immigrants in the country next to the Anglos, and their battle for civil rights followed a pattern established by other migrants who had peopled the continent. It was, in ef-

fect, a struggle to colonize the country they lived in—that is to acquire property and to use the law and government to safeguard what they owned.

Inevitably, therefore, the battle split into two, emphasizing either the influence of ownership or the guarantees of government. Booker T. Washington, founder of the Tuskegee Institute in Alabama, stressed that the campaign
should evolve from the bottom up, from black education and black-owned
businesses—"a dairy farm or industrial skills," as he put it in 1895—and
only then to political power. But by 1900 W. E. B. Du Bois estimated that
black Americans owned one million acres of land and property worth $12
million, and that without votes they still had no security against Jim Crow
legislation. To safeguard property rights, however, black Americans like
those before them had to have an influence in government. Consequently
more lives were lost and more blood shed in the battle to register voters
than in any other phase of the campaign to win equal rights.

No statistic underlines more starkly how fiercely the exclusive freedom of
whites was defended than the 4,733 lynchings that occurred between 1882
and 1959. Not all victims were black—a resurgent Ku Klux Klan targeted
Jews, Catholics, and Communists after the First World War—but the great
majority were, and the nature of a lynching made it the ultimate demonstration of social power against those who offended its norms by not knowing their place. The number of killings dropped rapidly in the 1920s and
1930s, from more than seventy a year to about ten, but that they continued,
together with the prevailing fear they induced, pointed up the critical importance of political power.

More than two hundred antilynching bills were introduced during the
first half of the twentieth century, but all failed, a record for which the
U.S. Senate formally apologized in 2005. Many were killed off during the
New Deal, a period when the interventionist power of the federal government reached a peak not seen in peacetime since Reconstruction. President
Franklin D. Roosevelt never concealed that he could not support laws
against lynching because he needed the solid block of southern Democratic
votes in the Senate and House to support his New Deal legislation. "If I
come out for the antilynching bill now," he told a delegate from the National Association for the Advancement of Colored People in 1934, "[the
South] will block every bill I ask Congress to pass to keep America from col-
lapsing. I just can't take that risk."

What virtually ended lynching and made the goal of equal rights a practical possibility was the Second World War. Pitted against Japanese veneration of the emperor and Nazi doctrines of the Teutonic *Übermensch*, the idea of universal rights to life, liberty, and the pursuit of happiness became a goal worth fighting for. Yet the most far-reaching effect of the war was simply one of dispersal. At home, factories operating at full capacity to meet wartime production targets created unprecedented opportunities for African-American workers outside the south, luring more than one million to cities such as Chicago in the north and Los Angeles in the west. They departed the south in such numbers that the population of North Carolina became predominantly white for the first time since the eighteenth century.

The vast wartime migration to the north and west introduced the city-based children of the 1900s immigrants to the formerly hidden world of black America. Jewish-Americans in New York and Italian-Americans in Chicago provided the earliest white audiences for jazz. City dwellers such as them were the first to be aware of the colonizing influence of African-Americans, some finding it a threat to the values and material gains for which they had striven, others welcoming it as a match with their own urban, progressive outlook. For each side on the racial divide, the encounter provided a first glimpse of the other as citizens rather than as the children of slaves and owners.

The transforming effect on national values was illustrated by the almost universal outburst of revulsion against the brutal lynchings of two black couples in Georgia in July 1946. That same year, the Civil Rights branch of the Justice Department succeeded for the first time in having a member of a lynch mob brought to trial and found guilty. Two years later, President Harry Truman banned segregation in both the army and the federal government, a decision forced on the administration by the requirements of the Universal Declaration of Human Rights prohibiting racial discrimination, but approved of by voters.

The tipping point came when Thurgood Marshall persuaded the Supreme Court in 1954 to reach beyond state lines and rule that the public provision of "separate but equal" facilities for blacks and whites according to the *Plessy* ruling was unconstitutional. Although the decision in *Brown v. the Board of Education of Topeka* only concerned public education, the principle applied to the provision of every kind of service, including hospitals, transport, and housing.

Among the pictures of the desegregation era, one stands out—the 1957 image of troopers from the 101st Airborne Division, sent by their Second World War commander, President Dwight D. Eisenhower, with their Second World War rifles on their shoulders, escorting nine black students into Little Rock Central High School in Arkansas. The moment represented the boundary between old and new. It harked back to Reconstruction, the last time that the federal government attempted to impose Lincoln's inclusive Constitution on the south by force, but it also pointed forward to the post–Civil Rights future, when it would be normal to expect all Americans, of every race, creed, and gender, to enjoy equal rights.

The critical piece of legislation turned out to be the 1965 Voting Rights Act striking down the legal niceties of "grandfather" clauses, literacy tests, and tax payments that prevented African-Americans from voting. The results were startling; in Mississippi alone the ratio of African-Americans registered to vote jumped from barely 6 percent to more than 66 percent, and nationwide the number of black voters almost tripled to nine million. It was not the end of discrimination, but the crucial watershed in the journey undertaken by everyone else who had crossed the frontier. Once African-Americans could make their voting power felt, they could ensure that the constitutional guarantees of personal and economic freedom were not subverted by some new version of Jim Crow legislation.

What made the black American demand for their share of liberty different from that of other immigrants was that throughout Anglo-American history their inferior status had been inseparable from the exclusive freedom enjoyed by other Americans. So long as they, who had arrived almost with the first colonists, were denied equality, the privileged nature of the freedom enjoyed by all others would not have changed.

The Civil Rights legislation of the 1960s that guaranteed equality of rights to African-Americans signaled a turning point of immeasurable significance. It enacted the measures needed to bring about Lincoln's inclusive freedom, and its consequences have permeated every section of U.S. society ever since. Native Americans, not even recognized as citizens until 1924, asserted their rights in the 1975 Self-Determination Act to educate their children in their own way free of the Bureau of Indian Affairs. Women, who had secured the vote in 1920 to safeguard their interests, now used the legislation to extend their rights as individuals. They were followed by other sections, defined by gender, ability, or interests, who felt themselves discriminated against.

What it has produced is a paradox. The liberty that should be an inalienable human right has only become available to everyone within the United States as a result of an intricate mixture of constitutional, political, and legal forces driven for generations by an equally rich cocktail of courage, optimism, and a stubborn belief in human dignity. The evolution of American freedom runs through the country's history and represents its crowning achievement. But it could not exist beyond the borders of the United States.

CHAPTER 14

THE END OF FRONTIERS?

All persons born or naturalized in the United States, and
subject to the jurisdiction thereof, are citizens of the United
States and of the State wherein they reside.
FOURTEENTH AMENDMENT, U.S. Constitution, 1868

A YELLOW LINE in the highway between Tijuana and San Diego marks
the point at which the United States ends and Mexico begins. After
nearly an hour trapped in the middle of seven lanes of traffic inching toward
the immigration and customs channels at the San Ysidro crossing, it feels
as though the transition from one country to the other should be more mo-
mentous. So much has been invested in maintaining the difference—border
patrols, security cameras, fences, identity checks, computer systems, and
enough uniforms to clothe a small army—and then . . . just a lick of paint.

When William Emory and José Salazar first marked it out, this stretch of
the line would have run through dry scrubland identical on either side. Now
it cuts across the metropolitan area of San Diego–Tijuana, home to around
four million inhabitants, most of whom live in the same combination of
concrete high-rises and rancho-style villas, choose between the same fast-
food chains offering burgers or frijoles, and work for the same borderland
economy offering transport, warehousing, and financial services. The division of this part of North America into Mexico and the United States
seems artificial compared to its obvious unity. It begs the question whether
the old importance attached to frontiers, as inviolable limits of sovereignty,
is now becoming misplaced.

A century ago, when the imperial frenzy was at its height and new boundaries were being drawn wherever an industrialized power could impose itself, Britain's George Curzon, a former viceroy of India, could declare, "Frontiers are indeed the razor's edge on which hang suspended the modern issues of war and peace, of life or death to nations." Just seven years later, the razor slipped when the German army crossed Belgium's frontier and the world's empires tumbled into the carnage of the First World War. In 1939 Adolf Hitler's decision to march the Wehrmacht across the Polish frontier triggered Britain's declaration of war against Nazi Germany and the start of the Second World War. Two years later, the violation of the U.S. frontier at Pearl Harbor catapulted her into war with Japan and Germany. And all through the Cold War, the moment when missiles crossed into national airspace would have unleashed the program of Mutually Assured Destruction. But when the Berlin Wall came down, literally the most concrete representation of the divisive boundary in the world, the influence of economic, technological, and political forces all contrived to undermine the significance of national frontiers.

In his widely quoted, much misunderstood 1989 essay "The End of History?" Francis Fukuyama provided a philosophical background for the way he thought the world might develop. With the end of the Cold War, the old clash of ideologies that had marked history—the battles between empires and monarchies, between communism, fascism, and democracy—would end and be replaced in the long term by acceptance that the world was developing toward a single model. "The state that emerges at the end of history," he wrote, "is liberal insofar as it recognizes and protects through a system of law man's universal right to freedom, and democratic insofar as it exists only with the consent of the governed."

Just a year later, the economist Kenichi Ohmae claimed in *The Borderless World* that the global economy "made traditional national borders almost disappear, and pushed bureaucrats, politicians, and the military toward the status of declining industries." Since then the effects of globalization have become commonplace, so that it is hardly surprising to find that an electric toothbrush sold around the world by Philips, a Dutch company, is actually assembled in Snoqualmie, Washington, from components made in China, Japan, Malaysia, France, Germany, and Sweden.

Driven by the logic of separating manufacture from assembly, global trade grew in the five years up to 2005 by nearly one third to $9.12 trillion. Fifteen years after Ohmae's original thesis, Thomas L. Friedman argued in *The World Is Flat* that the growth of Chinese and Indian corporations into world companies had created additional forces to weaken the concept of national sovereignty. International supply chains—to companies such as Philips and Wal-Mart, and from providers such as the Indian computer giant Infosys or the Chinese auto-parts maker Wanxiang—now dominated international relations. "No two countries that are part of the same global supply chain will ever fight a war," Friedman predicted, "as long as they're each still part of that supply chain."

In Europe, for centuries the cockpit of warring nation-states, growing economic integration has led to greater political harmony, with effects that are immediately visible. Since 2001, the Schengen Agreement among most of the nations in the European Union has made it possible to drive from Cádiz in the south of Spain to Norway's North Cape crossing seven international frontiers but without encountering a single border control. And at San Ysidro almost fifty thousand people a day commute to jobs, schools, and entertainment that happen to be on the other side of a border that barely registers in their daily routine.

It has become a commonplace to say that "everything changed" on September 11, 2001, but nowhere was it more true than in people's feelings about the frontier. Quite suddenly a line that had been virtually ignored and deemed beyond assault was shown to be terrifyingly fragile. "Protecting borders was not a national security issue before 9/11," the national commission report on Al Qaeda's attack stated succinctly. In the years since, border protection has become the single most important security issue in the war on terror.

At home it underpinned the introduction of a blizzard of measures to strengthen security, including putting the Department of Homeland Security in charge of border crossings. Abroad, as President George W. Bush repeatedly made clear, the need to protect the frontier justified a wide range of actions far beyond the actual boundary of the United States, including the war on terror and the Iraq campaign. "We cannot find security by abandoning our commitments and retreating within our borders," he argued in

The border crossing between the United States and Mexico at San Ysidro

his State of the Union address in January 2006. "If we were to leave these vicious attackers alone, they would not leave us alone. They would simply move the battlefield to our own shores." Yet the sense of vulnerability persists, and the conservative commentator Glynn Custred, for example, still maintains that "the longest undefended border in the world now looks like a 4,000-mile-long portal for terrorists."

Yet for many Americans, anxiety about terrorists comes second to fears about illegal immigration. The estimated eleven million illegal Hispanic immigrants pose a more insidious danger because, it is claimed, they threaten to subvert the very identity of the United States. Images of lines of illegal migrants heading through the scrub, led in some cases by organized criminals also shipping in drugs, produce a deep unease even among those who recognize the human instinct that drives ordinary people to risk everything in the hope of a better life. There is a sense of chaos breaking in, and the overrunning of the frontier represents the undermining of order within the United States itself.

Contributors to Internet discussion groups often quote the words of Mexican author Elena Poniatowski—"Mexico is recovering the territories yielded to the United States by means of migratory tactics"—and they draw the violent conclusion that illegal crossing of the frontier amounts to "a declaration of war." Echoing their sentiments, Harvard's Professor Samuel Huntington found in the level of Mexican migration "a unique, disturbing, and a looming challenge to our cultural integrity, our national identity, and potentially to the future of our country." The great swath of the Southwest, sometimes known as MexAmerica, home to five hundred radio stations and more than a hundred newspapers whose first language is Spanish, would seem to provide powerful supporting evidence.

Nevertheless, the history of Mexican-American immigration has very much followed the pattern set by other nationalities entering the United States. While almost twenty-eight million Americans speak Spanish at home, the majority are first-generation immigrants. Follow-up studies in Los Angeles indicate that almost three quarters of second-generation immigrants prefer to speak English at home, rising to 97 percent among third generation. That is a classic transition that was experienced and mourned by German speakers in the 1880s, by Italian and Polish speakers in the early twentieth century, and by Yiddish speakers in the 1950s. The difference today, according to Professor Rubén Rumbaut of the University of California, is that exposure to the Internet and other types of English-language technology is bringing about the change to English faster than before. Among more than fifty-two hundred second-generation immigrant children studied in the Miami and San Diego school systems in 2005, 99 percent spoke fluent English, and less than one third remained fluent in their parents' tongue by the age of seventeen.

"The fate of all these languages is to succumb to rapid assimilation," Rumbaut commented. "Demography will take care of the problem itself—it is not really a policy issue."

In the past, fears of cultural change have sprung from the assumption that the United States was formed by a single set of unchanging values, an assumption implicit in Huntington's question "Will the United States remain a country with a single national language and a core Anglo-Protestant culture?" Set in this static context, the identity and culture of the United States inevitably appear fragile and vulnerable to any sort of change. Yet throughout history, the reverse has been true. The core values of American society have evolved through a dynamic, often confrontational, process, directly affected by those already inside the frontier who naturally wish to preserve what is there, and those who want to cross the frontier and will inevitably alter the existing state of things.

Huntington's alarmist note bears an uncanny resemblance to the fears expressed by his Harvard predecessors in the 1880s when they threw their academic weight behind the Immigration Restriction League. At the end of the nineteenth century the United States faced a choice, according to the league, between being "peopled by British, German and Scandinavian stock, historically free, energetic, progressive, or by Slav, Latin and Asiatic races, historically down-trodden, atavistic and stagnant." Since there was no precedent for such large-scale immigration of non-English speakers with an alien culture, the nineteenth-century doomsayers had some reason for apprehension. Indeed, the 1890 census indicated that the proportion of Americans unable to speak English was about three times as great as it is today. Late-nineteenth-century American values were undoubtedly changed by their arrival, but they remain unmistakably American.

Seen against the long perspective of the frontier's history, the process of Americanization becomes clear. Ever since Andrew Ellicott drew the first national boundary enclosing the fractious inhabitants of Natchez, immigrants have become American by a process of reciprocity—a constitutional guarantee of individual rights that could be secured only in exchange for participation in government. For all the tensions that the process entails, it has worked to awesome effect for more than two centuries.

That long history suggests that a modern Frederick Jackson Turner might take the 2000 census as a starting point for a new frontier theory. Reviewing the main patterns thrown up by the census, the former director of the Census Bureau, Kenneth Prewitt, concluded, "The U.S. has become home to people from, literally, every civilization and of every nationality, and speaking almost every language. Not in recorded history has there been a nation so demographically complex. So it falls to us, the American citizens of the 21st century, to fashion from this diversity history's first 'world nation.'"

The frontier of the United States has never been the outer defense of Fortress America. Its purpose has always been to mark the extent of a system of government, law, and individual rights unlike any other in the world.

The tensions will always exist between immigrants and existing citizens, between new demands for equality and the protection of old habits. But the unparalleled commitment to democracy and individual liberty, and the values of inclusion, for which so much blood was spilled, have proved capable of creating Americans from every nationality under the sun.

ENVOI

BEFORE THE SNOWS of 1819 came, Andrew Ellicott left the forty-fifth parallel where he had been running the frontier with Canada and returned to the familiar discipline of West Point signaled by drums and marching cadets in smart gray uniforms, braided vests, and tall shakos. His health remained sound—he boasted to Sally that on the Canadian border he had maintained the arduous schedule of late-night observations and daylight calculations without fatigue, but his young assistants "could perform the laborious duty of sleeping eighteen hours out of 24 if not interrupted." With Thayer, Mansfield, and with increasing frequency his son-in-law Douglass, he drew up the regulations that molded the academy's future—no admissions except on ability decided by exam, promotions strictly on merit, two months' camp in the summer, no winter vacation, and at Douglass's insistence the self-regulating honor code that guided cadets' personal lives. In West Point as on the frontier, the rule of law had taken the place of wayward savagery.

In the summer of 1820 as Ellicott returned on the steamboat from New York to West Point, he was felled by a massive stroke. A doctor on board looked after him and he was still alive when the boat reached West Point, where his wife, Sally, took him up the hill to their house. "Everything that skill & tenderness could devise was afforded but without the wished for effect," his son-in-law wrote on August 28. "He died this morning (Monday) 1/2 past 12 o'clock & will be interred tomorrow afternoon. I am surrounded by affliction which added to my own is beyond expression."

Ellicott was buried near the northeast corner of the bluff overlooking the Hudson River, a place of savage beauty. A military funeral was read over his

Andrew Ellicott's grave at West Point

coffin, and a cadet honor guard fired a volley of shots as it was lowered into the grave. He would have liked the wildness of his resting place and the precision of the ceremony, but the raised gray slab that marks his grave is not his true memorial. That is to be found in the very fabric of the United States. The lines he drew in the wilderness did not simply define its states and its frontiers, they carried values of government and order and public service that molded his country's identity.

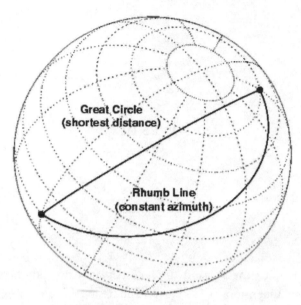

A Great Circle and Rhumb Line

constructed in the 1720s, zenith sectors abruptly changed the parameters of accuracy in stargazing. The largest examples were up to twenty-five feet long and suspended vertically so that the viewer had to lie on the ground staring upward, but their magnifying power and concentrated view of stars when they were directly overhead and most clear of refraction almost immediately brought about two discoveries: that the earth wobbles on its axis, and that in the time a star's light takes to reach earth, a star will have shifted its position slightly. Minute though these distortions were, once they had been eliminated, observation of the stars could achieve new levels of precision. One immediate payoff was the discovery in 1736 by the French astronomer Pierre-Louis de Maupertuis, using a zenith sector in Lapland, that the earth was not round but, as Isaac Newton had predicted, flattened at the poles likes a squashed orange. That Mason and Dixon were equipped with a six-foot-long zenith sector specially built for them by John Bird of London, with such added improvements as a micrometer screw that allowed adjustments to the nearest half second of arc, indicated their status. It was, as Thomas Penn remarked with some pride, "a very well executed and most curious Instrument," which had cost him three times as much as the inferior one provided by Lord Baltimore.

Appendix

Great Circle

In two dimensions the shortest distance between two points is a straight line. In three dimensions it is a curve. The basic problem this presents can be seen by comparing a conventional map with a globe. On the map, it may seem that the shortest distance from London to New York, for example, is a straight line running southwest across the Atlantic, but in three-dimensional reality, as transatlantic travelers quickly notice, the shortest route actually takes a northerly course passing close to Greenland. Hence the sight of glaciers from an aircraft window and, in an earlier age, the tragic fate of the *Titanic*. This route, known as a Great Circle, is a circumference of the earth. Extended beyond New York, it passes through the Gulf of Mexico and the Pacific to New Zealand on the far side of the globe and returns through Asia to London.

It was this paradox that Mason and Dixon used to check that their line really did run east-west along a parallel. Instead of following a compass bearing of 90° due west from their starting point, Charles Mason calculated that they should follow a Great Circle directed at 89°55′51″ west of north. This would bend away to the north from the parallel but recross it after about twelve miles. The separation at its widest point ought to be no more than twenty feet. At every mile an offset, or perpendicular line from the Great Circle, would be measured out to the parallel, and at the point of intersection elaborate checks using a zenith sector, or vertically aligned telescope, were undertaken to establish longitude and latitude.

The quality of the science was reflected in the instrument they used. First

The stars also provided the direction that Pennsylvania's boundary was to take. Each night, as they appeared to move from east to west across the heaven, they were tracked with a transit, or rotating telescope. When the selected star reached the angle of 89°55′51″ west of north, the telescope was locked in position so that it could swing no farther, then was tipped vertically down toward the horizon where an assistant stood about half a mile away with a lantern in his hand. Shouted commands sent him right or left until he was located precisely in the crosshairs of the telescope. The spot was marked, and in daylight a line was laid out in that direction. Several stars would be tracked in the same way to reduce the chance of error, but in the morning the lantern markers were usually found to be within inches of one another.

At the point where the Great Circle intersected with the parallel, further meticulous observations and calculations taking up to a week established the precise latitude and longitude. Once any corrections had been made, a visto or avenue through the trees was cleared along the line of the parallel back to the previous intersection point with marker stones inserted at every mile.

RHUMB LINE

To confuse matters further, Andrew Ellicott devised in 1785 a method of determining a parallel that relied on a third view of what constituted due east-west. Sailors found it more convenient to follow a constant compass bearing, for example 90 degrees (due east) or 270 degrees (due west). This line, known as a rhumb line, appears on the ground as a slight upward (in the northern hemisphere) curve. The curve occurs because the vertical meridians are in fact converging toward the north pole, and cutting each at right angles imperceptibly pulls the traveler along a circle. Ellicott's method, whose accuracy depended on multiple celestial observations (Ellicott estimated that at six different points he had made a total of 366 timed sightings) at the meridianal cutting point, became the model for the running of most east-west state lines, and of the U.S.-Canadian border.

Running a meridian or north-south line presented fewer problems. Such lines make a circumference of the whole earth, converging at the north and south poles. Thus a straight line heading due north or south will automatically follow the line of a Great Circle.

Finally, to end on a note of existential anxiety, all geographical terms, including *north*, *south*, *east*, and *west*, are merely conventions, and we can never be absolutely and precisely sure where we are in the real world. Even the center of the earth, the given point for celestial navigation, shifts, because variable densities of mass below the earth's surface change the direction of the gravitational pull toward it depending on when and where the force is measured. Indeed to modern geodesists, able to detect the daily rise and fall of oceans and mountains in millimeters, the earth appears as a gigantic, pulsing, pustulating, irregular globule. To make sense of it, they assume that it takes the form of a perfect earth-shape, known as a geoid, round which a series of related but artificial coordinates can be plotted. The most commonly used system, known as WGS 84, is based on the Global Positioning System, but around the world and in different parts of the United States, regional systems using different geoids and coordinates are employed because they produce more useful local results. When questions over the precise line of boundaries in areas of conflict such as the Middle East can result in violence and bloodshed, this is not a reassuring thought.

NEVIL MASKELYNE

To safeguard the ships of the Royal Navy, Parliament offered in 1711 a prize of £20,000 (about $90,000 in an era when $300 a year would keep a family) for the most effective way to work out longitude. The answer had to be a timepiece of utter reliability so that commanders could compare the time at Greenwich, London's port, with their local time and estimate by the number of hours' difference how many degrees they had traveled to the east or west. Famously the answer was provided by the self-taught genius John Harrison, whose watches lost barely one second a day. By taking two chronometers, one keeping Greenwich time, the other adjusted to local time, a sailor could estimate his longitude after weeks at sea to within a few miles. To mariners, the villain of the piece was Britain's astronomer royal, the Reverend Nevil Maskelyne, whose machinations denied Harrison the money until shortly before his death. In the navigation of the American wilderness, however, the dry, driven, perfectionist Maskelyne is the hero because his method of celestial navigation was more precise than anything achieved with Harrison's watches.

In 1766 Maskelyne brought together a series of star maps built up by himself, and former astronomers royal such as John Flamsteed and Edmond

Halley, and combined the results with the lunar tables produced by Tobias Mayer, a German mapmaker. The results were published in the *Nautical Almanac*, and for the next forty-five years, Maskelyne personally supervised its annual production. To help navigators, he also brought out four volumes of *Tables Requisite to be used with the Nautical Ephemeris for finding the latitude and longitude at sea*, containing formulas and calculations for use with the almanac. In all these works, Maskelyne based his calculations on the time at Greenwich.

STATE FINANCES

It is notoriously difficult to arrive at accurate figures for state finances between independence and the assumption of states' debts by the federal government in 1790. Taxes were paid, at least in part, in depreciated paper money, and often a year or more late. In Pennsylvania, the numbers are especially confused due to the Enron-like accounting practices of John Nicholson, the state comptroller and financial dictator from 1782 to 1794. Nevertheless, it is clear that wherever borders were run, the states increased their revenues, largely from taxes and duties, but also from land sales.

ACKNOWLEDGMENTS

I should like to thank the Society of Authors for generously providing financial assistance in the writing of this book. The great expert in the field of early American measurement in general, and on the life of Andrew Ellicott in particular, is Silvio Bedini, formerly deputy director of the National Museum of American History at the Smithsonian Institution. I am deeply grateful for his friendship, his generosity with advice and expertise, and his kindness in making available the fruit of his own research. I thank my friend Dr. Tom Schmiedeler of Washburn University, Kansas, for his encouragement and for sharing his enthusiasm for midwestern geography. I benefited enormously from the advice and assistance of Jack Ericson, archivist at the Daniel A. Reed Library, State University of New York at Fredonia, New York, concerning the background of the Ellicott family in New York and the wider history of the Seneca. I also thank for their help Edwin Danson, whose *Drawing the Line* is the definitive account of the running of the Mason and Dixon Line; Roger Woodfill of the Surveyors' Historical Society; Dr. Penry Williams, emeritus fellow of New College, Oxford University; Alan Smith, John Roberts, and Lyn Cole. I am profoundly grateful to George Gibson of Walker & Company, who has read, criticized, and tirelessly encouraged far beyond the call of duty. As always, I am indebted to my agent, Deborah Rogers, for her enthusiasm and unwavering support. And to my wife, Marie-Louise, my eternal thanks for her loving support throughout the research and writing.

I acknowledge with gratitude the professional assistance of the staff at the London Library, the British Library, the Library of Congress, the District of Columbia Historical Society, the Massachusetts Historical Society, the American Philosophical Society, the West Point Military Academy Library, the New York Public Library, the Daniel A. Reed Library, the National Archives and Records Administration in Washington, D.C., and the National Institute of Standards and Technology in Gaithersburg, Maryland.

NOTES

FORESIGHT

2 "stretched along the western border like a cord of union": "The Significance of the Frontier in American History" (paper presented to the American Historical Association at the 1893 World's Columbian Exposition in Chicago, Illinois).

3 The scene on top of Mount Welcome is described by Andrew Ellicott (AE) in a letter to his wife, Sally (SE), July 30, 1784, quoted from *Andrew Ellicott: His life and letters* by Catherine Van Cortlandt Matthews (New York: Grafton Press, ca. 1908) (referred to as *AE Life*).

8 John Cotton's sermon "The Divine Right to Occupy the Land" (London, 1630).

9 "I never Saw the inside of a School": *The Memoirs of Rufus Putnam*, ed. Rowena Buell (Marietta, OH: Houghton Mifflin, 1904).

9 "A doubloon is my constant gain": Draft letter in George Washington's journal, 1748. Quoted in *George Washington* by Henry Cabot Lodge, vol. 1, reprint of 1898 edition (New York: AMS Press, 1972).

10 The so-called Yankee-Pennamite War, in reality rarely more than skirmishes, lasted from 1754 to 1775. Connecticut's claim to the valley was based on its 1662 royal charter allocating it all the land from "Norrogancett [Narragansett] Bay on the East to the South Sea [Pacific Ocean] on the West parte." This battle saw the seven hundred Pennsylvania militia under Colonel William Plunkit defeated by about three hundred Connecticut settlers under Colonel Zebulon Butler, with, however, only one casualty.

11 Treaty of Westphalia: Despite the tendency to downplay Westphalia's significance in the development of the nation-state, it remains the most convenient moment from which to date the growing importance of territory over person as the chief symbol of the state. This trend is reflected in the different emphases offered by Hugo Grotius's 1625 *De jure belli et pacis* and by Emmerich de Vattel in *The Laws of Nations or the Principles of Natural Law* in 1758. www.lonang.com/exlibris/vattel/index.html.

12 "many are the waking Hours": Andrew Ellicott to Sarah Ellicott, September 11, 1785, *AE Life*.

12 "to support a government I venerate": Andrew Ellicott to Timothy Pickering, June 19, 1799, Papers of Andrew Ellicott, Library of Congress, control number mm 75019679 (referred to as Papers).

13 "he has the appearance of an antient [sic] athlete": entry in Ellicott's personal journal, *AE Life*.

14 "Here, every citizen": Morris Birkbeck, *Letters from Illinois* (1818).

14 " 'Twas they who rode the trackless bush": "Pioneers" by Andrew Barton "Banjo" Paterson, first published in *Town and Country Journal*, December 19, 1896.

15 "Asia for us is that same America": Quoted in *Natasha's Dance: A Cultural History of Russia* by Orlando Figes (London: Allen Lane, 2002).

Chapter 1

17 The summer of 1784: "Meteorological Imaginings and Conjectures" by Benjamin Franklin (May 1784), printed in *Memoirs of the Literary and Philosophical Society of Manchester* (London, 1819).

18 "If we can have clear Weather": Personal journal entry, November 12, 1784, *AE Life*.

20 "laudable example": Bk. 1, chap. 18, "Of the Establishment of a Nation in a Country," *The Laws of Nations or the Principles of Natural Law* by Emmerich de Vattel (1758), www.lonang.com/exlibris/vattel/index.html.

21 The history of Solebury Township can be found in chap. 18, *The History of Bucks County, Pennsylvania* by W. H. Davis (Philadelphia, 1905).

21 The Ellicott family history was assembled by AE's great-niece Martha E. Tyson in *A Brief Account of the Settlement of Ellicott's Mills. With fragments of history therewith connected* (Baltimore: Maryland Historical Society, Peabody Fund Publications no. 4, 1867). Joseph Ellicott Sr., AE's father, inherited ten run-down houses in Devon, England, in 1767. A typescript record of his journey to sell them and invest the proceeds in clockmaking tools can be found in his Journal to England from December 18, 1766, to September 21, 1767, Holland Land Company records, Reel 15, Buf 17, Daniel A. Reed Library, SUNY Fredonia (referred to as HLC). The will of Samuel Blaker revealed a feud with his son-in-law over a loan of $200 and near disinheritance of his daughter, Judith. She had good grounds for her shortness of temper.

23 "I would wish thee": Judith Ellicott to Joseph Ellicott, June 5, 1804, HLC, Reel 5.

23 "I never was caught in bed": AE to James Wilkinson, April 4, 1801, Papers.

23 "I never went to bed": AE to Thomas Pickering, January 31, 1799, Papers.

23 "I do not like the Country": AE to SE, July 2, 1784, *AE Life*.

24 "bold and indigent strangers": *The Conquest of the Old Southwest* by Archibald Henderson (New York: Century Company, 1920).

24 "those mad People": Benjamin Franklin to Dr. Dadwaldr Evans, July 13, 1765.

24 Thomas Cresap: *Thomas Cresap: Maryland Frontiersman* by Kenneth P. Bailey (Boston: Christopher Publishing House, 1944). AE's meeting: May 17, 1785, *AE Life*. Meeting with George Washington: March 17, 1747–48, *The Diaries of George Washington*, vol. 1, ed. Donald Jackson (Charlottesville: University Press of Virginia, 1976).

27 "The greatest Estates we have": Washington to John Posey, June 24, 1767. George Washington Papers.

28 Charles Mason and Jeremiah Dixon: The complications of Mason and Dixon's methods are lucidly explained and illustrated in *Drawing the Line: How Mason and Dixon Surveyed the Most Famous Border in America* by Edwin Danson (New York: John Wiley & Sons, 2001). *Mason & Dixon* by Thomas Pynchon (New York: Henry Holt, 1997). A. H. Mason, ed., *Journal of Charles Mason (1728–1786) and Jeremiah Dixon (1733–1779)*, Memoirs of the American Philosophical Society, vol. 76 (Philadelphia: American Philosophical Society, 1969).

31 "You were in your young days": AE to Robert Patterson, March 23, 1800.

31 "[Pennsylvania] is my native country": Note in personal journal, December 6, 1785, *AE Life*.

32 Almanacs: "The Maryland Press, 1777–1790" by Joseph Towne Wheeler (Baltimore: Maryland Historical Society, 1938). "The Archives of Maryland," vol. 0438, p. 0103.

32 "the most despised": *A History of American Literature* by Moses Coit Tyler (New York: Putnam & Sons, 1881).

34 "The old Gentleman had always too much": *David Rittenhouse* by Brooke Hindle (Princeton: Princeton University Press, 1964).

35 The results showed that the Mount Welcome observatory: Ibid.

CHAPTER 2

38 David Rittenhouse: Hindle, *Rittenhouse*.

40 "Conceive a Country": AE to SE, June 20, 1785, *AE Life*.

40 Running Pennsylvania's western border and the conditions encountered come from AE's journal and letters in *AE Life*.

41 Modern Pennsylvania measures just over forty-five thousand square miles. Of this, the northerly wedge claimed by Connecticut and New York between the Delaware River and Lake Erie accounted for almost five thousand square miles. The western slice claimed by Virginia would have removed close to one thousand square miles south of the Ohio River, and almost twice as many more to the north of it would have gone to the United States. Many different reasons are advanced for Pennsylvania's nickname, the Keystone State: the fixing of its boundaries along with those of six of the original states—New York, Connecticut, New Jersey, Delaware, Maryland, and Virginia—seems the most plausible contender.

42 Pennsylvania's economy: Only Germany after the First World War compares with the economic roller coaster that took the United States from hyperinflation to hypodeflation between 1775 and 1785. Within that general picture, the shortage of cash from the early 1780s in the northern states exacerbated the problem there. From Charles A. Beard's *An Economic Interpretation of the Constitution of the United States* (New York: Macmillan, 1935) by way of Forrest Macdonald's *We the People: The Economic Origins of the Constitution* (Chicago: University of Chicago Press, 1958) to David B. Robertson's *The Constitution and America's Destiny* (St Louis: University of Missouri, 2005), the literature on the economic effect upon constitutional reform is intense and combative. That the deliberations in Philadelphia generated an inspired dynamic is undeniable, but they did so against a background created by the economic power and ruthlessness of the states.

42 "Very few in this Town": "A Road Closed: Rural Insurgency in Post-Independence Pennsylvania" by Terry Bouton, *Journal of American History* 87, no. 3 (December 2000).

42 "these cursed hungry caterpillars": "A Serious Address to the Inhabitants of Granville County, containing an Account of our deplorable Situation we suffer . . . and some necessary Hints with Respect to a Reformation" by George Sims, June 6, 1765, quoted in Henderson, *Conquest of Old Southwest*.

42 The Regulators: "The North Carolina Regulation, 1766–1776: A Class Conflict" by Marvin L. Kay, in *The American Revolution: Explorations in the History of American Radicalism*, ed. Alfred F. Young (De Kalb: Northern Illinois University Press, 1976).

42 "How long will ye": *An Impartial Relation of the First Causes of the Recent Differences in Public Affairs Etc* by Herman Husband (New Bern, 1770), http://www.historymatters .gmu.edu/d/6233/.

44 "New Jersey is *our* country": "Obstacles to the Constitution" by Chief Justice Warren E. Burger, Supreme Court Historical Society 1987 Yearbook.

45 Thomas Jefferson's emotional devastation at Martha's death was widely noted. Patsy's account and Randolph's are cited in *Understanding Thomas Jefferson* by E. M. Halliday (New York: HarperCollins, 2001). I incline to the view of his biographer Joseph P. Ellis that in his grief Jefferson learned "he would rather be lonely than be vulnerable." *American Sphinx* by Joseph P. Ellis (New York: Knopf, 1997).

46 "Nature intended me": Jefferson to P. S. Dupont de Nemours, Washington, March 2, 1809, *The Letters of Thomas Jefferson: 1743–1826*, http://odur.let.rug.nl/~usa/P/tj3/ writings/brf/jeflxx.htm.

47 "proposed to lay off every county": *Autobiography* by Thomas Jefferson, in *Thomas Jefferson: Writings: Autobiography, Notes on the State of Virginia, Public and Private Papers, Addresses, Letters* (1984).

48 "if we can obtain an indisputed title": Thomas McKean to Samuel Adams, August 6, 1782, *Letters of Delegates to Congress, 1774—1789*, ed. Paul H. Smith et al. (Washington, D.C.: Library of Congress, 1976–2000).

49 by his estimate it could be run: "Report on the Reduction of the Civil List," March 4, 1784, *The Works of Thomas Jefferson*, ed. Paul L. Ford (New York and London: G. P. Putnam's Sons, 1904–5).

50 "leave it to [the other delegations] to come forward": Thomas Jefferson to Benjamin Harrison, governor of Virginia, March 3, 1784, ibid.

50 "the democratic principle is contained": *Origins of the American rectangular land survey system, 1784–1800* by W. D. Pattison (University of Chicago, Department of Geography Research Paper 50, 1957).

CHAPTER 3

53 Although the 1790 census recorded the population of the city of Philadelphia as only 28,522, the number more than doubled with the addition of the rest of Philadelphia County. According to the census, Baltimore contained 13,503 inhabitants. Benjamin Franklin was responsible for such prewar innovations in Philadelphia as the fire service, municipal cleaning, public library, etc., and postwar Philadelphia was home not only to the American Philosophical Society, but to painters such as Gilbert Stuart, Benjamin West, and Charles W. Peale.

54 AE's state of mind emerges both in his letters to SE, and in a personal journal kept during this period. *AE Life.*

55 "If you are not in fashion": Chesterfield's *Letters to His Son* went through twenty-nine full editions between 1775 and 1800. Its popularity in the United States led to the publication of nine exclusively American editions during the same period. More than a hundred abridgments and adaptations also appeared, many in the United States, occasionally bound in with Benjamin Franklin's homelier precepts. Chesterfield's advice heavily influenced numerous manners books, such as John Gregory's popular *A Father's Legacy to His Daughters*, that were published in the United States in the late eighteenth and early nineteenth centuries. See "Authorship, Print and Public in Chesterfield's Letters to His Son" by Ann C. Dean, *Studies in English Literature, 1500–1900* 45, no. 3 (2005).

56 The Wyoming Valley dispute is well described in Alfred Van Dusen's *Connecticut* (New York: Random House, 1961), and in the folksy *History of Luzerne County*, ed. H. C. Bradley (Pennsylvania: SB Nelson & Co., 1893).

58 AE's new method of running a guideline is described in *AE Life*, and in greater depth in AE's "A Letter . . . to Robert Patterson," *Transactions of the American Philosophical Society* 4 (1799): 32–51.

59 "My dear, In consequence of your distresses": AE to SE, June 12, 1786, Papers.

61 "This circumstance must be": AE to SE, May 29, 1787, *AE Life.* For Wyoming Valley, see Bradley, ed., *History of Luzerne County.*

62 The distorting effects of paper money on the political and economic society of the United States appear in John Ferling's excellent *A Leap in the Dark: The Struggle to Create the American Republic* (New York: Oxford University Press, 2003). Earlier and opposite perspectives come from Beard and the nineteenth-century commentator Alexander del Mar in *History of Money in America from the Earliest Times to the Establishment of the Constitution* (Hawthorne, CA: Omni, 1966 reprint of 1899 edition). The most authoritative modern source on taxation is Woody Holton's " 'From the Labours of Others': The War Bonds Controversy and the Origins of the Constitution in New England," *William & Mary Quarterly* 61, no. 2 (April 2004).

62 Index of wholesale prices: *Wholesale Prices in Philadelphia, 1780–1861* by Anne Bezanson, Robert D. Gray, and Miriam Hussey (Philadelphia: University of Pennsylvania Press, 1936).

62 "I lent the old Congress": Benjamin Franklin, February 1788, quoted in the preface to 1935 edition of *An Economic Interpretation of the Constitution of the United States* by Charles A. Beard (New York: Macmillan Company, 1962).

63 There is no modern work on boundaries and land sales, but contemporary references indicate that the connection between establishing secure borders and selling land to raise revenue and soak up paper money was taken for granted. The citizens of the "town of Glocester," for example, petitioned the Rhode Island General Assembly in 1786 "to hit upon some mode to cause the back Lands to be Settled in such a manner: as it can be done: as will Discharge the Public Debt."

64 "These lands might enable us to pay off ": North Carolina delegates Hugh Williamson and William Blount to Alexander Martin, October 22, 1782, *Letters of Delegates to Congress: Volume 19, August 1, 1782–March 11, 1783* by Paul Smith et al., eds.

64 The most complete account of early land sales in Pennsylvania is to be found in the Pennsylvania State Archives, Land Records, http://www.phmc.state.pa.us/bah/dam/landrec .htm. The essential guide is Donna Munger's *Pennsylvania Land Records: A History and Guide for Research* (Wilmington, DE: Scholarly Resources, 1991). Donation Lands were intended for the redemption of paper money paid to officers and soldiers in lieu of cash. Depreciation Lands were intended to compensate for the falling value of paper money. The 1780 Depreciation Act set the face value of its certificates as equal to gold and silver. The falling value of paper was reflected in subsequent acts that increased the ratio of paper to cash from 3:1 up to 75:1 in 1781—at which level a cash-rich buyer could make a killing.

64 "All I am now worth": Beard, *An Economic Interpretation.*

65 Distress in western Pennsylvania is the subject of Terry Bouton's moving "A Road Closed: Rural Insurgency in Post-Independence Pennsylvania," *Journal of American History* 87, no. 3 (December 2000).

65 figures issued by Alexander Hamilton: Alexander Hamilton, "A General Statement of the Domestic Debt, according to the Returns Made to the Treasury by the Several Commissioners Authorized to Issue Certificates of the Public Debt," *American State Papers: Finance* (Washington, DC, 1832), 1:239.

66 In 1786, Pennsylvania simply ignored: Burger, "Obstacles to the Constitution."

66 The fiscal weakness of the Continental Congress is underlined by Holton's " 'From the Labours of Others.' "

67 "almost the whole of the Specie": Board of Treasury Report, *Journal of the Continental Congress,* September 29, 1786.

67 The definitive history of the U.S. Public Land Survey is C. Albert White's *A History of the Rectangular Survey System* (Washington, DC: Government Printing Office, 1982). See also W. D. Pattison, *The Beginning of the American Rectangular Land Survey System* (Ohio Historical Society, 1970), and *Dividing the Land: Early American beginnings of our private property mosaic* by Edward T. Price (Chicago: University of Chicago, 1995). Andro Linklater's *Measuring America* (New York: Walker Books, 2002) presents the survey as the hidden infrastructure of western expansion.

68 the United States sold fewer than one hundred thousand acres: Pattison, *Beginning of the American Rectangular Land Survey*.

68 "Nothing occurs as a probable mode of relief ": Treasury Report, September 29, 1786.

68 The strength of the secessionist movement in New England is explored in *A Wilderness So Immense: The Louisiana Purchase and the Destiny of America* by Jon Kukla (New York: Knopf, 2003).

69 The nature of Shays's Rebellion remains hotly debated. The traditional context, that subsistence farmers were protesting the arrival of the cash economy, was put forth by David Zatmary in *Shays' Rebellion: The Making of an Agrarian Insurrection* (Amherst: University of Massachusetts Press, 1980); but Leonard L. Richards makes a convincing case for a particular cause, the pressure of taxation to pay bondholders, in *Shays's Rebellion: The American Revolution's Final Battle* (Philadelphia: University of Pennsylvania Press, 2002). However, the rebels' name and the nature of their demands also offer obvious connections to the prewar Regulators and the later Whiskey Rebellion.

80 For Washington's correspondence concerning Shays's Rebellion with Henry Knox and James Madison, see *The Papers of George Washington: Confederation Series*, vol. 4, ed. W. W. Abbot (Charlottesville and London: University Press of Virginia, 1995).

CHAPTER 4

72 AE's encounter with the Seneca is described in his report "Observatory on the West Side of the Conawango," August 29, 1787, to the President and Supreme Executive Council of Pennsylvania, and in a letter to SE, September 13, 1787, Papers.

73 "with chain and compass": *Thirty Thousand Miles with John Heckewelder*, ed. Paul A. Wallace (Pittsburgh: University of Pittsburgh Press, 1958).

74 The competition between New York and the United States for control over the Iroquois lands emerges from *The Divided Ground: Indians, Settlers and the Northern Borderland of the American Revolution* by Alan Taylor (New York: Knopf, 2006), and Max M. Mintz's *Seeds of Empire: The American Revolutionary Conquest of the Iroquois* (New York: New York University Press, 1999).

79 "it is in our United capacity we are known": George Washington to his brother John Augustine Washington, June 15, 1783, George Washington Papers.

79 "all the parts combined": George Washington, Farewell Address, September 17, 1796, George Washington Papers.

79 "that all business between them": George Washington to Timothy Pickering, September 4, 1790, George Washington Papers.

81 "It will be fortunate": George Washington to Thomas Jefferson, April 1, 1791, George Washington Papers.

81 "The States individually": George Washington to Alexander Hamilton, April 4, 1791, George Washington Papers.

82 Unfortunately no reliable biography of John Nicholson has yet been published. The details of the accusations against him as comptroller general are taken from *The Pennsylvania state trials: containing the impeachment, trial, and acquittal of Francis Hopkinson, and John Nicholson, esquires* (Philadelphia: printed by Francis Bailey, 1794).

83 "This Mr Gorham": AE to SE, August 15, 1789, Papers.

84 "I have long known Mr Andrew Ellicott": Manuscript reproduced in *AE Life*.

84 AE's report to Washington, January 15, 1790.

86 James Madison's extensive, unofficial notes are the source for the flavor of debates in the Constitutional Convention.

87 "the U.S. are sovereign": Oliver Ellsworth, August 20, 1787, James Madison's "Notes on Debates."

89 "The moment the idea is admitted": John Adams, "A Defense of the American Constitutions," 1787.

90 "Down this chasm": *AE Life*.

CHAPTER 5

91 In the 1890s, when Washington, D.C., was being stripped of its nineteenth-century clutter to bring it back to the original design, Pierre L'Enfant was romantically portrayed as the tragic genius who had single-handedly brought the city into being. The contributions of Washington, Jefferson, and the commissioners were largely pushed aside, and AE was ignored or vilified. Later scholarship has redressed some of the balance, as in *Thomas Jefferson and the National Capital*, ed. Saul K. Padover (Washington: Government Printing Office, 1946), and Kenneth R. Bowling's *Creation of Washington, D.C.: The Idea and Location of the American Capital* (Fairfax: George Mason University Press, 1991); the Library of Congress's unrivaled collection of maps is invaluable; and the Mary Ann Overbeck Capitol Hill History Project—www.capitolhillhistory.org/index.html—offers particularly useful ideas about the forces involved.

91 Report in the *Georgetown Weekly Ledger*, March 12, 1791: quoted in "The Survey of the Federal Territory," in *With Compass and Chain: American Surveyors and Their Instruments* by Silvio Bedini (Frederick, MD: Professional Surveyor Publishing, 2001).

92 Jefferson had discussed the exact site in "Notes on the Permanent Seat of Congress," April 13, 1784, Ford, ed., *Works of Thomas Jefferson*.

93 AE's work and instruments: Bedini, *With Compass and Chain*.

94 The most reliable biography of Benjamin Banneker is Silvio Bedini's *The Life of Benjamin Banneker* (New York: Scribner, 1972).

95 Pierre L'Enfant has been the subject of innumerable biographies and articles. The most useful are Elizabeth S. Kite's *L'Enfant and Washington, 1791–1792* (Baltimore: Johns Hopkins Press, 1929); and H. Paul Caemmerer, *The Life of Pierre Charles L'Enfant, Planner of the City of Washington* (New York: Da Capo Press, 1950).

96 "'The plan should be drawn'": L'Enfant to George Washington, September 11, 1789, Caemmerer, *Life of L'Enfant*.

97 Correspondence between George Washington and Thomas Jefferson, L'Enfant and the commissioners, is to be found in "The George Washington Papers at the Library of Congress," http://memory.loc.gov/ammem/mgwquery.html.

99 "If the commissioners live near the place": Thomas Jefferson, "Opinion on the Capital," November 29, 1790, Ford, ed., *Works of Thomas Jefferson*.

101 On the influence of Versailles, see *The Making of America: A history of city planning in the United States* by John W. Reps (Princeton: Princeton University Press, 1965).

101 AE's help to L'Enfant, see Bedini, "Survey of the Federal Territory."

107 L'Enfant's dismissal and the growing interference of the commissioners emerges from Washington's correspondence. See "George Washington Papers" and Bowling's *Creation of Washington*.

109 The evidence for AE's responsibility for naming Pennsylvania Avenue lies in the maps. Much ink has been spent in identifying one or another map as L'Enfant's or AE's, but since L'Enfant could not draw a scale map, the December map is manifestly a collaboration. The February map is AE's.

110 The deterioration of relations between AE and the commissioners emerges in his letters to SE, *AE Life*; his correspondence with Jefferson, in Ford, ed., *Works of Thomas Jefferson*; and the commissioners' correspondence with George Washington, in Padover, ed., *Thomas Jefferson and the National Capital*.

114 For the effect of the capital's failure on urban developments in the United States, see Reps, *Making of America*.

CHAPTER 6

117 The battle of wills between the president and the state of Pennsylvania emerges from his correspondence and journal. See "George Washington Papers."

117 "The President of the United States": Henry Knox to Thomas Mifflin, May 24, 1794, "Papers relating to the Establishment at Presqu' Isle," in John B. Lynn and William Egle, eds., *Pennsylvania Archives*, second series (Harrisburg, 1890).

117 "The interference of the General Government": *AE Life*.

118 the Whiskey Rebellion: see Bouton, "A Road Closed"; and Thomas P. Slaughter's *Whiskey Rebellion: Frontier Epilogue to the American Revolution* (New York: Oxford University Press, 1986).

120 The background to the San Lorenzo Treaty is covered in Kukla's *Wilderness So Immense*.

121 "The people of this region": *The Conquest of the Old Southwest* by Archibald Henderson (New York: The Century Company, 1920).

121 "This country will in a few years Revolt": Kukla, *Wilderness So Immense*.

123 AE's accounts of his work in demarcating the boundary with Spain come from his *Journal of Andrew Ellicott*; his correspondence with Timothy Pickering and other official letters held by the Library of Congress, Papers; and his letters to SE, *AE Life*. For his chief adversary, see *Gayoso: The Life of a Spanish Governor in the Mississippi Valley, 1789–1799* by Jack D. L. Holmes (Baton Rouge: Louisiana State University Press, 1965).

125 Brief notes on Natchez personalities appear in Professor Kenneth Stampp's introduction to the *Records of Ante-Bellum Southern Plantations from the Revolution Through the Civil War* (Frederick, MD: University Publications of America, 1985).

127 Albert James Pickett's *History of Alabama and incidentally of Georgia and Mississippi from the earliest times* (1851), now online—http://homepages.rootsweb.com /~cmamcrk4/pktfm.html—is dated but has firsthand memories and accounts of events.

128 James Wilkinson's character emerges most clearly from his self-serving autobiography, *Memoirs of My Own Times* (Philadelphia: Abraham Small, 1816). The opposite view comes from Daniel Clark's devastating exposé, *Proofs of the Corruption of General James Wilkinson and of His Connexion with Aaron Burr* (Philadelphia: Hall & Pierie, 1809), http://history.hanover.edu/hhr/98/hhr98_1.html. Jon Kukla offers a modern interpretation in *A Territory So Immense*, and James Savage's online essay "Spaniards, Scoundrels, and Statesmen: General James Wilkinson and the Spanish Conspiracy, 1787—1790," http://history.hanover.edu/hhr/98/hhr98_1.html, gives a useful summary.

131 "to leave it to the discretion": John Adams, "Message to the Senate and House," June 12, 1797.

131 Blount's letter is quoted in William Masteron's *William Blount* (Baton Rouge: Louisiana State University Press, 1954).

134 For Lintot's warning about "the Distribution of Land," see Papers.

135 "That domestic slavery is wrong": *Journal*.

136 "I feel a consciousness": AE to Pickering, October 18, 1797, Papers.

136 William Dunbar's life is covered in *Life, Letters and Papers of William Dunbar* by Mrs. Dunbar Rowland (Jackson: Press of the Mississippi Historical Society, 1930). His letters to AE are in Papers.

137 "I would not by this": AE to Daniel Clark, September 15, 1797, Papers.

138 For the inheritance of Margaret Gayoso, see U.S. Supreme Court docket, *Robinson v. Minor*, 51 U.S. 627 (1850).

139 "By a packet just arrived": Gayoso to AE, January 10, 1798, Papers.

139 "My Love": AE to SE, February 8, 1798, Papers.

CHAPTER 7

141 The sources for AE's account of his onerous running of the boundary and dramatic journey are his *Journal*, Papers, and *AE Life*.

141 "The situation of our encampment": *Journal*.

142 "It is a pleasing and interesting reflection": AE to Gayoso, May 22, 1798, Papers.

143 "This mode tho' less scientific": AE to Pickering, July 12, 1798, Papers.

143 The account of the mutiny is contained only in letters in Papers.

145 The discovery of Wilkinson's treachery is referred to in the *Journal*, *AE Life*, and AE's letter to Daniel Clark in 1808.

147 "When you consider": AE to Pickering, January 12, 1799, Papers.

148 "When you look at the picture": AE to SE, February 17, 1799, *AE Life*.

149 The fullest picture of Benjamin Hawkins comes from *The Collected Works of Benjamin Hawkins, 1796–1810*, ed. Thomas Foster (Tuscaloosa: University of Alabama Press, 2003).

150 The voyage of *The Sally* is well told in the *Journal*, which deserves reading for that if for no other reason.

154 AE's bizarre meeting with Bowles and Lieutenant James Woolridge appears in the *Journal*. Woolridge's career in the Royal Navy reached its apogee in 1809 when, as captain of a fireship, he steered with suicidal bravery into the midst of a French fleet, throwing himself overboard just before it exploded, and destroyed four enemy frigates, a feat for which he was awarded a gold chain, one hundred guineas, and a ceremonial sword.

156 "a mound of earth thrown up": Ellicott's Mound became famous when the dispute between Florida and Georgia about their border was finally resolved in 1872 with both sides agreeing that since it was the one obvious point their surveyors could identify, the border should run from the Mound rather than the center of the swamp.

CHAPTER 8

159 AE's domestic life back in Philadelphia is covered by letters to his daughters and wife in *AE Life* and Papers. His correspondence with Jefferson is in Papers and Ford, ed., *Works of Thomas Jefferson*.

160 "I have been obliged": AE to James Wilkinson, April 13, 1800, Papers.

162 From the wide-ranging literature on the Burr conspiracy, the most useful for this study has been Jonathan Daniels's *Ordeal of Ambition: Jefferson, Hamilton, Burr* (Garden City, NY: Doubleday Co., 1970). But Daniel Clark Jr.'s *Proofs of the Corruption of General James Wilkinson* is indispensable.

163 "[I] always shall be designated by the number 13": William R. Shepard, "Wilkinson and the Beginnings of the Spanish Conspiracy," *American Historical Review* 9 (1903–4). But even by 1808, his secret was sufficiently well-known for Clark to allude to him as "Number Thirteen" in the *Proofs*.

163 The betrayal of Lewis and Clark came in the "Reflections," offered by Wilkinson to Folch, *Southwestern Historical Quarterly* 1 (July 1913).

165 "I fear you will meet with an attack": Jackson to Claiborne, November 12, 1806, cited in "James Wilkinson: a defense by his grandson" by James Wilkinson, *Louisiana Historical Quarterly* vol. 1, no. 2, 1918.

167 For the response to the Louisiana Purchase, see Kukla, *Wilderness So Immense.*

168 Louisiana Purchase as a gigantic reservation: Thomas Jefferson explored the idea in various forms but most clearly in a letter of August 12, 1803, to John Breckinridge: "The best use we can make of the country for some time, will be to give establishments in it to the Indians on the East side of the Missipi [sic], in exchange for their present country."

169 The growth of the Public Land Survey, Putnam's failings, and Mansfield's strengths are covered in my *Measuring America.*

170 Lincoln's reasons for the family's move to Illinois were given to John L. Scripps of the *Chicago Press and Tribune.*

171 almost 80 percent of the population occupied just 4 percent: Wilma A. Dunaway, "Speculators and Settler Capitalists," in *Appalachia in the Making: The Mountain South in the Nineteenth Century*, Mary B. Pudup, et al., eds. (Chapel Hill: University of North Carolina Press, 1995).

172 The results of AE's astronomy were consistently reported in the *Transactions of the American Philosophical Society* from 1804 through 1809.

173 AE's contributions to the Wilkinson trial are taken from Papers; his letters are also included in Clark's *Proofs.*

176 The reception for James Monroe in 1817 is explored in " 'Look on This Picture . . . And on This!' Nationalism, Localism, and Partisan Images of Otherness in the United States, 1787–1820" by Andrew W. Robertson, *American Historical Review* 106.4 (October 2001).

177 Andrew Jackson and the law: The background comes from David Hackett Fischer's *Albion's Seed: Four British Folkways in America* (New York: Oxford University Press, 1991).

177 "treated property offenders much more harshly": Edward L. Ayers, *Vengeance and Justice: Crime and Punishment in the Nineteenth-Century American South* (New York: Oxford University Press, 1984).

178 The paid sheriff was introduced by Jackson's ordinance proclaimed in Pensacola on July 21, 1821.

CHAPTER 9

180 John Quincy Adams's fifty-one volumes of diaries, kept at the Massachusetts Historical Society and now online, are the prime source for his life. See http://www .masshist.org/jqadiaries/.

180 The problems of the eastern portion of the Canadian frontier were well documented in an exhibition, "John Mitchell's Map: An Irony of Empire," on April 21, 1997, at the Osher Map Library and Smith Center for Cartographic Education, University of Southern Maine. See http://www.usm.maine.edu/~maps/mitchell/.

181 AE's demarcation of the Georgia–North Carolina border, and his days at West Point are covered in *AE Life* and Papers.

184 The Monroe Doctrine and Adams's subsequent congressional career are best explained in Samuel Flagg Bemis's two volumes, *John Quincy Adams and the Foundations of American Foreign Policy* (New York: Knopf, 1949) and *John Quincy Adams and the Union* (New York: Knopf, 1956).

186 Adams's version of manifest destiny is quoted in Walter A. McDougall's *Promised Land, Crusader State: The American Encounter with the World Since 1776* (New York: Houghton Mifflin, 1997).

187 "If the Union must be dissolved": Adams's diary, 1819.

187 AE's reaction to western preachers: May 17, 1785, *AE Life*.

188 For Dow's preaching style, see "'Liquid Fire Within Me': Language, Self and Society in Transcendentalism and Early Evangelicalism, 1820–1860" by Ian Frederick Finseth (master's thesis in English, University of Virginia, August 1995).

189 The legend of the turtle-snapping Davy Crockett began with Matthew St. Clair Clarke's *Life and Adventures of Colonel David Crockett of West Tennessee* (Cincinnati, 1833).

189 John Melish's comment on the Public Land System appears in my *Measuring America*. Edward Gibbon Wakefield's reaction was more influential than Melish's, because his writing spread the idea throughout the British empire that the distribution of land could radically influence the type of society that grew up subsequently.

191 Among the many authorities on the influence of slavery on U.S. history, one dominant theme came from David Brion Davis's broad view of it as a cultural rather than purely economic phenomenon in *Slavery and Human Progress* (New York: Oxford University Press, 1984). It was counterbalanced by James L. Houston's overtly economic and property-based views in *Calculating the Value of the Union: Slavery, Property Rights, and the Economic Origins of the Civil War* (Chapel Hill: University of North Carolina Press, 2003).

194 "We cultivate certain great staples": John C. Calhoun's "South Carolina Exposition and Protest," December 19, 1828.

197 Unequivocally if repellently, any doubts about the profitability of slavery were removed by Robert W. Fogel and Stanley L. Engerman's *Time on the Cross: The Economics of American Negro Slavery* (reissue edition, New York: W. W. Norton and Company, 1995).

198 Timothy Flint's comments came in his *Recollections of the Last Ten Years, Passed in Occasional Residences and Journeyings in the Valley of Mississippi* (Boston: Cummings, Hilliard and Company, 1826).

198 Ashbel Smith's remark, made in a letter December 28, 1843, was quoted in Harriet Smither's "English Abolitionism and the Annexation of Texas," *Southwestern Historical Quarterly* 32 (1929).

199 Henry Adams's remark comes in his autobiography, *The Education of Henry Adams* (Boston: Houghton Mifflin, 1918).

201 The attitude of some New Yorkers appears in Samuel J. May's *Some Recollections of Antislavery Conflict* (Boston, 1869).

201 Harriet Martineau's comment was made in her *Autobiography of Harriet Martineau* (reprint, London: Virago, 1983).

202 Grant expressed his characteristically blunt opinion that the purpose of the Mexican War was to increase the number of slave states in his autobiography, *Personal Memoirs of U. S. Grant* (New York: Charles L. Webster & Company, 1885–86).

202 Calhoun's reasons for opposing the Mexican War were put forward in a Senate speech on January 4, 1848.

203 The despair in Adams's reference to the "Utopian daydream," in "Address of John Quincy Adams to his Constituents," September 17, 1842, colored much of his public utterance in old age.

CHAPTER 10

205 Woodrow Wilson's remarks on the random creation of states in the nineteenth century appeared in "The Making of the Nation," *Atlantic Monthly*, July 1897.

205 The House of Representatives set up its Committee on Territories in 1825, followed by the Senate in 1844. The latter became Stephen Douglas's power base.

206 The Beloit College archives published online at http://www.beloit.edu/~libhome/ Archives/papers/beloitbegin.html contain Horace White's memoir of the settlement's foundation.

209 Memories of harboring slaves and of the start of the Free Soil movement in Beloit are recorded in William Fiske Brown's "In Lincoln's Time: Our College Loyalty to Union and Freedom," *Round Table*, February 10, 1911.

211 Douglas's speaking style: *Memoirs of John Quincy Adams*, vol 11, ed. Charles F. Adams (12 vols; Philadelphia, 1874–77).

211 The Senate Committee on Territories, founded in the year that Douglas entered the Senate, was dominated by him. Although the House committee was longer established, its acquiescence in his intricate deal-making indicates that during Douglas's chairmanship the Senate committee took the lead, although poor record-keeping fails to show how this was achieved.

212 Douglas's expansionist vision: *Stephen Douglas: A study in American Politics* by Allen Johnson (New York: Macmillan Company, 1908).

213 The dealings of the Committee on Territories are detailed in Johnson's *Stephen Douglas*.

215 Douglas's comment about the burning effigies is recorded in F. H. Hodder, "Stephen A. Douglas," *Chautauquan* 29 (August 1899).

215 The story of Sherman Booth is recorded in "Rescue of Joshua Glover, a Runaway Slave," in *Leading Events of Wisconsin History* by Henry E. Legler (Milwaukee: Sentinel Company, 1898).

216 Thoreau's call for resistance came in a speech, "Slavery in Massachusetts," delivered at Framingham, Massachusetts, July 4, 1854. "The less government" is from Ralph Waldo Emerson's *Politics*, published in 1844. Walt Whitman's comment was sent to Mikhail Bakunin. Thoreau's disowning of American government was made in his 1849 essay "On Civil Disobedience."

217 Angelina Grimke's reference to *"human* rights" comes in "Letter XII Human Rights Not Founded on Sex," addressed to Catherine E. Beecher, October 2, 1837.

217 David Walker's *Appeal to the Colored Citizens of the World*, September 1829, http://docsouth.unc.edu/nc/walker/walker.html.

218 Lincoln's attack on the Know-Nothings was made in a letter to Joshua F. Speed, August 24, 1855, in *The Collected Works of Abraham Lincoln*, vol. 2, ed. Roy P. Basler (New Brunswick, NJ: Rutgers University Press, 1953).

219 AE's fight to reform West Point Military Academy is contained in the collection of Ellicott papers held at the academy's library. They include correspondence with James Monroe, General Joseph Swift, Sylvanus Thayer, and Jared Mansfield.

219 The history of the Corps of Topographical Engineers and its predecessor, the Bureau of Topographical Engineers, is told by Henry P. Beers in the "History of the U.S. Topographical Engineers, 1818–1863," *Military Engineer* 34 (June 1942).

220 Stephen Douglas as the promoter of railroads is the topic of Hodder's "Stephen A. Douglas."

221 The outrage created in the north by the Kansas-Nebraska Act was expressed by the Ohio senators and representatives who signed the "Address to the People," dated January 19, 1854.

221 The bloodthirsty threats by pro- and antislavers in the rush for Kansas are quoted in William G. Cutler's *History of the State of Kansas* (Chicago: Andreas, 1883).

222 The birth of Lawrence, Kansas, is detailed in the Reverend Richard Cordley's *A History of Lawrence, Kansas* (Lawrence: Lawrence Journal Press, 1895).

223 The Lincoln-Douglas debates: See *In the Name of the People: Speeches and Writings of Lincoln and Douglas in the Ohio Campaign of 1859*, ed. Harry V. Jaffa and Robert Johannsen (Columbus: Ohio State University Press, 1959).

227 Henry Adams's description of Washington, D.C., appears in *The Education of Henry Adams*.

CHAPTER 11

230 Chase's ruling was delivered in the case of *State of Texas v. White*, 74 U.S. 700, December 1868.

232 In his speech of December 18, 1865, when Stevens put this argument that the secessionist states were outside the Union, he also referred to them as "dead carcasses."

233 The title of Ralph Korngold's biography *Thaddeus Stevens: A Being Darkly Wise and Rudely Great* (New York: Harcourt, Brace and Company, 1955) says much about his character. What set Stevens apart was not his shrewd legal brain or his relentless political maneuvering, but his capacity for what Allan Nevins in *The War for the Union: War Becomes Revolution, 1862–1863* (New York: Charles Scribner's Sons, 1960) called "a frenzy of anger." His furious passion for equality, honed by a background of poverty, found its cause in the fight for the abolition of slavery and its target in the hierarchical south.

234 "Admit the right of the seceding states": *What They Fought For, 1861–1865* by James M. McPherson (New York: Anchor Books, 1994).

234 "everywhere a rigid spirit of caste": "Three Months among the Reconstructionists," *Atlantic Monthly*, February 1866.

235 Edward Thomas's comments were made in his autobiography, *Memoirs of a Southerner* (Savannah, 1912), http://docsouth.unc.edu/fpn/thomas/thomas.html.

236 The material achievements of Reconstruction are contained in Eric Foner's admirable *Reconstruction: America's Unfinished Revolution* (New York: Harper & Row, 1988).

237 Hiram C. Whitley's dubious adventures are recounted in *A Standard History of Kansas and Kansans* by William E. Connelley (Topeka: Kansas State Historical Society, 1918).

238 Senator William Fulbright's remarks were expressed in *The Arrogance of Power* (New York: Random House, 1966).

238 The spread of Jim Crow laws is described in Foner's *Reconstruction*.

238 John Marshall Harlan's dissenting opinion was expressed in *Plessy v. Ferguson*, 163 U.S. 537 (1896).

239 Henry Adams's portrait of William H. Seward appeared in *The Education of Henry Adams*.

239 "I look off on Prince Rupert's Land and Canada": *The Life of William H. Seward* by Frederic Bancroft (New York: Harper and Brothers, 1900).

239 Seward's speech at Sitka, made on August 12, 1869, is online at the Library of Congress's page "Meeting of Frontiers."

241 The most vivid account of Sumner's attempt to lever Canada inside the U.S. frontier is Henry Adams's in his *Education of Henry Adams*.

242 Prime Minister Macdonald's desire to leave the west a wilderness was expressed in a letter dated March 27, 1865, to Sir Edward W. Watkin, now held in the National Archives of Canada.

243 "every drop of the blood": Congressman Wise's comments are recorded in *Niles' National Register*, February 5, 1842.

243 "One held one's breath": See *Education of Henry Adams*.

244 Mahan's question "What harm can we do Canada?" expresses eloquently the depth of the strategic rivalry with the British empire.

244 "I went down on my knees": *First Great Triumph: How Five Americans Made Their Country a World Power* by Warren Zimmermann (New York: Farrar, Straus & Giroux, 2002).

245 Theodore Roosevelt's Berkeley speech is quoted in David McCullough's *Mornings on Horseback: The Story of an Extraordinary Family, a Vanished Way of Life, and the Unique Child Who Became Theodore Roosevelt* (New York: Simon & Schuster, 1982).

246 Mahan's remark comparing the Philippines with Britain's Boer War appeared in his essay "The Transvaal and the Philippine Islands," *Independent* 52 (February 1900).

247 The evidence of atrocities in the Philippines was quoted in a petition addressed to Secretary of War Elihu Root, dated February 4, 1902, and signed by, among others, Mark Twain.

248 The judgment of Justice Edward White and the dissent of Justice John Marshall Harlan were given in the case of *Dorr v. United States*, 195 U.S. 138 (1904).

CHAPTER 12

250 Frederick Jackson Turner's thesis continues to tower like a battle-scarred colossus over the history of the west, however much its shortcomings are exposed. It seems useful, therefore, to be reminded of the context in which it was originally made, and how confrontational it must have sounded.

252 Woodrow Wilson responded in his essay "The Making of the Nation," *Atlantic Monthly*.

253 The artistic response to the frontier can be found in *American Sublime: Landscape Painting in the United States, 1820–1880* by Andrew Wilton and Tim Barringer (Princeton: Princeton University Press, 2003).

253 The literary response emerges generally in *Main Currents in American Thought: An interpretation of American Literature from the beginning to 1920* by Vernon Louis Parrington (New York: Harcourt Brace & Co, 1930); a more focused source is another classic, *Virgin Land: The American West as Symbol and Myth* by Henry Nash Smith (Cambridge: Harvard University Press, 1950, 1978). The mythic reality of Kit Carson is well covered in *Virgin Land*.

255 Edwin Godkin is quoted in Parrington's *Main Currents*.

256 The values of the new western school of history were brought together in *Under an Open Sky: Rethinking America's Western Past*, ed. William Cronon, George Miles, and Jay Gitlin (New York: W. W. Norton, 1992).

258 Dawes's 1887 speech: Angie Debo, *And Still the Waters Run* (New York: Gordian, 1966).

259 Mayor T. C. Henry's opinion of Wild Bill Hickok: "Myths and Realities of Frontier

Violence: A Look at the Gunfighter Saga" by Rainer Eisfeld, *Journal of Criminal Justice and Popular Culture* 3, no. 5 (1995): 106–22.

259 The realities of the Chisholm Trail and other cattle drives are revealed in numerous interviews with cowboys, held in the Library of Congress. Entitled "The Chisholm Trail," they are also available online at http://www.thechisholmtrail.com/boy1.htm.

CHAPTER 13

261 The intolerance of the Puritans toward Catholics was the major reason why French Canadians failed to join in the revolution against British rule despite a personal plea by Benjamin Franklin.

261 Franklin's own protests against German immigration came in his pamphlet "Observations Concerning the Increase of Mankind."

262 Ellis Island records reveal unequivocally that among the crowd of Irish immigrants who disembarked from the *Nevada*, Ellie King was first, and the more newsworthy Annie Moore came next with her brothers.

262 The role of the railroads in encouraging settlement in the west is covered in my *Measuring America*.

263 The articles in *New York Independent* were clearly rewritten, but the details have a firsthand authenticity. They have been republished in *The Life Stories of Undistinguished Americans, as Told by Themselves* by Hamilton Holt (New York: Routledge, 2000).

265 The appendix to Israel Zangwill's *Melting Pot* is worth quoting if only because it is almost invariably ignored.

265 James Michael Curley's 1914 comments about the Irish making Massachusetts were delivered against the background whir of thousands of Puritans turning in their graves; he is quoted in William V. Shannon's "Boston's Irish Mayors: An Ethnic Perspective," in *Boston, 1700–1980: The Evolution of Urban Politics*, ed. Ronald P. Formisano and Constance K. Burns (Westport, CT: Greenwood Press, 1984).

267 The Du Bois–Washington split is significant in demonstrating that African-Americans had to accept the same dynamics as that of other outside groups intent on sharing power. The statistics of lynching compiled by the Tuskegee Institute are evidence of how the civil rights movement differed in the ferocity with which it was resisted.

267 President Roosevelt's meeting with Walter White of the NAACP had been arranged by Eleanor Roosevelt. The result of FDR's conservative approach to civil rights was the internment of Japanese-Americans in 1941 and the decision to go to war with a segregated army.

268 The postwar civil rights movement is covered in *Race, Reform and Rebellion: The Second Reconstruction in Black America, 1945–1982* by Manning Marable (Jackson: University Press of Mississippi, 1984).

CHAPTER 14

271 The growth of barriers on either side of the San Ysidro crossing, and awareness of the intensity of the immigration debate, make the banality of the actual frontier even more striking.

272 Curzon's observation that "frontiers are indeed the razor's edge" was made in the 1907 Romanes Lecture delivered at Oxford University.

272 Francis Fukuyama's 1989 essay "The End of History?" was published in the *National Interest*.

272 Kenichi Ohmae's *The Borderless World: Power and Strategy in the Interlinked Economy* (New York: Harper Business, 1990).

273 Thomas L. Friedman's *The World Is Flat: A Brief History of the Twenty-first Century* (New York: Farrar, Straus & Giroux, 2005).

275 Elena Poniatowski's remarks were made in an interview in Venezuela, August 15, 2001.

275 Professor Samuel P. Huntington's warnings came first in his article "The Hispanic Challenge," *Foreign Policy*, March/April 2004, and were later amplified in his book *Who Are We?: The Challenges to America's National Identity* (New York: Simon & Schuster, 2004).

275 Professor Rubén Rumbaut, codirector of the Center for Research on Immigration, Population, and Public Policy at the University of California, Irvine; his conclusions appear in the recently updated and expanded *Immigrant America: A Portrait*, written with Alejandro Portes (Berkeley: University of California Press, 2006).

ENVOI

278 The account of AE's final years is derived from the West Point archive and letters in Papers.

SELECT BIBLIOGRAPHY

Andrew Ellicott's own writing is to be found in the following forms:

Papers of Andrew Ellicott—the Library of Congress's archive collection of correspondence, maps, charts, and reports of astronomical observations, chiefly concerning Ellicott's work in surveying the boundary between the United States and Florida under the San Lorenzo Treaty (1795) and also his surveys of the city of Washington, the boundary between Georgia and North Carolina, the town of Presque Isle (later Erie), Pennsylvania, and the boundary between the United States and Canada under the Treaty of Ghent (1814). LC Control Number: mm 75019679. Original papers in the Manuscript Division, 1975: MSS19679. Microfilm edition available: no. 16,232.

The Journal of Andrew Ellicott, late Commissioner on behalf of the United States . . . for determining the boundary between the United States and the possessions of his Catholic Majesty in America . . . With six maps . . . To which is added an appendix containing all the astronomical observations made, etc. Philadelphia, 1803.

Transactions of the American Philosophical Society (TAPS) from 1793 through 1818:

—"Accurate Determination of the Right Ascension and Declination of b Bootes, and the Pole Star: In a Letter from Mr. Andrew Ellicott to Mr. R. Patterson." *TAPS* 3 (1793): 116–18.

—"A Letter from Mr. Andrew Ellicott, to Robert Patterson; In Two Parts. Part First Contains a Number of Astronomical Observations. Part Second Contains the Theory and Method of Calculating the Aberration of the Stars, the Nutation of the Earth's Axis, and the Semiannual Equation." *TAPS* 4 (1799): 32–66.

—"A Letter from Mr. Andrew Ellicott, to Mr. Robert Patterson. A Method of Calculating the Eccentric Anomaly of the Planets." *TAPS* 4 (1799): 67–69.

—"Miscellaneous Observations Relative to the Western Parts of Pennsylvania, Particularly Those in the Neighbourhood of Lake Erie." *TAPS* 4 (1799): 224–30.

—"Observations Made on the Old French Landing at Presqu' Isle, to Determine the Latitude of the Town of Erie. In a Letter from Andrew Ellicott, to Robert Patterson, Secretary of the Society." TAPS 4 (1799): 231–32.

—"Astronomical, and Thermometrical Observations, Made at the Confluence of the Mississippi, and Ohio Rivers." TAPS 5 (1802): 162–202.

—"Astronomical, and Thermometrical Observations, Made on the Boundary between the United States and His Catholic Majesty." TAPS 5 (1802): 203–311.

—"A Short and Easy Rule for Finding the Equation for the Change of the Sun's Declination When Equal Altitudes Are Used to Regulate a Clock or Other Time Keeper. Communicated by Andrew Ellicott Esq" (in Part I). TAPS 6 (1809): 26–28.

—"Improved Method of Projecting and Measuring Plane Angles by Mr. Robert Patterson Communicated by Mr. Andrew Ellicott" (in Part I). Robert Patterson and Andrew Ellicott. TAPS 6 (1809): 29–32.

—"Astronomical Observations Made at Lancaster, Pennsylvania, Chiefly with a View to Ascertain the Longitude of That Borough, and as a Test of the Accuracy with Which the Longitude May Be Found by Lunar Observation; In a Letter from Andrew Ellicott to Robert Patterson" (in Part I). TAPS 6 (1809): 61–69.

—"Continuation of Astronomical Observations, Made at Lancaster, Pennsylvania. In a Letter from Andrew Ellicott, Esq. to R. Patterson" (in Part I). TAPS 6 (1809): 113–19.

—"The Geographical Position of Sundry Places in North America, and in the W. Indies, Calculated by J. J. de Ferrer" (in Part II). Jose Joaquin de Ferrer, Andrew Ellicott, Julian Ortis de Canelas, and M. Mechain. TAPS 6 (1809): 221–32.

—"Continuation of the Astronomical Observations Made at Lancaster, in Pennsylvania" (in Part II). TAPS 6 (1809): 233–35.

—"Observations of the Eclipse of the Sun, June 16th, 1806; Made at Lancaster" (in Part II). TAPS 6 (1809): 255–60.

—"Astronomical Observations, &c. Communicated by Andrew Ellicott, Esq." TAPS n. s., 1 (1818): 93–101.

Catherine Van Cortlandt Matthews. Andrew Ellicott. His life and letters. New York: Grafton Press, 1908. This contains many of the letters and personal journals contained in the Papers of Andrew Ellicott.

Other unpublished Ellicott family records are contained in the Holland Land Company archive held in the Daniel A. Reed Library, State University of New York at Fredonia. Archives of the Holland Land Company, 1789–1869. Microform/HD/195/H64/H6, 1984. 202 reels. This contains correspondence of Joseph Ellicott, agent of the Holland Land Company, with Andrew Ellicott, Benjamin Ellicott, Sally Ellicott, Judith

Ellicott, and other relatives. It also contains a typescript account of Joseph Ellicott Sr.'s "Journal to England from December 18, 1766, to September 21, 1767." Microfilm HD/195/H64/H65 /1986a/guide. 25 reels.

Published Ellicott Family Records

Evans, Charles W. *Biographical and Historical Accounts of the Fox, Ellicott and Evans Families*. Buffalo: Baker Jones, 1882.

Tyson, Martha E. *A Brief Account of the Settlement of Ellicott's Mills. With fragments of history therewith connected*. Baltimore: Maryland Historical Society. Peabody Fund Publication no. 4. 1867.

Published Works Directly Referring to Andrew Ellicott

Bedini, Silvio. "Ellicott and Banneker." *Washington History* 3, no. 1 (1991).

———. *The Life of Benjamin Banneker*. New York: Scribner, 1972.

Crim, R. D. *Andrew Ellicott and the North Georgia Boundary of 1811*. Paper submitted to the ACSM/FIG Conference in April 2002 in Washington, D.C.

Davies, N. M. *Andrew Ellicott: Astronomer, mathematician, surveyor*. Lewis and Clark Trail Heritage Foundation, Philadelphia Chapter, 2001.

Gallalee, Jack C. *Andrew Ellicott and the Ellicott Stone. Alabama Review* 18, no. 2 (1965).

Register, Robert. "Andrew Ellicott's Observations While Serving on the Southern Boundary Commission: 1796–1800." *Gulf Coast Historical Review* 12, no. 2 (1997).

Van Horne, John C. "Andrew Ellicott and Natchez." *Journal of Mississippi History* 45, no. 3 (1983).

General Works

Abernethy, Thomas P. *Western Lands and the American Revolution*. New York: Appleton-Century Co., 1937.

Adams, Charles F. *Memoirs of John Quincy Adams*, vol. 11. 12 vols. Philadelphia, 1874–77.

Adams, Henry. *The Education of Henry Adams*. Boston: Houghton Mifflin, 1918.

Anderson, Benedict. *Imagined Communities: Reflections on the Origin and Spread of Nationalism*. London: Verso Press, 1983.

Bailey, Kenneth P. *Thomas Cresap: Maryland Frontiersman*. Boston: Christopher Publishing House, 1944.

Beard, Charles A. *An Economic Interpretation of the Constitution of the United States*. New York: Macmillan, 1935.

Bedini, Silvio. *With Compass and Chain: American Surveyors and Their Instruments*. Frederick, MD: Professional Surveyor Publishing, 2001.

Bemis, Samuel Flagg. *John Quincy Adams and the Foundations of American Foreign Policy.* New York: Knopf, 1949.

——. *John Quincy Adams and the Union.* New York: Knopf, 1956.

Bezanson, Anne, Robert D. Gray, and Miriam Hussey. *Wholesale Prices in Philadelphia, 1780–1861.* Philadelphia: University of Pennsylvania Press, 1936.

Bowling, Kenneth R. *The Creation of Washington, D.C.: The Idea and Location of the American Capital.* Fairfax: George Mason University Press, 1991.

Boyd, Julian P., ed. *The Papers of Thomas Jefferson.* Princeton: Princeton University Press, 1950 onward.

Buchanan, Allen, and Margaret Moore, eds. *States, Nations and Borders: The ethics of making boundaries.* Cambridge, UK: Cambridge University Press, 2003.

Caemmerer, Hans Paul. *The Life of Pierre Charles L'Enfant.* New York: Da Capo Press, 1970.

Clark, Daniel. *Proofs of the Corruption of General James Wilkinson and of His Connexion with Aaron Burr.* Philadelphia: Hall & Pierie, 1809.

Clark, Thomas D., and John W. Guice. *Frontiers in Conflict: The Old Southwest, 1795–1830.* Albuquerque: University of New Mexico Press, 1989.

Cronon, William, George Miles, and Jay Gitlin, eds. *Under an Open Sky: Rethinking America's Western Past.* New York: W. W. Norton, 1992.

Danson, Edwin. *Drawing the Line: How Mason and Dixon Surveyed the Most Famous Border in America.* New York: John Wiley & Sons, 2001.

Davis, David Brion. *Slavery and Human Progress.* New York: Oxford University Press, 1984.

Davis, W. H. *The History of Bucks County, Pennsylvania.* Philadelphia, 1905.

Dusen, Alfred Van. *Connecticut.* New York: Random House, 1961.

Ellis, David M., ed. *The Frontier in American Development: Essays in Honor of Paul Wallace Gates.* Ithaca: Cornell University Press, 1969.

Ellis, Joseph. *American Sphinx.* New York: Knopf, 1997.

Ferling, John. *A Leap in the Dark: The Struggle to Create the American Republic.* New York: Oxford University Press, 2003.

Fischer, David Hackett. *Albion's Seed: Four British Folkways in America.* New York: Oxford University Press, 1991.

Flint, Timothy. *Recollections of the Last Ten Years, Passed in Occasional Residences and Journeyings in the Valley of Mississippi.* Boston: Cummings, Hilliard and Company, 1826.

Fogel, Robert W., and Stanley L. Engerman. *Time on the Cross: The Economics of American Negro Slavery.* Reissue edition, New York: W. W. Norton and Company, 1995.

Ford, Paul L., ed. *The Works of Thomas Jefferson.* New York and London: G. P. Putnam's Sons, 1904–5.

Foster, Thomas, ed. *The Collected Works of Benjamin Hawkins, 1796–1810.* Tuscaloosa: University of Alabama Press, 2003.

Friedman, Thomas L. *The World Is Flat: A Brief History of the Twenty-first Century*. New York: Farrar, Straus & Giroux, 2005.

Gates, Paul W. *History of the Public Land Law Development*. Washington, DC, 1968.

Grant, Ulysses S. *Personal Memoirs of U. S. Grant*. New York: Charles L. Webster & Company, 1885–86.

Guy, Donna J., and Thomas E. Sheridan, eds. *Contested Ground: Comparative Frontiers on the Northern and Southern Edges of the Spanish Empire*. Tucson: University of Arizona Press, 1998.

Hall, Basil. *Travels in North America in the Years 1827 and 1828*. Philadelphia, 1829.

Halliday, E. M. *Understanding Thomas Jefferson*. New York: HarperCollins, 2001.

Harris, Michael. *Origin of the Land Tenure System in the United States*. Ames, Iowa: Iowa State College Press, 1953.

Henderson, Archibald. *The Conquest of the Old Southwest*. New York: Century Company, 1920.

Hindle, Brooke. *David Rittenhouse*. Princeton: Princeton University Press, 1964.

Holmes, Jack D. L. *Gayoso: The Life of a Spanish Governor in the Mississippi Valley, 1789–1799*. Baton Rouge: Louisiana State University Press, 1965.

Houston, James L. *Calculating the Value of the Union: Slavery, Property Rights, and the Economic Origins of the Civil War*. Chapel Hill: University of North Carolina Press, 2003.

Jackson, Donald, ed. *The Diaries of George Washington*. Charlottesville: University Press of Virginia, 1976.

Jaffa, Harry V., and Robert Johannsen, eds. *In the Name of the People: Speeches and Writings of Lincoln and Douglas in the Ohio Campaign of 1859*. Columbus: Ohio State University Press, 1959.

Johnson, Allen. *Stephen Douglas: A Study in American Politics*. New York: Macmillan Company, 1908.

Jones, Landon Y. *The Essential Lewis and Clark*. New York: ECCO Press; HarperCollins, 2000.

Kite, Elizabeth Sarah. *L'Enfant and Washington, 1791–1792*. Baltimore: Johns Hopkins Press, 1929.

Korngold, Ralph. *Thaddeus Stevens: A Being Darkly Wise and Rudely Great*. New York: Harcourt, Brace and Company, 1955.

Kukla, Jon. *A Wilderness So Immense: The Louisiana Purchase and the Destiny of America*. New York: Knopf, 2003.

Linklater, Andro. *Measuring America: How an Untamed Wilderness Shaped the United States and Fulfilled the Promise of Democracy*. New York: Walker, 2002.

Macdonald, Forrest. *We the People: The Economic Origins of the Constitution*. Chicago: University of Chicago Press, 1958.

Mar, Alexander del. *History of Money in America from the Earliest Times to the Establishment of the Constitution*. Hawthorne, CA: Omni, 1966.

Marable, Manning. *Race, Reform and Rebellion: The Second Reconstruction in Black America, 1945–1982*. Jackson: University Press of Mississippi, 1984.

Martineau, Harriet. *Autobiography of Harriet Martineau*. Reprint, London: Virago, 1983.

Masteron, William Henry. *William Blount*. Baton Rouge: Louisiana State University Press, 1954.

McDougall, Walter A. *Promised Land, Crusader State: The American Encounter with the World Since 1776*. New York: Houghton Mifflin, 1997.

Mintz, Max M. *Seeds of Empire: The American Revolutionary Conquest of the Iroquois*. New York: New York University Press, 1999.

Munger, Donna. *Pennsylvania Land Records: A History and Guide for Research*. Wilmington, DE: Scholarly Resources, 1991.

Nobles, Gregory H. *American Frontiers: Cultural Encounters and Continental Conquest*. New York: Hill & Wang, 1997.

Padover, Saul K., ed. *Thomas Jefferson and the National Capital, 1783–1818*. Washington, DC: Government Printing Office, 1946.

Parrington, Vernon Louis. *Main Currents in American Thought: An interpretation of American Literature from the beginning to 1920*. New York: Harcourt Brace & Co., 1930.

Reps, John W. *The Making of America: A history of city planning in the United States*. Princeton: Princeton University Press, 1965.

———. *Monumental Washington: The Planning and Development of the Capital Center*. Princeton: Princeton University Press, 1967.

Richards, Leonard L. *Shays's Rebellion: The American Revolution's Final Battle*. Philadelphia: University of Pennsylvania Press, 2002.

Robertson, David B. *The Constitution and America's Destiny*. St. Louis: University of Missouri Press, 2005.

Rutman, Darrett B., ed. *The Old Dominion: Essays for Thomas Perkins Abernethy*. Charlottesville: University Press of Virginia, 1964.

Slaughter, Thomas P. *The Whiskey Rebellion: Frontier Epilogue to the American Revolution*. New York: Oxford University Press, 1986.

Smith, Henry Nash. *Virgin Land: The American West as Symbol and Myth*. Cambridge: Harvard University Press, 1950, 1978.

Smith, Paul, et al., eds. *Letters of Delegates to Congress, 1774–1789*. Washington, DC: Library of Congress, 1976–2000.

Taylor, Alan. *The Divided Ground: Indians, Settlers and the Northern Borderland of the American Revolution*. New York: Knopf, 2006.

Tyler, Moses Coit. *A History of American Literature*. New York: Putnam & Sons, 1881.

Wallace, Paul A., ed. *Thirty Thousand Miles with John Heckewelder*. Pittsburgh: University of Pittsburgh Press, 1958.

White, C. Albert. *A History of the Rectangular Survey System.* Washington, DC: Government Printing Office, 1982.

Wilkinson, James. *Burr's Conspiracy exposed and General Wilkinson vindicated against the slanders of his enemies on that important occasion.* Washington, 1811.

———. *Memoirs of My Own Times.* Philadelphia: Abraham Small, 1816.

Wilton, Andrew, and Tim Barringer. *American Sublime: Landscape Painting in the United States, 1820–1880.* Princeton: Princeton University Press, 2003.

Wyckoff, William. *The Developer's Frontier: The Making of Western New York.* New Haven: Yale University Press, 1988.

Young, Alfred F., ed. *The American Revolution: Explorations in the History of American Radicalism.* De Kalb: Northern Illinois University Press, 1976.

Zatmary, David. *Shays' Rebellion: The Making of an Agrarian Insurrection.* Amherst: University of Massachusetts Press, 1980.

JOURNALS

Beers, Henry P. "History of the U.S. Topographical Engineers, 1818–1863." *Military Engineer* 34 (June 1942).

Bouton, Terry. "A Road Closed: Rural Insurgency in Post-Independence Pennsylvania." *Journal of American History* 87, no. 3 (December 2000).

Brown, William Fiske. "In Lincoln's Time: Our College Loyalty to Union and Freedom." *Round Table*, February 10, 1911.

Burger, Warren E. "Obstacles to the Constitution." Supreme Court Historical Society 1987 Yearbook.

Dunaway, Wilma A. "Speculators and Settler Capitalists." In *Appalachia in the Making: The Mountain South in the Nineteenth Century.* Chapel Hill: University of North Carolina Press, 1995.

Eisfeld, Rainer. "Myths and Realities of Frontier Violence: A Look at the Gunfighter Saga." *Journal of Criminal Justice and Popular Culture* 3, no. 5 (1995): 106–22.

Finseth, Ian Frederick. "'Liquid Fire Within Me': Language, Self and Society in Transcendentalism and Early Evangelicalism, 1820–1860." Master's thesis in English, University of Virginia, August 1995.

Fukuyama, Francis. "The End of History?" *National Interest*, 1989.

Hodder, F. H. "Stephen A. Douglas." *The Chautauquan* 29 (August 1899).

Holton, Woody. "'From the Labours of Others': The War Bonds Controversy and the Origins of the Constitution in New England." *William & Mary Quarterly* 61, no. 2 (April 2004).

Johnson, Samuel. "Observations on the Present State of Affairs." *Literary Magazine* 4 (July 15–August 15, 1756). In Donald J. Greene, ed., *Political Writings* (New Haven: Yale University Press, 1971).

Robertson, Andrew W. "'Look on This Picture . . . And on This!' Nationalism, Localism, and Partisan Images of Otherness in the United States, 1787–1820." *American Historical Review* 106.4 (October 2001).

Shepard, William R. "Wilkinson and the Beginnings of the Spanish Conspiracy." *American Historical Review* 9 (1903–4).

Smithers, Harriet. "English Abolitionism and the Annexation of Texas." *Southwestern Historical Quarterly* 32 (1929).

Wheeler, Joseph Towne. "The Maryland Press, 1777–1790." Baltimore: Maryland Historical Society, 1938.

Wilson, Woodrow. "The Making of the Nation." *Atlantic Monthly,* July 1897.

INDEX

Adams, Henry, 199, 204, 227–28, 239, 241, 243
Adams, John, 48, 89, 131, 136, 160, 166, 167, 186
Adams, John Quincy, 13, 180, 184–87, 189, 193–94, 199–204, 211, 212, 229, 238
Adams–Onís Treaty (1819), 13, 185–86, 196
Alabama, 120, 192
Alaska, 203, 239–41, 242, 244
Alien and Sedition Acts (1798), 166–67
almanacs, 4, 31–32, 54, 94, 95, 102–3. *See also specific almanac*
American Philosophical Society, 46, 53, 95, 142, 155, 172, 173, 175
American Revolution, 3, 28, 31, 44, 55, 57, 62, 63, 71, 77, 120, 176, 242
"American System," 193–94
Annapolis conference (1786), 68
Arizona, 220, 224
Arkansas, 193, 196, 229, 269
army, U.S., 175, 218–19. *See also specific person*
Articles of Confederation, 9, 10, 11, 44, 49, 66, 68–69, 71, 74, 86, 231, 234
astronomy, 18–19, 29, 32–33, 37–38, 124, 136, 164, 172–73, 183

banks, 55, 190, 196, 266
Banneker, Benjamin, 94–95, 102–3, 107, 137
Beloit College, 208, 209
Beloit, Wisconsin, 206–8, 209, 210, 221, 223
Benton, Thomas Hart, 192
Bill of Rights, 127
black Americans: and "black codes," 232; citizenship for, 233–34; civil rights for, 266–70; education for, 236, 268; free, 210, 216, 217, 236; inferiority of, 95, 102–3, 235, 269; and Jim Crow laws, 238, 267, 269; land occupation by, 171; and law and order, 267; as legislators, 237; lynchings of, 267–68;

property rights of, 236, 267; during Reconstruction, 232, 233–34, 236–37; voting rights for, 232, 234, 235, 236, 237, 269. *See also* Fugitive Slave Act; slavery; *specific person*
Blodgett's Settlement. *See* Beloit, Wisconsin
Blount, William, 131–32, 134, 149, 161, 175
Boone, Daniel, 125
Booth, Sherman, 210, 215
Boston, Massachusetts, 70, 198, 262, 265–66
boundaries/borders: benefits of, 61–62; characteristics of, 27; in Europe, 6, 10; as force in U.S. foreign and domestic policy, 15; as frontiers, 1; impact on states of creation of, 44–45; importance/functions of, 6, 7, 9–10, 15–16, 30, 218, 279; and "ingredients" of states, 230; and law and order, 13–14; as means for control of citizens, 30; security at, 1, 273–74; types of, 9; and uniqueness of U.S., 2, 3. *See also* frontier(s); *specific boundary or state/territory*
Bourbon County, Georgia, 131, 166
Brant, Joseph, 77, 80, 81
Briggs, Isaac, 102, 103, 111, 171
Brown, John, 145, 223, 224
Brown v. Board of Education of Topeka (1954), 268
Bucks County, Pennsylvania, 19, 21–22, 24
Bureau of Indian Affairs, U.S., 258, 259, 269
Burr, Aaron, 146, 160, 162–65, 173, 175
Burr Conspiracy, 146, 162–65, 173
Bush, George W., 273–74

Calhoun, John C., 193, 194, 195, 197, 199, 202, 203, 210, 211, 213, 216, 228, 234
California, 13, 120, 199, 202, 213–14, 224, 230, 266
Calvert family, 5, 20, 28, 29, 30